W9-BOP-739

LOCKE

SELECTIONS

LOCKE
SELECTIONS

EDITED BY

STERLING P. LAMPRECHT

CHARLES SCRIBNER'S SONS New York

1 3 5 7 9 11 13 15 17 19 M/P 20 18 16 14 12 10 8 6 4 2

ISBN 0-684-14825-0

Printed in the United States of America

INTRODUCTION

I

John Locke was born on the 29th of August, 1632, at Wrington, a small town seven or eight miles south of Bristol, England. He died at Oates, some twenty miles north of London, on October 28th, 1704.

Locke lived through one of the most troubled periods in English history. He witnessed the hard struggles between Charles I and Parliament, the rise to power of the Presbyterians and Independents, the execution of Charles, the rule of Cromwell, the Restoration and reigns of Charles II and James II, the Glorious Revolution of 1688 and the constitutional settlement under William and Mary. He dealt in his writings with many of the public issues at stake in the conflicts of the closing decades of the seventeenth century. He had the gift of grasping the broad principles involved in the immediate issues. And he had the perseverance of thinking through the rival claims of the warring parties and of formulating a general philosophical position in rational defence of his own political, religious, and social convictions. While he raised many of the problems which have busied philosophical thinkers for more than two centuries, he approached these problems, not as so many academic questions, but as vital and pressing matters of crucial importance. The perennial interest of Locke's writings is largely due to the contact of his thinking with the realities of social life in one of the most creative periods of English history.

Locke's family was intimately involved in the turmoils of the revolution. His father was a country attorney who, as clerk for justices of the peace in his district of Somersetshire, was called on to act as agent in collecting the "ship-money" which King Charles I and his ministers sought to levy upon the seaport towns. This "ship-money" was a device for getting funds without the consent of Parliament for new taxes. The device rested upon an ancient custom which required all seaport towns to contribute vessels, or money for building vessels, for the naval forces which defended British shipping. Bristol was of course the chief seaport town of the southwest of England, and was forced to pay large sums of this "ship-money" to the Crown. The King and his ministers proceeded to use the money for any purpose which they had in hand, often against the interest of the Parliamentary party. Thus the impost seemed highly unjust to advocates of Parliamentary control over national policies and expenditures. Locke's father adhered to the expression of disapproval of the impost which Parliament issued in 1642; and soon afterwards, when armed rebellion broke out, he became captain of a troop of horse on the side of the Parliamentary forces. We do not know of the course of his military fortunes. But we do know that, when he resumed his legal practice at the conclusion of the civil wars, he had suffered the loss of a large part of his estate.

Locke himself continued his education without interruption in spite of the chaotic conditions in England during his boyhood and youth. He spent six years at Westminster School which had been entrusted by Parliament to a committee of Parliamentary sympathizers. He doubtless received his scholarship here as the son of a man identified with the Parliamentary cause, and probably associated wholly with boys from families of like political persuasion. The school work consisted almost entirely of exercises in the grammar, translation, and composition of the Greek and Latin languages. The pedantry of this work led Locke later to protest in his *Some Thoughts concerning Education.* As he then wrote: "A great part of the learning now in fashion in the schools of Europe and that goes ordinarily into the round of education, a gentleman may in a good measure be unfurnished with, without any great disparagement to himself or prejudice to his affairs."

In 1652 Locke went up to Oxford and matriculated at Christ Church College. His connection with Christ Church, first as student and then as fellow, lasted for more than thirty years, until in 1684 he was deprived of his fellowship by mandate of Charles II. He was in residence at Oxford for most of the first ten years of this period. The regular course of studies proved most distasteful to him. Besides further work in the classics he was expected to spend much time on the traditional Aristotelian philosophy in its scholastic form and on public disputations. Both of these pursuits impressed Locke as quite unprofitable, as is indicated by the two following passages from the earliest biography of Locke (written by LeClerc in French and translated into English in 1706.) "Although Mr. Locke had gained such a reputation in the university, he has been often heard to say of the first years of his being there, that he found so little satisfaction in the method that was prescribed them for their studies that he has wished his father had never sent him to Oxford, when he found that what he had learnt there was of little use to him to enlighten or enlarge his mind and to make him more exact in his reasonings." Again: "Mr. Locke did not acquire this great reputation he had at Oxford (as Mr. Tyrrell says) by his performances in the public disputations; for he was ever averse to these and always looked upon them as no better than wrangling, and that they served only for a vain ostentation of a man's parts and not in the least for the discovery of truth and advancement of knowledge."

Two influences, however, had a great constructive effect upon Locke during his Oxford days. One of these was his personal contact with John Owen, dean of Christ Church College and vice-chancellor of the university. Owen owed his appointment to the favor of the Independents in Parliament and of Cromwell himself. He was a man of strong Puritan sympathies but of a very tolerant temper. Even when he found his own religious party in the ascendancy, he pleaded for mutual respect of diverse religious beliefs and opposed the resort to political penalties for differences of theological opinion. Indeed he stood out as one of the few real defenders of toleration among the warring sects of the century. And this spirit found worthy expression in Locke too. Locke was by nature a compromiser, seeking a middle ground on which all parties of moderate mind could unite. Locke remained a sponsor of toleration for all but certain extreme groups even though he changed over about this time from the Independents (to whom both John Owen and his own father belonged) to the Church of England. His reason for the change was the conviction that no single sect could hope to restore theological peace to England, and that the Church of England had a much better chance than any non-conformist group of becoming an inclusive and comprehensive church. He desired an ecclesiastical organization within which wide diversities of opinion could harmoniously exist. In joining the church body which stood nearest to the historic traditions of the centuries he yet remained firm in his belief that other religious groups had an equal right to respect and to a free exercise of their independent organizations. Thus in departing from the non-conformist group to membership in the Church of England he carried over Owen's tolerant spirit, only changing his idea as to the most effective means whereby to work for the desired end. And especially after the Restoration, his judgment concerning the relative value of non-conformity and of a comprehensive establishment was probably a sound one. He played a large part in making the Church of England the broad, inclusive national religious body which it increasingly became.

The second important constructive influence on Locke during his Oxford days was the philosophy of Descartes. Locke told his friends later in life that the first books which gave him a relish for philosophical reading were those of Descartes. He differed profoundly from Descartes in many respects. He lacked Descartes's confidence in the power of human reason and the ability of reason to determine the nature of things by resort to "clear and distinct" ideas; he was unwilling to identify the soul with the activity of thought; he rejected the supposition that matter was essentially extension. But none the less he found Descartes's writings lucid, intelligible, and relevant to genuine human concerns. And hence he rated them as superior to the traditional Aristotelian metaphysics of the schools and to the philosophy taught in the universities. In several important respects Descartes left deep traces on his philosophical system. Locke incorporated Descartes's proof for the existence of the self as the most indubitable of all truths; he repeated (with slight modifications) Descartes's cosmological argument for the existence of God; he is one with Descartes in taking the immediate content of consciousness to be, not externai objects, but effects produced in the individual mind by external objects. Even more than these specific points, the general temper of Descartes exercised a determining influence on him. Philosophy grew for Descartes out of the state of the physical sciences, and it was compelled to describe reality in terms harmonious with the scientific concepts of the day. The assumption of such a world order as was implied by seventeenth-century science was in the background of Locke's speculations; and though Locke was later on more inclined to the Newtonian than to the Cartesian version of the physical sciences, yet Descartes proved to Locke in his Oxford days that philosophy could still grapple with the problems of life in such a world as the sciences had discovered and could analyze these problems so as to permit answers on many points. The traditional text-book on the history of philosophy speaks of Descartes and Locke as two contrasted types of rationalist and empiricist respectively. And while there is much truth in such a view, the great indebtedness of Locke to Descartes is likely to be overlooked.

Locke's choice of a profession proved to be a difficult matter for him. For a short time he acted as a tutor at Oxford; but he had no inclination to continue that work. He was designed by his father for the church, and often himself considered that calling; but he seems to have felt sincerely a possibility that he was not fitted therefor (even aside from consideration of his liberal views upon theological questions). Meanwhile his interest in experimental science led him to a serious study of medicine. He began this study, not with the intention of preparing himself for the practice of medicine, but from a sheerly intellectual curiosity in natural science. In 1668 Locke was elected a Fellow of the Royal Society; but for some years antecedent to that time he had frequented the company of men of scientific attainments. Robert Boyle, the chemist, was the central figure in the group which indeed often met at his lodgings. Locke made some meteorological observations; he urged Boyle on to investigate the nature of the atmosphere; and he it was who in 1691, upon the death of Boyle, edited Boyle's *General History of the Air*. His interest and his general competence in the whole field of the natural sciences are reflected in his *Elements of Natural Philosophy* (written as a guide in educating boys in science), which contains a summary of the current scientific views of the physical world. Locke did not receive his degree as Bachelor of Medicine until 1674 (largely because of failing to comply with certain residence requirements at Oxford); and he seldom practiced his profession either before or after receiving his degree. Yet he seems to have had considerable skill. At least he is said to have saved the life of the Earl of Shaftesbury by an operation. He was always glad to make suggestions and give medical advice and prescribe drugs for families with whom he was on terms of friendly intimacy. But on the whole it may be said that Locke was interested in medicine as a branch of experimental science, wherein he could satisfy his intellectual thirst for knowledge and could secure confirming evidence of the value of the methods which under the influence of Bacon and Descartes were taking possession of all branches of science.

In 1666 Locke met Lord Ashley who became the first Earl of Shaftesbury. The two men found an unusual satisfaction in each other's society and became close friends. For the next fifteen years Locke's life was largely bound up with the fortunes of the Shaftesbury family. Locke even became a rather constant member of the Shaftesbury household. During these years he found himself drawn into many enterprises of a public nature, dealing with finance, the value of money, political organization, and the relation of church and state. He held a number of minor offices when Shaftesbury was in power in the government. He participated in drawing up *The Fundamental Constitutions for the Government of Carolina,* though the provisions of this document were never actually put into force in the colony. He was private adviser to Shaftesbury while the latter as lord chancellor was dealing with the question of the legal status of dissenters and the right of freedom of religious worship. In all the matters dealt with in this period he revealed the wise tolerance of one who aimed at security, useful compromise of conflicting claims, and moderation.

An amusing anecdote (told in LeClerc's biography) makes clear the place which Locke held in the Shaftesbury circle. "The freedom which he used with persons of this rank had somewhat which I cannot express, that agreed very well with his character. One day three or four of these lords being met together at my Lord Ashley's, rather for their diversion than business, after the usual compliments were over, the cards were brought when little or no discourse had passed between them. Mr. Locke took notice of the game for some time, and then taking out his pocket-book, he set himself to write somewhat with very great seriousness. One of the lords having observed it asks him what it was that he was writing. My lord, he says, I endeavor to get as much as I can in your good company, and having waited with impatience the honour of being present at a meeting of the wisest and most ingenious men of the age and enjoying at length this happiness, I thought it was best to write your conversation. And I have accordingly set down the substance of what has been said within this hour or two. There was no need for Mr. Locke to read much of this dialogue. These lords perceived the banter and diverted themselves a while with improving the jest. They left their play and entered into conversation more agreeable to their character and so spent the rest of the day."

Locke's associations with Shaftesbury eventually led to his going into voluntary exile. Towards the end of the reign of Charles II there were many conspiracies concerning the succession to the throne. Shaftesbury was bold and open in his opposition to the King's brother, the Duke of York, on account of the latter's allegiance to the Catholic faith. Locke seems to have had no part in these conspiracies. But as an intimate friend and frequent member of the household of Shaftesbury, he naturally fell under suspicion. After the death of Shaftesbury in 1682 and the loss of the protection of this powerful patron, Locke prudently withdrew to the continent. He lived in various cities in Holland, fearful at times of arrest at the instance of the government of James II who peacefully ascended the throne in 1685. He was indeed mentioned at the end of a list of eighty-four Englishmen whose surrender was demanded from the Dutch government for participation in an abortive rebellion in favor of the succession of the Duke of Monmouth. He was soon offered a free pardon; but he rejected the offer on the ground that one who had not committed a crime could not have need for pardon. He moved about quietly among the houses of his Dutch friends, keeping his exact location as secret as possible. None the less he was in constant touch with the men whom he wished to know. He saw much of LeClerc, and became one of the editors of and a frequent contributor to LeClerc's *Bibliothèque Universelle* (one of the earliest periodicals devoted to criticism in Europe). He associated with Limborch, a liberal-minded professor of theology at Amsterdam, who was virtual leader of the Remonstrants, the group of those who protested against the extreme Calvinism of the Synod of Dort and the more orthodox party in the Protestant Church. He thus became deeply interested in theological problems as well as in the correlated practical problems of getting hostile sects to live in peace with each other.

The Glorious Revolution of 1688 and the accession of William and Mary greatly changed Locke's prospects. Instead of being suspect by the government he was now in the highest favor. He even returned to England in 1689 on the ship on which the Queen made the crossing. He was proffered various posts of honor under the new government. He declined most of the offers, partly because for some years his health had not been good, and partly because he wanted a quiet life with time for writing and study. He did accept some minor positions which would not engross his full time. But after his return to England he was occupied chiefly with bringing out a series of philosophical works and in defending them against the attacks of various pamphleteers and critics.

Early in 1691 Locke took up his residence at Oates in the household of Sir Francis Masham. This move is described for us in LeClerc's biography. "He had made some visits at different times to Sir Francis Masham, who lived at Oates, a little more than twenty miles from London, where he found the air so good that he thought there was none could suit better with his constitution. Besides, the agreeable company that he found at Sir Francis Masham's, which would beautify the most melancholy place, was one great motive no doubt, to incline him to desire that gentleman to receive him into his family, that he might settle there and expect his death, in applying himself to his studies as much as his weak health would allow. He was received on his own terms, that he might have his entire liberty there and look upon himself as at his own house. And it was in this pleasant society that he passed the rest of his life, and from which he was absent as little as possible, because the air of London grew more and more troublesome to him. He went thither only in the summer for three or four months; and if he returned to Oates anything indisposed, the air of the country soon recovered him." And so, contributing his share to the expenses of running the establishment and having his own apartments to which he could retire, he yet was happily surrounded by friends who were solicitous to care for him. Lady Masham was a daughter of the Cambridge Platonist, Ralph Cudworth; and Locke frequently spoke of her in his letters as affording him excellent company both on account of her intellectual attainments in theology and philosophy and on account of her tender regard for his comfort. Thus he spent his last years in the kind of peace he had sought throughout his whole lifetime.

One further friendship of Locke's closing years should be noted. He had probably met Isaac Newton (who became Sir Isaac Newton in 1708) during the 1670's when both men were members of the Royal Society. He thought most highly of Newton's scientific work and also respected his competence in the field of theology. He often referred to Newton in his writings as "the incomparable Mr. Newton." After 1690 he was in frequent correspondence with Newton on theological, astronomical, and chemical questions. An unfortunate misunderstanding in 1692 and 1693 (doubtless connected with the mental derangement under which Newton seems for a time to have suffered) broke off their relationship. But Newton's apology and Locke's kindly forgiveness restored the friendship. Locke thereafter submitted part of his lengthy *Third Letter for Toleration* to Newton's approval in advance of publication, and sought Newton's opinion on some exegetical points in his notes on St. Paul's epistles. In 1702 Newton paid Locke a visit at Oates. In 1703 Locke wrote in a letter to his cousin Lord King: "Mr. Newton is really a very valuable man, not only for his wonderful skill in mathematics, but in divinity too, and his great knowledge in the Scriptures, wherein I know few his equals."

Locke's first published work appeared in 1689. But he had been engaged in literary activity for nearly two decades before that time. The famous *Essay concerning Human Understanding* owed its inception to a discussion which Locke had with some intimate friends in about the year 1670. As Locke tells us in *The Epistle to the Reader* at the beginning of the *Essay,* he became interested in the problem of knowledge because he and his friends were unable to reach definite conclusions about the subjects they were discussing. These subjects (as we are informed by James Tyrrell) were the "principles of morality and revealed religion." Locke and his friends agreed to turn from consideration of these principles to a preliminary examination of the methods and nature of knowledge. Locke undertook to treat the problem of knowledge at the next meeting of the group and prepared a brief paper on this topic. During the ensuing years of semi-public work under Shaftesbury and of exile from England, these considerations continued to interest him. The disputes in theology, the dogmatic claims of partisan politics, the unjustifiable fervor with which some contestants asserted their opinions as certain dogmas, these and such facts impressed upon him the desirability, indeed the necessity, of a preliminary formulation of the origin, nature, and limits of knowledge. Thus, as he himself tells us, the work was "begun by chance, continued by entreaty, written by incoherent parcels, and after long intervals of neglect resumed again as humour or occasions permitted." The year following his return from exile to England the work appeared. In style it is imperfect, and in arrangement it is faulty. Locke's desire to speak the language of the common man and thus to avoid the arid technicalities of "the schools" led him to use words of ill-defined import, and unwittingly introduced many ambiguities and obscurities into his thought. His manner of writing resulted in many repetitions, in much needless overlapping of parts, and in serious lack of proportion in the treatment of various topics. None the less the work was momentous. It was directly relevant to the theological quarrels of the time and it was based upon current scientific suppositions. Locke had so much respect for the empirical procedure of contemporary science (particularly as contrasted with the dogmatism and verbalisms of current theology and metaphysics) that he sought to make out of the method of science a general theory of knowledge for all fields of inquiry. Thereby he revealed unsuspected difficulties in the very preconceptions of science and stumbled upon problems which have been a concern of modern philosophy ever since his time.

Though the *Essay* is the work on which Locke's reputation primarily rests, it was not his first work to appear in print. In 1689 there appeared, first in Latin and then in English translation, *A Letter concerning Toleration.* And in 1690 there was published the *Two Treatises of Government.* The first of these writings had been completed by 1685, and in its Latin form was dedicated to Limborch. The latter probably was composed partly in Holland before the Glorious Revolution, but was revised and completed after the actual accession of William. They both take their point of departure from conditions such as prevailed in England at that time, and deal directly with issues which were conspicuously pressing upon the occasion of the overthrow of James II and the crowning of William and Mary. But the underlying principles had been in Locke's mind for several decades and were relevant to the whole century of troubled religious and political life through which England had been passing. As early as 1667 Locke wrote a considerable outline of a projected essay on toleration in his Common-place Book. And in repeated literary fragments of the years from 1660 on, the principles of government received attention from his pen.

The closing decade at Oates witnessed the appearance of a large number of further writings. Some of these were contributions to new fields of inquiry; while others were controversial discussions in which the original works were defended against attacks. The most important of the former group were *Some Thoughts concerning Education, Some Consideration of the Consequences of the Lowering of Interest and Raising the Value of Money,* and *The Reasonableness of Christianity. An Essay for the Understanding of St. Paul's Epistles* revealed the piety of Locke's attitude towards Scripture, but has ceased long since to have any but an antiquarian interest for those concerned with the history of Biblical criticism. In the second group were three letters to Edward Stillingfleet, Bishop of Worcester, who charged the *Essay concerning Human Understanding* with being subversive of Christian faith and morals, two further letters (and an unfinished *Fourth Letter*) in defence of the principles of toleration, and two vindications of the theological position set forth in *The Reasonableness of Christianity*. These controversial writings at times add materially to an understanding of Locke's original writings; but, like most of the controversial writings of the age, they are dull and wearisome to the modern reader, and can be appreciated only by those who are keenly alive to the issues of thought in the closing decade of the seventeenth century.

II

The key-note of Locke's thought is the desire for peace through generous toleration of mutual differences. The spirit of his work is one of compromise.

A famous passage from his hand in 1660 illustrates this desire for peace and readiness to compromise. "I no sooner perceived myself in the world, but I found myself in a storm which has lasted almost hitherto; and I therefore cannot but entertain the approaches of a calm with the greatest joy and satisfaction. And this, methinks, obliges me both in duty and gratitude to endeavor the continuance of such a blessing by disposing men's minds to obedience to that government which has brought with it the quiet settlement which even our giddy folly had put beyond the reach not only of our contrivance but hopes. And I would men would be persuaded to be so kind to their religion, their country, and themselves, as not to hazard again the substantial blessings of peace and settlement in an over-zealous contention about things which they themselves confess to be little and at most are but indifferent. . . . All the freedom I can wish my country or myself is to enjoy the protection of those laws which the prudence and providence of our ancestors established and the happy return of his Majesty has restored." Locke was referring in this passage to the Restoration of Charles II. He soon found that the rule of the Stuarts did not mean the happy religious tranquillity and civil peace he anticipated. But the longing for security and the moderation of spirit were typical of his entire life.

In all the fields in which he worked and wrote he attempted to adjust the institutions of the time to the needs of the new world which had been ushered in by the renaissance and developed under the influence of modern science. Old methods of conducting the schools, old laws requiring conformity to established creeds, old forms of government, old standards of faith were still strongly entrenched in the organization of society. And the crying need of the time seemed to be a total transformation of practice in these diverse fields. The transformation had been delayed beyond endurance because of the lack of a systematic and reasoned body of principles to guide the process of adjustment. Such a body of principles it was Locke's aim to furnish. Locke had a dread of chaos; he feared the confusion of aimless revolt; he realized the danger of losing the values of civilized living through the anarchy and violence of unintelligent revolt. He was by nature timid and retiring. He would never consent to lend his endeavors to any hit-and-miss experimenting with even the unsatisfactory procedure of current institutions. But he was also keenly aware of the imperative necessity of welcoming a radical transformation of social affairs. The spirit of protest was too strong to be suppressed and too justifiable to be ignored. Years of political upheaval and of theological strife convinced him of the inevitability of rapid changes in the customs of the body politic. The immediate future lay between two alternatives, either violence and mutual persecution and the destructive effects of mere agitation, or far-sighted programs of rational adjustment and deliberate reform on the basis of compromise and mutual conciliation.

Thus the two evils he most steadily combatted were the dogmatic retention of traditional forms and the fevered clamor of sectarian bias. That is, he particularly fought stolidity and "enthusiasm." Stolidity was insistence upon what was established just because it was established, even though it was not based upon rational principles. "Enthusiasm" was rhapsodic allegiance to fancies of subjective origin without a shred of objective evidence. In neither case was there the carefully reasoned understanding of principle which could win wide support and become the foundation of a new and better social order. So Locke set himself to show the difference between what we know through satisfactory proof and what we may believe in the absence of any vestige of proof. We are, as rational human beings, capable of agreement with each other in all those matters where proof gives knowledge. Beyond the limits of our knowledge we may if we desire believe many things; but we have no moral right to impose our beliefs on other persons or erect our beliefs into official creed.

It is thus no accident that the earliest published work from Locke's pen is *A Letter concerning Toleration*. And it is significant that it was followed by two elaborate defences against attack and that a final defence was in course of composition when death put an end to his writing. Much that Locke said in his plea for toleration has been so widely adopted in the practice of subsequent European and American life that the casual reader to-day may fail to appreciate both the courage and the originality of the vigorous argument. The chief principle is a distinction between the spheres of church and state. The state is a means adopted to secure life, liberty, health, freedom of person, and security of property. It is essentially a temporal or secular device for the better enjoyment of the goods available in this world.

It is not concerned with "the care of souls." It is not designed, nor is it competent, for the work of preparing men for salvation in the world to come. All religious organizations are voluntary associations for the worship of God according to the manner and form preferred by a certain group of men. No church has the right to exclusive protection from the government; no church has the right to impose its ritual or its creed on those unwilling to associate themselves voluntarily with it. The state is necessarily one, and can compel obedience to its lawful regulations. But churches may be many; and because of the diverse possibilities of belief in the realm which lies beyond human experience, they are sure to be many. And these many churches, however much they may require conformity of their members, have neither authority to compel membership nor the right to use civil penalties in the endeavor to secure or retain members. State and church have different functions. And whereas the state owes protection to all churches in the security of their properties and the freedom of their worship, it must not exhibit political favor or make membership in any one church a prerequisite to civil preferment or public office.

Toleration, however, has its just limits. Neither church nor individual can properly demand absolute license. Whereas there is no purely speculative opinion which is dangerous to the civil liberty and worldly prosperity of one's fellow-citizens, there are some practical opinions as to right conduct with which the state is necessarily concerned. The state should not tolerate opinions which are destructive of society; it need show no generosity towards those who, under cover of religion, seek to gain control over the state for their sectarian advantage. Furthermore it can not tolerate those religious groups that profess allegiance to a foreign prince of authority supreme above that of the state. And finally it can not tolerate atheists. Two of these limitations of toleration require special comment. The refusal to tolerate religious groups that owe allegiance to a foreign prince was due to anti-Catholic fears. It would of course operate against Mohammedans and other sects with an ecclesiastical authority in foreign countries. But the motivation of this limitation was fear of the Catholic Church. The days of the Reformation were not yet far behind, and the association of Catholicism with the political absolutism of the Stuarts was fresh in all English minds. Locke felt the threat which the papal control over men's consciences made against the self-determination of the English people in their own affairs. As to the refusal to tolerate atheists, Locke gave for reason that moral obligation is obedience to the will of God, and therefore disbelief in God removes all sense of obligation and destroys the basis of morality. This theological sanction for morality is not the only form of ethical theory which appears in the pages of Locke's writings; but it is the opinion to which he constantly returned as final and indubitable. He was himself a devout person, given to deriving his moral rules from the meditative reading of Scripture. And he seems to have been unsympathetic towards a secular or sanctionless theory of morals.

The motivation of Locke's plea for toleration is further visible in his theological discussion in *The Reasonableness of Christianity*. While Locke had a strong and simple faith in God and in Jesus as Messiah, he both distrusted the dogmatic claims of conflicting parties in the various churches of the time and hated the agitated atmosphere and open struggle between these conflicting parties. His great desire was to discover a broad basis of fundamentals on which reasonable men of all parties could agree, and then to permit as many variations of further doctrinal belief as men might privately hold. Uniformity of belief on all matters he regarded as impossible; for human reason does not give us knowledge beyond a few preliminary matters. Divergences of belief are inevitable and legitimate; but persecution or ostracism for holding to such divergence is unjust. While men have no right to affirm on faith a single point which is in opposition to what reason can prove to be true, they may well accept on faith many a doctrine which lies beyond the province of reason. Only it is to be firmly maintained that such matters of faith beyond what is established by reason are personal hazards which no one has a right to impose on others.

The compromising spirit which characterized Locke's discussion of religion is shown in a fragment of a letter which in 1685 he wrote to Limborch. In this letter he commented upon a recent book which expressed sympathy with the advanced critical views of Spinoza on the literature of the Old Testament. He said: "Though I admit the argument is modestly put forward and cautiously worked out, I think it is one that cannot be too carefully discussed. If everything in the sacred books is to be indiscriminately adopted by us as divinely inspired, great opportunity will be given to philosophers for doubting our faith and sincerity. If on the other hand any part is to be regarded as of merely human composition, what becomes of the divine authority of the Scriptures, without which the Christian religion falls to the ground? What is to be the criterion? what the rule?" All extremes must be avoided in getting a broad platform of moderate opinion as a basis of union for all reasonable men.

The three essentials of Christian faith which Locke could not permit to be questioned were the existence of God, the messiahship of Jesus, and the principles of morality as he found them set forth in the Bible. Two of these he considered to be capable of perfect demonstration, namely the existence of God and the principles of morality. The messiahship of Jesus he sought to prove by elaborate use of Scriptural texts. The two demonstrable doctrines form the content of *natural religion,* i.e. of the religion which all rational minds will come to accept if they pay proper attention to the evidences in nature and the connection of their own ideas. Most men, however, are so corrupt in their impulses and lazy intellectually that they fail to note the truths within their powers. Hence revelation became essential to recall their minds to God and virtue. Jesus was the bearer of this revelation. His teaching re-established the natural religion and then added the further requirement that men should accept him as the divinely appointed leader or Messiah. Christianity is thus built around natural religion, but has positive elements which natural religion does not contain.

In addition to the three essentials of Christian faith, Locke believed that many further doctrines could be demonstrated by judicious use of the Scriptures. But such doctrines are neither requisite to salvation nor clear to all men. They should hence be a subject for peaceful debate among the learned, but not a requirement for fellowship in a comprehensive church. Experience only too well proved that bitterness results from attempts to add dogmas to the three essentials of the simple Christian faith. Original sin, justification by faith, endless punishment of the wicked in hell-fire, predestination, election, the nature of inspiration, the mode of Christ's sacrificial atonement,—these are matters of interest to certain scholars, but are immaterial to most men. On such matters we may speculate, but we do not clearly know. We may believe for ourselves, but we have no warrant to compel others to agree with us or to exclude from full civil equality and religious fellowship those who hold opposed beliefs on the same points.

Enthusiasm is the term which Locke, following the usage of the seventeenth century, gave to the too zealous partisanship of sectarian minds. Enthusiasm blinds men to the distinction between what reason enables them to know and what personal preference leads them to believe. And to the danger of enthusiasm Locke added the further danger of being misled by words, of taking abstract terms to stand for real beings, and of supposing real entities to exist where we only have ideas in our minds. At times he went so far as to insist that to assent to any proposition or doctrine which could not be proved was a mark of indifference to truth.

Thus it can be seen that back of Locke's plea for toleration lay two points which received stress in his developed theory of knowledge. One was the conviction that reason is able clearly to prove whatever is important for men to know for the successful pursuit of human affairs in this world and for adequate preparation of the soul for the next world. The other was the conviction that the contentions which divide men into warring sects and parties are both unimportant in themselves and unsusceptible of logical proof. Scepticism on most matters of theological and metaphysical speculation placed limits about the human understanding.

The historical influence of Locke's discussion of toleration and of the bare essentials of religion was to promote increasing scepticism. In the generation after his death his proof of God and his respect for Scripture as evidence of the messiahship of Jesus did not continue to receive the confident assent which he placed in them. And his emphasis on the impossibility of proving other points of doctrine in metaphysics and theology came to dominate the thought of radical groups. Whereas for Locke toleration was part of his program to effect a working compromise in church and state, it became for the next generation a by-product of intellectual confusion and religious indifference. Locke fostered religious doubts and disintegrated metaphysical speculation far beyond his intent and purpose.

III

Locke's contributions to political and educational theory were highly important.

In politics his aim was to show the fundamental principles behind the movement for a constitutional monarchy. He wrote his *Treatises of Government* in order "to establish the throne of our great restorer, our present King William" and "to justify to the world the people of England whose love of their just and natural rights, with their resolution to preserve them, saved the nation when it was on the very brink of slavery and ruin."

The basis of Locke's political philosophy is the theory of the transition from a state of nature to a state of political society by means of a binding social contract. Most of the ideas involved in this theory were current in the seventeenth century, but the form which Locke gave to them was largely original. And it was in their Lockian form that they became a potent political program of action during the following century.

The state of nature was conceived by Locke as the original condition in which men once existed prior to the formation of civil government. This state of nature he so described as to enable him to derive from it the kind of constitutional government he was seeking to defend. In it men were free from all external control; they were able to acquire property rights in the products of their own labors; they were grouped in families with mutual bonds of affection and duty. Above all they were under obligation to obey the moral law. Morality was not first created with the institution of government (in which case the nature of the government would have determined the kind of morals incumbent upon men to accept). Rather men were, merely as men, under obligation from the beginning to respect each other's rights. This pre-political morality was summed up in the phrase the *law of nature*. It is discoverable by reason. It consists in the recognition that each man has certain rights to life, liberty, property, and the pursuit of happiness, and that in exercising his rights he should infringe in no way upon the equal rights of all his fellows. But however much men are subject to the requirements of the law of nature, they often do not in the state of nature so act as to fulfil the dictates of that law. Rather they invade each other's rights, they seek special advantage, they seize property to which they are not entitled, they enslave others for their own selfish whims. The state of nature would be a state of peace, happiness, and goodwill if men were inclined of their own free accord to act in conformity to the law of nature. But unfortunately men are not exclusively under the control of reason: they are only too frequently dominated by greed, envy, laziness, and lust. The love of dominion over others is "the first original of most vicious habits." And thus the state of nature tends to degenerate into a state of war. Locke found the troubled times of his youth and manhood an effective illustration of what the state of war concretely meant.

In order to escape from the dangers of the state of nature, men deliberately form political societies. They "join in society with others who are already united or have a mind to unite, for the mutual preservation of their lives, liberties, and estates." The basis of this political society is the social contract. In the social contract men agree to give up some of their natural rights in order more effectually to secure their remaining rights. The rights they relinquish are the right to take into their own hands the task of defending themselves and their possessions and also the right to dispose freely of themselves and their goods. They agree to turn over to a central authority the maintenance of law and order, and they agree to submit to such direction of their activities and such taxation of their goods as are necessary to preserve and strengthen the established authority. This central and established authority is of course the state. The marks by which its presence is manifested are three: a known body of law as the basis for settling all controversies between members of the state, a known judge of impartial nature, and a recognized power to enforce the law and the decisions of the judge. In the state of political society men theoretically have fewer rights than in the state of nature; for they surrender some natural rights to the governing powers. But practically they find themselves possessed of more effective rights through the security which the government affords them in the exercise of the rights retained for themselves. Thus the state of political society is superior in value to the state of nature. Men lose little and gain much by establishing commonwealths.

The social contract was so formulated by Locke as to sanction only a constitutional government. An arbitrary and despotic rule (such as the tyranny of the Stuarts) would never have been set up by free men in fair covenant. A government has just those powers (and no others) which were surrendered to it under the terms of the social contract. Since men would never voluntarily surrender their rights to life, happiness, a certain freedom of action, and a control over the bulk of their estates, it can be surely known that the government of a commonwealth did not receive power to oppress its citizens on these scores. Tyranny is not a just government nor a legitimate government; it can not claim any moral support from the people. "No government can have a right to obedience from a people who have not freely consented to it." Tyranny is clear indication that a government has gone beyond the terms of the social contract upon which it was founded. Tyranny therefore dissolves the government, and makes of the tyrants one party to a state of war in which the people are free to act energetically in their own defence. "Using force upon the people without authority and contrary to the trust put in him that does so is a state of war with the people. . . . . In all states and conditions the true remedy of force without authority is to oppose force to it." As long as a government conducts affairs according to the terms of the social contract, no people could be morally justified in revolt. But once the government exceeds its due powers, it has acted contrary to the contract and thereby has destroyed itself.

Since no actual document could be pointed to as the social contract on which most European states of Locke's day rested, he made the terms of the social contract to fit what he wanted a government to be. And he could thus easily show how the Stuarts made themselves enemies of the people in a state of war, and he could point to the terms of settlement of William and Mary as the partial re-definition of the original social contract between the English people and their monarch. Particularly he could derive from his theory the right of the people to oppose a tyranny, to conspire freely together as to the best means to secure themselves from further invasion of their rights, to use force as well as passive resistance to gain their legitimate ends, and to set up a new government which would more faithfully carry out the original compact of their political society.

It is important to note that Locke did not use either the term *sovereignty* or the term *right of revolution.* No government for Locke possessed sovereignty in the sense of ultimate power or authority. A government is always limited to the powers delegated to it in the social contract. The community retains always the supreme power, and the government has "only a fiduciary power to act for certain ends." Likewise the people have no right to revolt, but only a right to defend themselves against a usurpation of illegitimate power. Locke was not inclined to give to any people a right to change their government at will; he was no lover of frequent or capricious change of political status. He emphasized the point that in resisting tyranny the people are in no sense rebels against constituted authority; he declared that they are in such a case on the defensive against unwarranted aggression. Locke was aiming, not to encourage revolt, but to discourage tyranny. He was interested to deny to rulers "the divine right to govern wrong." He was eager to point out to rulers that they were limited in their claims to authority, that the only basis of their continued rule was strict observance of the limitations of the social contract, that justice was the sole ground upon which their right to obedience could be maintained. Locke was not a radical, but a seeker of peace through compromise. He aimed, not to foment rebellion, but so to define the foundation of political society that governments would rule in accordance with constitutional provisions. He had of course to justify the particular revolution of 1688 which brought William and Mary to the throne and drove James II into exile. But he sought to render improbable the recurrence of political strife by making the government aware of its dependence upon specific agreements.

Throughout his discussion of political philosophy Locke showed an underlying rationalism. He was never content to point out that a principle was justified by its successful working. He did not set up a utilitarian test of legitimate government. He did of course believe that his political principles would justify themselves in practice. But with a rather legalistic mind prone to appeal to law, he sought to find the basis of political rights and duties in an initial definition of the social contract. The fact that such a contract is, in the cases of most states, purely mythological did not disturb him, indeed it did not occur to him. It was the origin rather than the effects of a government which to him made it a right government. He defined justice by determining the source rather than the consequences of any exercise of power. In order to judge whether a people has a right to take a stand against a particular ruler, he would not examine what desirable or undesirable results would follow; rather he aimed to settle the question by appealing to the letter of the contract which lay behind the relations between a people and its government. Herein again his essential conservatism is evident.

Locke's work entitled *Some Thoughts on Education* is not a systematic treatise on educational theory. It is rather a body of shrewd reflections, designed to give practical guidance to a friend who sought advice on how to educate his son. It is futile to seek to classify Locke's educational ideas under any one of the catch words by which educational theories are to-day distinguished from each other. His discussion of education will be best understood by remembering two points: first, that he had himself been exposed to a particularly useless schooling, and secondly, that he viewed education, not as an ornament for the leisure hours of an idle social class, but as a training to fit men for the place they would occupy in the world. Milton had said in 1644 that the schooling of an English boy was like "an asinine feast of sow-thistles and brambles." Locke felt no less strongly about his own experience. He wished to supplant the routine of reading and writing Latin prose and poetry with a series of studies of things related to current living in England. He wished to introduce boys to the results of the natural sciences which were making such amazing and significant progress in the seventeenth century. He wished to equip them with the social graces which would make them distinguished among their social equals. He would adjust the content of study to the prospects of the students, thus requiring Latin in the case of a gentleman whose status in society would furnish him with opportunities to profit from his knowledge of it, but refusing to waste time on it in the case of a tradesman's son who would never have occasion to utilize his smattering knowledge of the dead language. In other words Locke made a distinction between education and learning. Education is training for competence in the affairs of life; learning is the pursuit of a specialized group of scholars. And while he had the greatest respect for learning and achieved some excellence himself in scholarship, he would not have the needs of all sacrificed to the particular interests of the few. He saw how grievously mere pedantry reigned in the schools of his day and remembered the futility of his own school and college work. And as in his general philosophical work he sought to escape the fixed ideas and intellectual ruts which tradition had preserved from mediaeval times, so in the realm of education he endeavored to turn from what was merely outworn custom to what was vital and pregnant for new times and new modes of life. If Locke occasionally revealed a certain insensitivity to the charms of the fine arts, the critic may well enjoy a smile at his expense. It is amusing to read that a poet is no better than a gambler and idler, and that outward grace of bodily movement is to be valued for the "manly thoughts" which are alleged to accompany such a pleasing exterior. But Locke had withal a wholesome and sensible attitude towards games, diversion, and play as well as towards the acquisition of clarity and accuracy in language, the accumulation of a body of useful information about the world, and the training of the mind in critical powers of logical analysis. Though a bit stolid at times, he was eminently sane. And as elsewhere in his works, the idea of compromise and moderation is obvious in his writings on education. He lends himself to no single principle or dominating end, but seeks a well-integrated general scheme of training of the full man.

Locke emphasized the moral element as well as the intellectual element in a complete and adequate education. The educated man is one of high and noble character. He must have control over his impulses. He must have ready habits. He must be able to deny himself certain minor satisfactions for the sake of more difficult but more valuable ends. He must never be petulant in the face of adversity, but calm, brave, and persistent in effort. He must be sensitive to the esteem of his fellows, yet unwilling to lower his standards for the sake of popularity. Locke had no trust in the unguided exercise of natural impulses. He wanted rather the judicious moulding of impulses into an integrated character under the control of reason.

IV

Locke's most momentous contribution to philosophy is his theory of knowledge. This theory of knowledge is chiefly set forth in the *Essay concerning Human Understanding,* a product of nearly twenty years' reflection and piecemeal writing. In this work Locke sought to avoid the technical terminology of scholastic philosophy and to adopt colloquial language such as men ordinarily use in conversation. He succeeded thereby in putting forth a book which was more widely read than any philosophical work of its generation. But he fell naturally into two faults, first, the frequent use of words of ambiguous meaning which he never exactly defined and did not employ evidently in the same senses throughout, and secondly, the naïve adoption of certain uncriticised assumptions which were implicit in the scientific theories of the seventeenth century.

Since so much of modern philosophy has been influenced by Locke, it is perhaps best to consider his theory of knowledge under four points to which technical terms may be given. These are empiricism, dualism, subjectivism, and scepticism. What these terms mean as applied to Locke and in much later speculation will in turn be shown.

1. Locke approached the problem of the nature, origin, and extent of knowledge, as has already been noted in discussing his life, because of the difficulties of determining truth in matters of morality and revealed religion. He seems to have been deeply impressed with the contrast between the confusion and uncertainty in theology and ethics on the one hand and on the other hand the precision and accuracy in natural science. In the former realm of human interest he found unverified and arrogant claims to ultimate truths; in the latter

realm he found considerable experimental evidence and cautious generalizations. He sought to introduce into theology and ethics, into metaphysics and politics, the same method of obtaining knowledge which was proving so fruitful in the sciences of astronomy, optics, physics, and medicine. Perhaps it should be added that even in the sciences he detected a sharp contrast of methods. For some scientific writers were endeavoring to deduce certain knowledge from alleged first principles and were using vague terms of no clear empirical meaning. Even the great Descartes, though a leader in experimental investigation, also spoke of "clear and distinct ideas" as a test of truth, and seemed to lend his authority to conceivability as a guide to determining matters of objective fact. However, the great scientific advance of the preceding century had come through careful observation by minds freed from preconceptions and fixed ideas. Locke was fairly familiar with the work of the continental scientists from Copernicus to Descartes. He was intimately acquainted with the results of the research of Harvey (who had discovered the circulation of the blood), of Boyle (who had enabled chemistry to throw aside the old assumptions of alchemy and formulated the law of the elasticity of the air), of Newton (whose great *Principia* had appeared several years before the completion of Locke's *Essay*), of Sydenham (who asserted that medical practice should abandon the explanation of diseases by reference to traditional axioms and discover by induction the best practical way to handle specific types of disease). As a member of the Royal Society Locke heard from time to time the results of various experiments of men who were taking the lead in the newer experimental methods.

An illustration of Locke's empiricism is to be found in two letters which he wrote in 1692-3. In the *Essay* he had written that "in the study of nature we must beware of hypotheses and wrong principles." That is, "general maxims" and "precarious principles" should give way to "particular experiments." In the letters referred to, he maintained that a physician might employ hypotheses provided that the hypotheses were subservient to careful observation. One might even safely use inconsistent and contradictory hypotheses with that restriction. If hypotheses are accepted too readily as the real truth about things, they are "but a sort of waking dreams" and lead to a "learned ignorance." If they are used as a working basis for detection of "the sensible effects" of certain methods of treating disease, they may help in the acquisition of "practical knowledge."

Turning to theology and metaphysics Locke found no use of empirical methods. He found rather that argument began with the assertion of first principles based upon an allegedly innate knowledge or upon self-evident insight. He saw that *enthusiasm* for one's own axioms replaced confirmation of tentative ideas by the observed outcome in practice. He recalled how utterly useless, how wholly verbal and unconnected with the content of experience, had been the philosophy of his student days at Oxford; and he denounced such philosophy as "cumbered with the learned but frivolous use of uncouth, affected, or unintelligible terms." The radicals in theology who would sweep away the bulk of Christian faith and the conservatives in theology who would persecute any one who departed from any of the established doctrines of orthodoxy, were, both of them, equally inclined to take their own fixed ideas as necessary principles of reason. Locke realized that most of the theological and metaphysical claims could neither be proved nor disproved by empirical methods. He wished to turn attention from the profitless jargon about hidden essences and unknowable entities to the pressing problems of reorganizing church and state according to principles which practice proved to result in general happiness.

Thus Locke began his famous *Essay* with an attack upon innate ideas and innate principles. His argument here was a necessary preface to his own statement of an empirical theory of knowledge. While Locke did not choose to mention many names of those he was opposing, we can see that he was rejecting all the theological, metaphysical, political, and ethical systems which appealed to necessary truths of reason and indubitable principles of the human mind.

2. Locke's empiricism led naturally, in the intellectual atmosphere of the seventeenth century, to a dualism of a radical sort. If he adopted the good features of the scientific method of his day, he also took over, and with what seems to have been not merely uncritical but also unconscious acceptance, certain assumptions of the scientific point of view of the seventeenth century. For more than a hundred years the notion had been gaining ground that the external world of real bodies was devoid of the sense qualities detected in immediate experience. Matter was extended substance; sometimes it was also believed to be solid, impenetrable, and analyzable into a certain number of ultimate units of stuff (or atoms). But colors, sounds, tastes, and smells were denied any status in the external world. These qualities were banished from the realm of real bodies, and were considered as effects produced by real bodies in the minds of men. Thus the scientific point of view involved a thoroughgoing dualism. On the one hand there were material bodies, and on the other hand there were knowing minds. The qualities of bodies were not identical with the way bodies appeared to the knowing minds. Nature and mind were two disparate kinds of being.

Now undoubtedly science was advancing rapidly in the use of this point of view. Nature as denuded of sense qualities lent itself to mathematical treatment and could be described in terms of accurate and universal laws. As an hypothesis for the further accumulation of knowledge and for the gaining of control, the point of view was most successful. As an interpretation of the ultimate reality of things it had never been adequately investigated. And it did not receive such investigation from Locke. What Locke did was to develop more fully than any others before him the view of mind which was here involved. Scientists and philosophers of the century before Locke had been concerned with external nature rather than with mind; they were content simply to have the realm of mind as a place in which to deposit whatever qualities they found no place for in the external world. Locke turned the attention of thinkers to the status of mind in this commonly accepted world theory. He asked how mind, so defined and so related to external objects, might gain knowledge of itself, of God, and of nature. That is, he began to make clear the latent implications of the current dualism for a theory of knowledge.

As long as the dualistic assumptions of this scientific method were used in the physical sciences, the theoretical difficulties which lurked in the point of view did not become manifest. Colors, sounds, tastes, and other sense qualities were granted to be effects of the ultimate material particles of which material bodies are composed, indeed to be correlated with the bulk, shape, contexture, and motion of these particles. Other thinkers had been anxious to deny the objective nature of these sense qualities. Locke made emphatic that these sense qualities were the original starting point of the mind in its efforts to gain knowledge. Though the sense qualities are merely effects in our minds of objects which have no such qualities, none the less they and they alone provide us with indications of the objects which cause them. Locke did not doubt that the sense qualities enable us successfully to adjust ourselves in practice to external things; but he began to doubt how much they enable us to know of the real nature of things.

Locke adopted the customary terminology of primary and secondary qualities. Primary qualities are those which bodies always have and are perceived by sense as they really exist in bodies, e. g. solidity, extension, figure, position, and motion. Secondary qualities are those which produce in us the colors, sounds, tastes, and smells, but which are in the bodies nothing but such an arrangement of its primary qualities as to produce such effects in us. These secondary qualities, even if not directly open to inspection and known to us only through effects unlike them, are supposedly powers in the bodies which science can discuss intelligently and utilize effectively. We may not know how the secondary qualities of bodies come to produce in us the colors, sounds, etc.; but ignorance on this point does not detract from "the certainty of the senses." Locke was prone to send men to their senses for information about the external world. Concerning the reality of these material bodies he said: "The greatest assurance I can possibly have, and to which my faculties can attain, is the testimony of my eyes, which are the proper and sole judges of this thing." That is, even though the secondary qualities are known only through their effects in us, we are primarily concerned with bodies in so far as they affect us. And so whatever difficulty there may be in the way of knowing the nature of things as they are apart from all relation to the human mind, at least we can from observation gain that kind and degree of knowledge of things with which as men we are primarily concerned. More abstract speculations we may well leave aside while we go about our main business of caring for our affairs, securing the comforts of life, gaining prosperity, and living in decent relations with our fellowmen.

And yet, however successful in the physical sciences and useful in social practice the dualistic assumptions of seventeenth century thought might be, the difficulties emerged more and more as attention was turned to the status of the mind. As Locke said at the outset of the *Essay,* all the immediate objects of the mind in thinking are ideas. We start, he explained, with the simple ideas which the senses give to us or which reflection on the operations of our minds presents. In other words, all the materials of knowledge are the ideas within our own minds, and can be traced back to the simple ideas with which sensation and reflection equip us. By compounding, abstracting, and comparing these initial ideas, we obtain further complex ideas. And knowledge, which is the perception of the agreement or disagreement of our ideas, can to an attentive mind penetrate as far as it has ideas. But by no such means can we ever hope to go beyond ideas to a direct contact with things. Whatever lies beyond our ideas can thus never be known.

3. Dualism thus led on to subjectivism. Originally the dualistic methodology of the natural sciences was a technique for ridding the external world of qualities with which the scientists did not wish to deal. But this methodology, turned into a general theory of knowledge, became increasingly aware of the way in which the mind was confined to its own ideas, to its own mental realm.

Locke was only too glad to point out the consequences of the method as applied to theology. The terms men used in discussing the trinity, the atonement, inspiration, justification, eternal punishment, and the like, stand, not for real beings, but for ideas in men's minds. Moreover they are very far removed from the simple ideas with which reasoning must begin, and are consequently highly abstract. Their objects, if there be such, lie beyond experience. The terms can be defined; but we can not tell, by contemplating the ideas, which of them are true and which are false. The ideas are a kind of screen between the mind and real objects; they tend rather to conceal than to disclose the objects beyond. Whereas in the natural sciences the ideas seem to be direct and adequate symbols for the realities which produce them, in theological speculations no such situation prevails. Locke found this subjectivism an aid in his warfare against dogmatism in theology and barren verbalisms in metaphysics. And he drove home forcefully the point that in such speculations men are arguing about their own ideas and are not coming in contact with reality at all.

But Locke was thoroughly honest in his theory of knowledge. And after he had once drawn out the theological consequences of his general theory, he applied the theory to all fields of human reflection. And he continually found that the ideas, instead of being tools for the knowledge of objects, tend to become an obstacle in the way of obtaining knowledge. In practical affairs the ideas may be means or instruments for effective control; but in theoretical affairs, they block the way to sure conclusions. He arrived at a serious predicament when he was driven to open the fourth book of the *Essay* with the words: "Since the mind, in all its thoughts and reasonings, hath no other immediate object but its own ideas, which it alone does or can contemplate, it is evident that our knowledge is only conversant about them." He adopted from Descartes's system of philosophy two points according to which knowledge of real objects is possible; first, we know directly or intuitively our own existence, and secondly, we know by necessary demonstration the existence of God. But all other objects are unknowable in their real natures. We can not seriously doubt of the real existence of external objects; for the ideas are obviously imprinted on our minds by external things. But we can only speculate by tentative and uncertain hypotheses about the nature of these objects. "We are so far from being admitted into the secrets of nature, that we scarce so much as ever approach the first entrance towards them."

4. The outcome was a genuine scepticism, at least in matters of ontological theory. We may know enough to get along well in the world and to save our souls; but we do not know the essence of a single object about us. Locke was so habituated to the prevailing scientific conception of matter as solid, extended, impenetrable stuff of atomic structure, that he did not find it possible entirely to relinquish that hypothetical notion. And he frequently wrote from the standpoint of such a scientific realism. But none the less he fully recognized the fact that from the standpoint of one who was confined to his own ideas no proof of the reality of matter was possible.

Locke's scepticism was further promoted through his acceptance of the mathematical ideal of knowledge which prevailed in the seventeenth century. We have what we can justly call knowledge when, and only when, we have complete certainty. Knowledge is to be distinguished from judgment on the basis of probability. And of the things which constitute the order of nature we can make no certain affirmations beyond the ideas present to the mind at the moment of judging, no certain affirmations at all of a universal character. "In the greatest part of our concernments, he [God] has afforded us only the twilight, as I may so say, of probability, suitable, I presume, to that state of mediocrity and probationship he has been pleased to place us in here." The relations we observe between our ideas do not give us the real essence of things. "After all, if we would have, and actually had, in our complex idea, an exact collection of all the secondary qualities or powers of any substance, we should not yet thereby have an idea of the *essence* of that thing." What we ordinarily call the essence of a thing is its *nominal* essence, not its *real* essence. That is, it is the appearance of the thing to us, not its own hidden nature, that we commonly call its essence.

The scepticism to which Locke was thus driven led him finally to conclude that no genuine science of nature is possible for us. "We are so far from being able to comprehend the whole nature of the universe, and all the things contained in it, that we are not capable of a philosophical knowledge of the bodies that are about us, and make a part of us. . . . As to a *perfect science* of natural bodies, (not to mention spiritual beings), we are, I think, so far from being capable of any such thing, that I conclude it lost labour to seek after it." Since natural science could not achieve the certainty which attaches to mathematics, it is not properly to be called knowledge. The ideal of human knowledge is too high to permit of realization in the investigation of nature as in the mysteries of theology.

Through all his scepticism Locke retained the seventeenth-century faith in the rational nature of the world. He believed there was an objective logical necessity in the processes of the world, even if we could not discover this necessity. "If we could discover the figure, size, texture, and motion of the minute constituent parts of any two bodies, we should know without trial several of their operations one upon another, as we do now the properties of a square or a triangle." The important phrase in this sentence is *without trial.* Nature is a machine, each part of which is related to each other part by a necessary and rational bond. All events "have a constant and regular connection in the ordinary course of things." Failure to obtain a science of nature is the fault, not of nature and its logical operations, but of the mind and its lack of access to real objects. We are not equipped with senses acute enough to detect the minute particles of which all objects are composed; and hence we must forever remain ignorant of "their mechanical affections" and "their properties and ways of operations."

The position which Locke thus held is an interesting point in the development of modern thought about the significance of science. Descartes had maintained both that the order of nature is a machine in which each element necessarily implies each other element, and also that the human mind was equipped to know what this order of nature is. Locke retained the first of these suppositions and rejected the second. Hume later rejected both of the Cartesian suppositions. Thus Locke held to the rationalistic ideal, but recognized the empirical basis of our actual human procedure. Rationalist he still was in large part. Reason it is that operates on the materials furnished by experience in order to produce knowledge; and without the exercise of reason no accumulation of the materials of experience can ever give us a scrap of knowledge. But reason is not competent to explore the universe; it can only look at the ideas within the mind. Reason is still ambitious; but it no longer possesses its original birthright of unlimited access to the full being of God, man, and nature. Reason has had its wings clipped. If it goes beyond the materials of experience it becomes fancy, it but indulges in vain hopes, it mistakes its own bias for information about things. Reason is narrowly limited to what sensation and reflection provide in the way of simple ideas. And though it may make out of these materials many further ideas of interest and significance, it can never hope to know how much its work mirrors the necessities which lie beyond its range of vision. Locke was in an uncomfortable position. He could not go back to a theological sanction for scientific procedure (such as Descartes used), to innate ideas, to unchecked deduction from first principles guaranteed by a supernatural authority. Neither had he thought through the nature of the empirical method he tried to formulate, so as to point clearly to the new inductive procedure which later centuries were to employ. But in terms of the current outlook of the age he built up a theory of knowledge which made evident the difficulties in the dualism of mind and material nature. Thereby he set many a problem for later philosophies to solve.

STERLING P. LAMPRECHT

LIST OF LOCKE'S PUBLISHED WORKS

Epistola de Tolerantia, 1689. Translated into English, 1689. Further defences of toleration appeared in 1690, 1692, 1706.

Two Treatises of Government, 1690.

An Essay concerning Human Understanding, 1690. 2nd ed., 1694; 3rd ed., 1695; 4th ed., 1700. The fourth edition contained many and important changes, and was the last revision Locke made of his chief work.

Some Considerations of the Consequences of the Lowering of Interest and Raising the Value of Money, 1691. A defence of this work appeared in 1695.

Some Thoughts concerning Education, 1695.

The Reasonableness of Christianity, 1695. Two defences of this work appeared in 1695 and 1697.

Three Letters to the Lord Bishop of Worcester concerning some passages in the Essay concerning Human Understanding, 1697, 1697, 1699.

A Paraphrase and Notes on the Epistles of St. Paul, 1705.

On the Conduct of the Understanding, 1706.

A Discourse on Miracles, 1706.

An Examination of P. Malebranche's Opinion of Seeing All Things in God, 1706.

Remarks upon some of Mr. Norris's Books, wherein he asserts P. Malebranche's Opinion of Seeing All Things in God, 1720.

Elements of Natural Philosophy, 1720.

Some Familiar Letters between Mr. Locke and several of his friends, 1706.

Letters to Anthony Collins, Samuel Bold, and others, 1720.

Original Letters of Locke, Algernon Sidney, and Anthony Lord Shaftesbury, 1830.

Lettres inédites de Locke à ses amis, 1913.

The Life of John Locke, with Extracts from his Correspondence, Journals, and Common-place Books. Edited by Lord King, 1829.

TABLE INDICATING THE SOURCE OF THE SELECTIONS PRINTED IN THIS VOLUME

Some Thoughts concerning Education. Sections 1, 32, 33, 38, 39, 47–51, 56, 57, 61, 67, 164–166, 174, 188–190, 192–194, 217.

The Dangers of Enthusiasm. From *Essay concerning Human Understanding,* Book IV, chapter 19, sections 1, 7–11.

Why Men Reason so Poorly. From *Conduct of the Understanding,* section 3.

Language and Its Proper Use. From *Essay concerning Human Understanding,* Book III, chapter 1, sections 1–3; chapter 2, sections 1–2, 7–8; chapter 3, sections 1–4, 6, 9, 11; chapter 10, sections 1–6, 9–10, 12, 14; chapter 11, sections 8–9, 11.

The Spirit of Toleration. From *Works* (11th edition, 1812), Vol. VI, pp. 4, 9–10, 13, 16–18, 20–21, 39–41, 43, 45–47, 49–50.

Liberalism in Religion. From *Works,* Vol. VII, pp. 135–140, 110–113, 105, 101–102, 156–158, 229–231.

Liberalism in Politics. From *Treatise of Civil Government,* sections 3, 4, 6, 7, 13, 25, 27, 28, 32, 36, 46–48, 50, 77, 87, 95–99, 123–127, 171, 202–204, 223–226, 229–230.

Locke's Theory of Knowledge as set forth in *Essay concerning Human Understanding:*

The Epistle to the Reader.

The general design and plan of the Essay. Introduction, sections 1–8.

Rejection of innate ideas and principles. Book I, chapter 1, sections 1–5, 15, 18; chapter 2, sections 1–4, 13; chapter 3, sections 8–11.

Origin of our ideas in experience. Book II, chapter 1, sections 1–5, 20, 22, 24–25.

A classification of our ideas. Book II, chapter 2, sections 1–3.

Simple ideas. Book II, chapter 3, sections 1–2; chapter 4, sections 1–3, 5–6; chapter 5, section 1; chapter 6, chapter 7, sections 1–3, 7–8, 10; chapter 9, sections 1–3, 11, 15; chapter 10, sections 1–3, 7–8; chapter 11, sections 1–2, 4–6, 8–9, 15–17.

Complex ideas. Book II, chapter 12, sections 1–8.

Simple modes. Book II, chapter 13, sections 1–5, 7, 11–14; chapter 14, sections 1, 3–4, 6, 17–19, 24, 27, 31; chapter 16, sections 1–4; chapter 17, sections 1–5, 7–8, 13; chapter 19, sections 1–2; chapter 20, sections 1, 4–13, 18; chapter 21, sections 1–2, 4–8, 11, 14, 17, 19–24, 73, 75.
Mixed modes. Book II, chapter 22, sections 1–4, 9–10.
Ideas of substances. Book II, chapter 23, sections 1–12, 15, 17–18, 29, 37.
Ideas of relations. Book II, chapter 25, sections 1, 4–5, 8, 11; chapter 26, section 1; chapter 27, sections 1–7, 9–10, 17, 25; chapter 28, sections 4, 7–10.
The relation of our ideas to the qualities of objects. Book II, chapter 8, sections 7–10, 15, 17, 19–20, 22–23, 26.
Relative value of our different ideas. Book II, chapter 29, sections 1–3; chapter 30, sections 1–2, 4–5; chapter 31, sections 1–3, 6, 13; chapter 32, sections 1, 4, 14, 17–18.
Danger of the association of ideas. Book II, chapter 33, sections 5–6, 9, 17–18.
The nature of knowledge. Book IV, chapter 1, sections 1–7.
The degrees of knowledge. Book IV, chapter 2, sections 1–4, 7, 14.
The extent of knowledge. Book IV, chapter 3, sections 1–14, 18, 20–28, 30.
The reality of knowledge. Book IV, chapter 4, sections 1–8, 11–12.
Knowledge of our own existence. Book IV, chapter 9, sections 2–3.
Knowledge of the existence of God. Book IV, chapter 10, sections 1–11, 13–16, 18–19.
Knowledge of the existence of other things. Book IV, chapter 11, sections 1–9, 11.
Knowledge of the nature or essence of the substances about us. Book III, chapter 3, sections 15–18; chapter 5, sections 3–6; chapter 9, sections 9, 11; chapter 6, sections 2, 6, 9–13, 20, 28; Book IV, chapter 6, sections 10–11; chapter 12, sections 9–12, 14.
Judgment and probability. Book IV, chapter 14; chapter 15, sections 1–4; chapter 16, sections 5–9, 12–13.
Reasoning. Book IV, chapter 17, sections 2, 4, 6.
Relation of faith and reason. Book IV, chapter 16, section 14; chapter 18, sections 1–2; chapter 17, section 24; chapter 18, sections 3–5, 7–8, 10.

Locke's Letters and Controversial Writings:
The nature of ideas. *Works,* Vol. X, pp. 248, 256.
The faculty of reason. *Works,* Vol. IV, pp. 65, 11–12, 134–135, 160.
The relation of reason and ideas in obtaining knowledge. *Works,* Vol. IV, pp. 130, 58–60, 70–72, 57, 54, 233.

The idea of substance. *Works,* Vol. IV, pp. 7–9, 448.
The idea of causation. *Works,* Vol. IV, pp. 61–62.
The association of ideas. *Conduct of the Understanding,* section 41.
Whether matter can think. *Works,* Vol. IV, pp. 460–461, 463–465.
The objectivity of knowledge. *Works,* Vol. IX, pp. 250–251.
The reality of knowledge. *Works,* Vol. IV, pp. 405–406.
Proof for the existence of God. *Works,* Vol. IV, pp. 62–63.
Criticism of theological speculation. *Works,* Vol. IV, pp. 68, 197, 466–467.
Nominal essence. *Works,* Vol. IX, pp. 305–306.
Contrast between nominal and real essence. *Works,* Vol. IV, pp. 87–88, 77–78, 7, 81–82.
An instance of empiricism. *Works,* Vol. IX, pp. 464–465.

CONTENTS

LOCKE'S GENERAL PHILOSOPHICAL POSITION

LOCKE'S GENERAL PHILOSOPHICAL POSITION

SOME THOUGHTS CONCERNING EDUCATION

A SOUND mind in a sound body is a short but full description of a happy state in this world. He that has these two has little more to wish for; and he that wants either of them will be but little the better for anything else. Men's happiness or misery is most part of their own making. He whose mind directs not wisely will never take the right way; and he whose body is crazy and feeble will never be able to advance in it. I confess there are some men's constitutions of body and mind so vigorous and well framed by nature that they need not much assistance from others; but by the strength of their natural genius they are from their cradles carried towards what is excellent, and by the privilege of their happy constitutions are able to do wonders. But examples of this kind are but few; and I think I may say, that of all the men we meet with, nine parts of ten are what they are, good or evil, useful or not, by their education. It is that which makes the great difference in mankind. The little, or almost insensible impressions on our tender infancies, have very important and lasting consequences. And there it is, as in the fountains of some rivers, where a gentle application of the hand turns the flexible waters in channels that make them take quite contrary courses; and by this direction given them at first in the source, they receive different tendencies and arrive at last at very remote and distant places.

If what I have said be true, as I do not doubt but

it is, *viz.* that the difference to be found in the manners and abilities of men is owing more to their education than to anything else, we have reason to conclude that great care is to be had of the forming children's minds, and giving them that seasoning early which shall influence their lives always after. For when they do well or ill, the praise and blame will be laid there; and when anything is done awkwardly, the common saying will pass upon them that it is suitable to their breeding.

As the strength of the body lies chiefly in being able to endure hardships, so also does that of the mind. And the great principle and foundation of all virtue and worth is placed in this: that a man is able to deny himself his own desires, cross his own inclinations, and purely follow what reason directs as best, though appetite lean the other way. This power is to be got and improved by custom, made easy and familiar by an early practice. If therefore I might be heard, I would advise that, contrary to the ordinary way, children should be used to submit their desires and go without their longings, even from their very cradles. The first thing they should learn to know should be, that they were not to have anything because it pleased them, but because it was thought fit for them. If things suitable to their wants were supplied to them, so that they were never suffered to have what they once cried for, they would learn to be content without it, would never with bawling and peevishness contend for mastery, nor be half so uneasy to themselves and others as they are, because from the first beginning they are not thus handled. If they were never suffered to obtain their desire by the impatience they expressed for it, they would no more cry for another thing than they do for the moon.

I say not this, as if children were not to be indulged in anything, or that I expected they should in hanging-sleeves have the reason and conduct of counsellors. I consider them as children, who must be tenderly used, who must play, and have playthings. That which I mean is that whenever they craved what was not fit for them to have or do, they should not be permitted it because they were little and desired it: nay, whatever they were importunate for, they should be sure, for that very reason, to be denied.

The usual lazy and short way by chastisement and the rod, which is the only instrument of government that tutors generally know, or ever think of, is the most unfit of any to be used in education, because it tends to both these mischiefs. First, this kind of punishment contributes not at all to the mastery of our natural propensity to indulge corporal and present pleasure, and to avoid pain at any rate, but rather encourages it, and thereby strengthens that in us which is the root from whence spring all vicious actions and the irregularities of life. Secondly, this sort of correction naturally breeds an aversion to that which it is the tutor's business to create a liking to. How obvious is it to observe that children come to hate things which were at first acceptable to them, when they find themselves whipped and chid and teased about them. This is natural to be so. Offensive circumstances ordinarily infect innocent things which they are joined with; and the very sight of a cup wherein any one uses to take nauseous physic turns his stomach, so that nothing will relish well out of it, though the cup be never so clean and well-shaped and of the richest materials. Thirdly, such a sort of slavish discipline makes a slavish temper. The child submits, and dissembles obedience, whilst the fear of the rod hangs over him. But when that is removed, and by being out of sight, he can promise himself impunity, he gives the greater scope to his natural inclination; which by this way is not at all altered, but on the contrary heightened and increased in him; and after such restraint breaks out usually with the more violence. Or, fourthly, if severity carried to the highest pitch does prevail and works a cure upon the present unruly distemper, it often brings in the room of it a worse and more dangerous disease, by breaking the mind; and then in the place of a disorderly young fellow, you have a low-spirited moped creature, who, however with his unnatural sobriety he may please silly people who commend tame and inactive children because they make no noise nor give them any trouble, yet at last will probably prove as uncomfortable a thing to his friends as he will be all his life an useless thing to himself and others.

The rewards and punishments then, whereby we should keep children in order, are quite of another kind, and of that force, that when we can get them once to work, the business, I think, is done and the difficulty is over. Esteem and disgrace are, of all others, the most powerful incentives to the mind, when once it is brought to relish them. If you can once get into children a love of credit and an apprehension of shame and disgrace, you have put into them the true principle, which will constantly work and incline them to the right. Children (earlier perhaps than we think) are very sensible of praise and commendation. They find a pleasure in being esteemed and valued, especially by their parents and those whom they depend on. If therefore the father caress and commend them when they do well, shew a cold and neglectful countenance to them upon doing ill, and this accompanied by a like carriage of the mother and all others that are about them, it will, in a little time, make them sensible of the difference; and this, if constantly observed, I doubt not but will of itself work more than threats and blows, which lose their force when once grown common, and are of no use when shame does not attend them.

Concerning reputation, I shall only remark this one thing more of it, that though it be not the true principle and measure of virtue, (for that is the knowledge of a man's duty, and the satisfaction it is to obey his maker, in following the dictates of that light God has given him, with the hopes of acceptation and reward) yet it is that which comes nearest to it. And being the testimony and applause that other people's reason, as it were by a common consent, gives to virtuous and well-ordered actions, it is the proper guide and encouragement of children, until they grow able to judge for themselves and to find what is right by their own reason.

Manners, as they are called, about which children are so often perplexed and have so many goodly exhortations made them by their wise maids and governesses, I think, are rather to be learnt by example than rules. And then children, if kept out of ill company, will take a pride to behave themselves prettily, after the fashion of others, perceiving themselves esteemed and commended for it. But if by a little negligence in this part, the boy should not pull off his hat nor make legs very gracefully, a dancing-master will cure that defect and wipe off all that plainness of nature, which the *a-la-mode* people call clownishness. And since nothing appears to me to give children so much becoming confidence and behaviour, and so to raise them to the conversation of those above their age, as dancing, I think they should be taught to dance as soon as they are capable of learning it. For though this consist only in outward gracefulness of motion, yet, I know not how, it gives children manly thoughts and carriage, more than anything. But otherwise, I would not have children much tormented about punctilios or niceties of breeding.

Latin I look upon as absolutely necessary to a gentleman; and indeed custom, which prevails over everything, has made it so much a part of education, that even those children are whipped to it and made spend many hours of their precious time uneasily in Latin, who, after they are once gone from school, are never to have more to do with it as long as they live. Can there be anything more ridiculous than that a father should waste his own money and his son's time in setting him to learn the Roman language, when at the same time he designs him for a trade, wherein he having no use of Latin fails not to forget that little which he brought from school, and which it is ten to one he abhors for the ill usage it procured him?

But how necessary soever Latin be to some, and is thought to be to others to whom it is of no account of use and service, yet the ordinary way of learning it in a grammar-school is that which having had thoughts about I cannot be forward to encourage. If a man could be got, who himself speaking good Latin would always be about your son, talk constantly to him, and suffer him to speak or read nothing else, this would be the true and genuine way, and that which I would propose, not only as the easiest and best, wherein a child might, without pains or chiding, get a language which others are wont to be whipt for at school six or seven years together, but also as that wherein at the same time he might have his mind and manners formed, and he be instructed to boot in several sciences, such as are a good part of geography, astronomy, chronology, anatomy, besides some parts of history, and all other parts of knowledge of things that fall under the senses and require little more than memory. For there, if we would take the true way, our knowledge should begin, and in those things be laid the foundation; and not in the abstract notions of logic and metaphysics, which are fitter to amuse than inform the understanding in its first setting out towards knowledge.

If these may be any reasons against children's making Latin themes at school, I have much more to say, and of more weight, against their making verses, verses of any sort. For if he has no genius to poetry, it is the most unreasonable thing in the world to torment a child and waste his time about that which can never succeed; and if he have a poetic vein, it is to me the strangest thing in the world that the father should desire or suffer it to be cherished or improved. Methinks the parents should labour to have it stifled and suppressed as much as may be; and I know not what reason a father can have to wish his son a poet, who does not desire to have him bid defiance to all other callings and business; which is not yet the worst of the case; for if he proves a successful rhymer and gets once the reputation of a wit, I desire it may be considered what company and places he is like to spend his time in, nay, and estate too. For it is very seldom seen that any one discovers mines of gold or silver in Parnassus. It is a pleasant air, but a barren soil; and there are very few instances of those who have added to their patrimony by any thing they have reaped from thence. Poetry and gaming which usually go together are alike in this too, that they seldom bring any advantage but to those who have nothing else to live on. Men of estates almost constantly go away losers; and it is well if they escape at a cheaper rate than their whole estates or the greatest part of them. If therefore you would not have your son the fiddle to every jovial company, without whom the sparks could not relish their wine nor know how to pass an afternoon idly; if you would not have him to waste his time and estate to divert others, and contemn the dirty acres left him by his ancestors, I do not think you will much care he should be a poet, or that his schoolmaster should enter him in versifying.

Rhetoric and logic being the arts that in the ordinary method usually follow immediately after grammar, it may perhaps be wondered that I have said so little of them. The reason is, because of the little advantage young people receive by them; for I have seldom or never observed any one to get the skill of reasoning well or speaking handsomely by studying those rules which pretend to teach it. And therefore I would have a young gentleman take a view of them in the shortest systems could be found, without dwelling long on the contemplation and study of those formalities. Right reasoning is founded on something else than the predicaments and predicables, and does not consist in talking in mode and figure itself.

If the use and end of right reasoning be to have right notions, and a right judgment of things, to distinguish betwixt truth and falsehood, right and wrong, and to act accordingly; be sure not to let your son be bred up in the art and formality of disputing, either practicing it himself or admiring it in others; unless, instead of an able man, you desire to have him an insignificant wrangler, opiniator in discourse, and priding himself in contradicting others; or, which is worse, questioning everything, and thinking there is no such thing as truth to be sought, but only victory in disputing. There gentleman, or any one who pretends to be a rational cannot be anything so disingenuous, so misbecoming a creature, as not to yield to plain reason and the conviction of clear arguments. Truth is to be found and supported by a mature and due consideration of things themselves, and not by artificial terms and ways of arguing. These lead not men so much into the discovery of truth as into a captious and fallacious use of doubtful words, which is the most useless and most offensive way of talking, and such as least suits a gentleman or a lover of truth as anything in the world.

Natural philosophy, as a speculative science, I imagine we have none; and perhaps I may think I have reason to say, we never shall be able to make a science of it. The works of nature are contrived by a wisdom and operate by ways too far surpassing our faculties to discover or capacities to conceive, for us ever to be able to reduce them into a science. Natural philosophy being the knowledge of the principles, properties, and operations of things as they are in themselves, I imagine there are two parts of it, one comprehending spirits with their nature and qualities, and the other bodies. The first of these is usually referred to metaphysics. But under what title soever the consideration of spirits comes, I think it ought to go before the study of matter and body, not as a science that can be methodized into a system, and treated of upon principles of knowledge, but as an enlargement of our minds towards a truer and fuller comprehension of the intellectual world, to which we are led both by reason and revelation. And since the clearest and largest discoveries we have of other spirits, besides God and our own souls,[1] is imparted to us from heaven by revelation, I think the information that at

[1] Locke thought that through reason men could reach a certain knowledge of the existence of God and their own souls: cf. p. 258. But for a knowledge of "other spirits" he depended wholly on revelation: cf. pp. 295, 315.

least young people should have of them should be taken from that revelation. To this purpose, I conclude, it would be well if there were a good history of the Bible for young people to read; wherein if everything that is fit to be put into it were laid down in its due order of time, and several things omitted which are suited only to riper age, that confusion which is usually produced by promiscuous reading of the Scripture, as it lies now bound up in our Bibles, would be avoided. And also this other good obtained, that by reading of it constantly there would be instilled into the minds of children a notion and belief of spirits, they having so much to do in all the transactions of that history, which will be a good preparation to the study of bodies. For without the notion and allowance of spirit, our philosophy will be lame and defective in one main part of it, when it leaves out the contemplation of the most excellent and powerful part of the creation.

The reason why I would have this premised to the study of bodies, and the doctrine of the Scriptures well imbibed before young men be entered in natural philosophy, is, because matter being a thing that all our senses are constantly conversant with, it is so apt to possess the mind and exclude all other beings but matter, that prejudice, grounded on such principles, often leaves no room for the admittance of spirits, or the allowing any such things as immaterial beings *in rerum natura;* when yet it is evident, that by mere matter and motion, none of the great phenomena of nature can be resolved; to instance but in that common one of gravity, which I think impossible to be explained by any natural operation of matter or any other law of motion, but the positive will of a superior Being so ordering it.

But to return to the study of natural philosophy, though the world be full of systems of it, yet I cannot say I know any one which can be taught a young man as a science, wherein he may be sure to find truth and certainty, which is what all sciences give an expectation of. I do not hence conclude that none of them are to be read. It is necessary for a gentleman in this learned age to look into some of them, to fit himself for conversation. But whether that of Descartes be put into his hands as that which is most in fashion, or it be thought fit to give him a short view of that and several others also, I think the systems of natural philosophy that have obtained in this part of the world are to be read more to know the hypotheses and to understand the terms and ways of talking of the several sects, than with hopes to gain thereby a comprehensive, scientifical, and satisfactory knowledge of the works of nature. Only this may be said, that the modern corpuscularians talk in most things more intelligibly than the peripatetics who possessed the schools immediately before them. But I would not deter any one from the study of nature because all the knowledge we have or possibly can have of it cannot be brought into a science. There are very many things in it that are convenient and necessary to be known by a gentleman; and a great many other that will abundantly reward the pains of the curious with delight and advantage. But these, I think, are rather to be found amongst such writers as have employed themselves in making rational experiments and observations than in starting barely speculative systems. Such writings therefore, as many of Mr. Boyle's are, with others that have writ of husbandry, planting, gardening, and the like, may be fit for a gentleman, when he has a little acquainted himself with some of the systems of the natural philosophy in fashion.

Though the systems of physics that I have met with afford little encouragement to look for certainty or science in any treatise which shall pretend to give us a body of natural philosophy from the first principles of bodies in general, yet the incomparable Mr. Newton has shown how far mathematics applied to some parts of nature may, upon principles that matter of fact justify, carry us in the knowledge of some, as I may so call them, particular provinces of the incomprehensible universe. And if others could give us so good and clear an account of other parts of nature as he has of this our planetary world and the most considerable phenomena observable in it, in his admirable book *Philosophiae Naturalis Principia Mathematica,* we might in time hope to be furnished with more true and certain knowledge in several parts of this stupendous machine than hitherto we could have expected. And though there are very few that have mathematics enough to understand his demonstrations, yet the most accurate mathematicians who have examined them allowing them to be such, his book will deserve to be read, and give no small light and pleasure to those, who, willing to understand the motions, properties, and operations of the great masses of matter in this our solar system, will but carefully mind his conclusions, which may be depended on as propositions well proved.

Though I am now come to a conclusion of what obvious remarks have suggested to me concerning education, I would not have it thought that I look on it as a just treatise on this subject. There are a thousand other things that may need consideration, especially if one should take in the various tempers, different inclinations, and particular defaults that are to be found in children, and prescribe the remedies. The variety is so great that it would require a volume; nor would that reach it. Each man's mind has some peculiarity, as well as his face, that distinguishes him from all others; and there are possibly scarce two children who can be conducted by exactly the same method. Besides that, I think a prince, a nobleman, and an ordinary gentleman's son should have different ways of breeding. But having had here only some general views in reference to the main end and aims in education, and those designed for a gentleman's son, whom, being then very little, I considered only as white paper or wax, to be moulded and fashioned as one pleases, I have touched little more than those heads which I judged necessary for the breeding of a young gentleman of his condition in general; and have now published these my occasional thoughts with this hope, that though this be far from being a complete treatise on this subject, or such as that every one may find what will just fit his child in it, yet it may give some small light to those whose concern for their dear little ones makes them so irregularly bold, that they dare venture to consult their own reason in the education of their children, rather than wholly to rely upon old custom.

THE DANGERS OF ENTHUSIASM

He that would seriously set upon the search of truth, ought in the first place to prepare his mind with a love of it. For he that loves it not, will not take much pains to get it, nor be much concerned when he misses it. There is nobody in the commonwealth of learning, who does not profess himself a lover of truth; and there is not a rational creature that would not take it amiss to be thought otherwise of. And yet for all this, one may truly say, that there are very few lovers of truth for truth-sake, even amongst those who persuade themselves that they are so. How a man may know whether he be so in earnest, is worth inquiry: and I think there is one unerring mark of it, *viz.* the not entertaining any proposition with greater assurance, than the proofs it is built upon will warrant. Whoever goes beyond this measure of assent, it is plain, receives not truth in the love of it; loves not truth for truth-sake, but for some other by-end. Whatsoever credit or authority we give to any proposition, more than it receives from the principles and proofs it supports itself upon, is owing to our inclinations that way, and is so far a derogation from the love of truth as such: which, as it can receive no evidence from our passions or interests, so it should receive no tincture from them.

Reason is natural revelation, whereby the eternal father of light, and fountain of all knowledge, communicates to mankind that portion of truth which he has laid within the reach of their natural faculties: revelation is natural reason enlarged by a new set of discoveries communicated by God immediately, which reason vouches the truth of, by the testimony and proofs it gives, that they come from God. So that he that takes away reason, to make way for revelation, puts out the light of both, and does much-what the same, as if he would persuade a man to put out his eyes, the better to receive the remote light of an invisible star by a telescope.

Enthusiasm, though founded neither on reason nor divine revelation, but rising from the conceits of a warmed or over-weening brain, works yet, where it once gets footing, more powerfully on the persuasions and actions of men, than either of those two, or both together: men being most forwardly obedient to the impulses they receive from themselves; and the whole man is sure to act more vigorously, where the whole man is carried by a natural motion. For strong conceit, like a new principle, carries all easily with it, when got above common sense, and freed from all restraint of reason, and check of reflection, it is heightened into a divine authority, in concurrence with our own temper and inclination.

Though the odd opinions and extravagant actions enthusiasm has run men into, were enough to warn them against this wrong principle, so apt to misguide them both in their belief and conduct; yet the love of something extraordinary, the ease and glory it is to be inspired, and be above the common and natural ways of knowledge, so flatters many men's laziness, ignorance, and vanity, that when once they are got into this way of immediate revelation, of illumination without search, and of certainty without proof, and without examination; it is a hard matter to get them out of it. Reason is lost upon them, they are above it: they see the light infused into their understandings, and cannot be mistaken; it is clear and visible there, like the light of bright sunshine; shows itself, and needs no other proof but its own evidence: they feel the hand of God moving them within, and the impulses of the spirit, and cannot be mistaken in what they feel. This light from heaven is strong, clear, and pure, carries its own demonstration with it; and we may as naturally take a glow-worm to assist us to discover the sun, as to examine the celestial ray by our dim candle, reason.

This is the way of talking of these men: they are sure, because they are sure: and their persuasions are right, because they are strong in them. For, when what they say is stripped of the metaphor of seeing and feeling, this is all it amounts to: and yet these similies so impose on them, that they serve them for certainty in themselves, and demonstration to others.

But to examine a little soberly this internal light, and this feeling on which they build so much. These men have, they say, clear light, and they see; they have awakened sense, and they feel; this cannot, they are sure, be disputed them. For when a man says he sees or feels, nobody can deny it him that he does so. But here let me ask: this seeing, is it the perception of the truth of the proposition, or of this, that it is a revelation from God? This feeling, is it a perception of an inclination or fancy to do something, or of the spirit of God moving that inclination? These are two very different perceptions, and must be carefully distinguished, if we would not impose upon ourselves. I may perceive the truth of a proposition, and yet not perceive that it is an immediate revelation from God. I may perceive the truth of a proposition in Euclid, without its being or my perceiving it to be a revelation: nay, I may perceive I came not by this knowledge in a natural way, and so may conclude it revealed, without perceiving that it is a revelation from God; because there be spirits, which, without being divinely commissioned, may excite those ideas in me, and lay them in such order before my mind, that I may perceive their connexion. So that the knowledge of any proposition coming into my mind, I know not how, is not a perception that it is from God. Much less is a strong persuasion, that it is true, a perception that it is from God, or so much as true. But however it be called light and seeing, I suppose it is at most but belief and assurance: and the proposition taken for a revelation, is not such as they know to be true, but take to be true. For where a proposition is known to be true, revelation is needless: and it is hard to conceive how there can be a revelation to any one of what he knows already. If therefore it be a proposition which they are persuaded, but do not know, to be true, whatever they may call it, it is not seeing, but believing. For these are two ways, whereby truth comes into the mind, wholly distinct, so that one is not the other. What I see I know to be so by the evidence of the thing itself: what I believe I take to be so upon the testimony of another: but this testimony I must know to be given, or else what ground have I of believing? I must see that it is God that reveals this to me, or else I see nothing. The question then here is, how do I know that God is the revealer of this to me; that this impression is made upon my mind by his Holy Spirit, and that therefore I ought to obey it? If I know not this, how great soever the assurance is that I am possessed with, it is groundless; whatever light I pretend to, it is but enthusiasm. For whether the proposition supposed to be revealed, be in itself evidently true, or visibly probable, or by the natural ways of knowledge uncertain, the proposition that must be well grounded, and manifested to be true, is this, that God is the revealer of it, and that what I take to be a revelation is certainly put into my mind by him, and is not an illusion dropped in by some other spirit, or raised by my own fancy. For if I mistake not, these men receive it for true, because they presume God revealed it. Does it not then stand them upon, to examine on what grounds they presume it to be a revelation from God? or else all their confidence is mere presumption: and this light, they are so dazzled with, is nothing but an *ignis fatuus* that leads them constantly round in this circle; it is a revelation, because they firmly believe it, and they believe it, because it is a revelation.

In all that is of divine revelation, there is need of no other proof but that it is an inspiration from God: for he can neither deceive nor be deceived. But how shall it be known that any proposition in our minds is a truth infused by God; a truth that is revealed to us by him, which he declares to us, and therefore we ought to believe? Here it is that enthusiasm fails of the evidence it pretends to. For men thus possessed boast of a light whereby they say they are enlightened, and brought into the knowledge of this or that truth. But if they know it to be a truth, they must know it to be so, either by its own self-evidence to natural reason, or by the rational proofs that make it out to be so. If they see and know it to be a truth, either of these two ways, they in vain suppose it to be a revelation. For they know it to be true the same way, that any other man naturally may know that it is so without the help of revelation. For thus all the truths, of what kind soever, that men uninspired are enlightened with, came into their minds, and are established there. If they say they know it to be true, because it is a revelation from God, the reason is good; but then it will be demanded how they know it to be a revelation from

God. If they say, by the light it brings with it, which shines bright in their minds, and they cannot resist: I beseech them to consider whether this be any more than what we have taken notice of already, viz. that it is a revelation, because they strongly believe it to be true. For all the light they speak of is but a strong, though ungrounded, persuasion of their own minds, that it is a truth. What readier way can there be to run ourselves into the most extravagant errours and miscarriages, than thus to set up fancy for our supreme and sole guide, and to believe any proposition to be true, any action to be right, only because we believe it to be so? The strength of our persuasions is no evidence at all of their own rectitude: crooked things may be as stiff and inflexible as straight: and men may be as positive and peremptory in errour as in truth.

WHY MEN REASON SO POORLY

Besides the want of determined ideas, and of sagacity, and exercise in finding out, and laying in order, intermediate ideas; there are three miscarriages, that men are guilty of, in reference to their reason, whereby this faculty is hindered in them from that service it might do, and was designed for. And he that reflects upon the actions and discourses of mankind, will find their defects in this kind very frequent, and very observable.

1. The first is of those who seldom reason at all, but do and think according to the example of others, whether parents, neighbours, ministers, or who else they are pleased to make choice of to have an implicit faith in, for the saving of themselves the pains and trouble of thinking and examining for themselves.

2. The second is of those who put passion in the place of reason, and, being resolved that shall govern their actions and arguments, neither use their own, nor hearken to other people's reason, any farther than it suits their humour, interest, or party; and these one may observe commonly content themselves with words, which have no distinct ideas to them, though in other matters, that they come with an unbiased indifferency to, they want not abilities to talk and hear reason, where they have no secret inclination, that hinders them from being intractable to it.

3. The third sort is of those who readily and sincerely follow reason; but, for want of having that, which one may call large, sound, round-about sense, have not a full view of all that relates to the question, and may be

of moment to decide it. We are all short-sighted, and very often see but one side of a matter; our views are not extended to all that has a connexion with it. From this defect I think no man is free. We see but in part, and we know but in part, and therefore it is no wonder we conclude not right from our partial views. This might instruct the proudest esteemer of his own parts, how useful it is to talk and consult with others, even such as come short of him in capacity, quickness, and penetration: for, since no one sees all, and we generally have different prospects of the same thing, according to our different, as I may say, positions to it; it is not incongruous to think, nor beneath any man to try, whether another may not have notions of things, which have escaped him, and which his reason would make use of, if they came into his mind. The faculty of reasoning seldom or never deceives those who trust to it; its consequences, from what it builds on, are evident and certain; but that which it oftenest, if not only, misleads us in, is, that the principles from which we conclude, the grounds upon which we bottom our reasoning, are but a part, something is left out, which should go into the reckoning, to make it just and exact.

In this we may see the reason, why some men of study and thought, that reason right, and are lovers of truth, do make no great advances in their discoveries of it. Errour and truth are uncertainly blended in their minds; their decisions are lame and defective, and they are very often mistaken in their judgments: the reason whereof is, they converse but with one sort of men, they read but one sort of books, they will not come in the hearing but of one sort of notions: the truth is they canton out to themselves a little Goshen, in the intellectual world, where light shines, and as they conclude, day blesses them; but the rest of that vast *expansum* they give up to night and darkness, and so avoid coming near it. They have a pretty traffic with known correspondents, in some little creek; within that they confine themselves, and are dexterous managers enough of the wares and products of that corner, with which they content themselves, but will not venture out into the great ocean of knowledge, to survey the riches that nature hath stored other parts with, no less genuine, no less solid, no less useful, than what has fallen to their lot, in the admired plenty and sufficiency of their own little spot, which to them contains whatsoever is good in the universe.

Every man carries about him a touchstone, if he will make use of it, to distinguish substantial gold from superficial glitterings, truth from appearances. And indeed the use and benefit of this touchstone, which is natural reason, is spoiled and lost only by assuming prejudices, overweening presumption, and narrowing our minds. The want of exercising it, in the full extent of things intelligible, is that which weakens and extinguishes this noble faculty in us.

To carry this a little farther: Here is one muffled up in the zeal and infallibility of his own sect, and will not touch a book, or enter into debate with a person that will question any of those things, which to him are sacred. Another surveys our differences in religion with an equitable and fair indifference, and so finds, probably, that none of them are in every thing unexceptionable. These divisions and systems were made by men, and carry the mark of fallible on them; and in those, whom he differs from, and till he opened his eyes, had a general prejudice against, he meets with more to be said for a great many things, than before he was aware of, or could have imagined. Which of these two, now, is most likely to judge right, in our religious controversies, and to be most stored with truth, the mark all pretend to aim at? All these men, that I have instanced in, thus unequally furnished with truth, and advanced in knowledge, I suppose of equal natural parts; all the odds between them has been the different scope that has been given to their understandings to range in, for the gathering up of information, and furnishing their heads with ideas, and notions and observations, whereon to employ their mind, and form their understandings.

LANGUAGE AND ITS PROPER USE

THE NATURE OF LANGUAGE

God, having designed man for a sociable creature, made him not only with an inclination, and under a necessity to have fellowship with those of his own kind; but furnished him also with language, which was to be the great instrument and common tie of society. Man therefore had by nature his organs so fashioned, as to be fit to frame articulate sounds, which we call words. But this was not enough to produce language; for parrots, and several other birds, will be taught to make articulate sounds distinct enough, which yet, by no means, are capable of language.

Besides articulate sounds therefore, it was farther necessary, that he should be able to use these sounds as signs of internal conceptions; and to make them stand as marks for the ideas within his own mind, whereby they might be made known to others, and the thoughts of men's minds be conveyed from one to another.

But neither was this sufficient to make words so useful as they ought to be. It is not enough for the perfection of language, that sounds can be made signs of ideas, unless those signs can be so made use of as to comprehend several particular things; for the multiplication of words would have perplexed their use, had every particular thing need of a distinct name to be signified by. To remedy this inconvenience, language had yet a farther improvement in the use of general terms, whereby one word was made to mark a multitude of particular existences: which advantageous use of sounds was obtained only by the difference of the ideas they were made signs of: those names becoming general, which are made to stand for general ideas, and those remaining particular, where the ideas they are used for are particular.

THE SIGNIFICANCE OF WORDS

MAN, though he has great variety of thoughts, and such, from which others, as well as himself, might receive profit and delight; yet they are all within his own breast, invisible and hidden from others, nor can of themselves be made appear. The comfort and advantage of society not being to be had without communication of thoughts, it was necessary that man should find out some external sensible signs, whereof those invisible ideas, which his thoughts are made up for, might be made known to others. For this purpose nothing was so fit, either for plenty or quickness, as those articulate sounds, which with so much ease and variety he found himself able to make. Thus we may conceive how words which were by nature so well adapted to that purpose, come to be made use of by men, as the signs of their ideas; not by any natural connexion that there is between particular articulate sounds and certain ideas, for then there would be but one language amongst all men; but by a voluntary imposition, whereby such a word is made arbitrarily the mark of such an idea. The use then of words is to be sensible marks of ideas; and the ideas they stand for are their proper and immediate signification.

The use men have of these marks being either to record their own thoughts for the assistance of their own memory, or as it were to bring out their ideas, and lay them before the view of others; words in their primary or immediate signification stand for nothing but the ideas in the mind of him that uses them, how imperfectly soever or carelessly those ideas are collected from the things which they are supposed to represent. When a man speaks to another, it is that he may be understood; and the end of speech is, that those sounds, as marks, may make known his ideas to the hearer. That then which words are the marks of are the ideas of the speaker: nor can any one apply them as marks, immediately to any thing else, but the ideas that he himself hath.

Though the proper and immediate signification of words are ideas in the mind of the speaker, yet because by familiar use from our cradles we come to learn certain articulate sounds very perfectly, and have them readily on our tongues, and always at hand in our memories, but yet are not always careful to examine, or settle their significations perfectly; it often happens that men, even when they would apply themselves to an attentive consideration, do set their thoughts more on words than things. Nay, because words are many of them learned before the ideas are known for which they stand; therefore some, not only children, but men, speak several words no otherwise than parrots do, only because they have learned them, and have been accustomed to those sounds. But so far as words are of use and signification, so far is there a constant connexion between the sound and the idea, and a designation that the one stands for the other; without which application of them, they are nothing but so much insignificant noise.

Words by long and familiar use, as has been said, come to excite in men certain ideas so constantly and readily, that they are apt to suppose a natural connexion between them. But that they signify only men's peculiar ideas, and that by a perfectly arbitrary imposition, is evident in that they often fail to excite in others (even that use the same language) the same ideas we take them to be the signs of: and every man has so inviolable a liberty to make words stand for what ideas he pleases, that no one hath the power to make others have the same ideas in their minds that he has, when they use the same words that he does. And therefore the great Augustus himself, in the possession of that power which ruled the world, acknowledged he could not make a new Latin word: which was as much as to say, that he could not arbitrarily appoint what idea any sound should be a sign of, in the mouths and common language of his subjects. It is true, common use by a tacit consent appropriates certain sounds to certain ideas in all languages, which so far limits the signification of that sound, that unless a man applies it to the same idea, he does not speak properly: and let me add, that unless a man's words excite the same ideas in the hearer, which he makes them stand for in speaking, he does not speak intelligibly. But whatever be the consequence of any man's using of words differently, either from their general meaning, or the particular sense of the person to whom he addresses them, this is certain, their signification, in his use of them, is limited to his ideas, and they can be signs of nothing else.

GENERAL TERMS

All things that exist being particulars, it may perhaps be thought reasonable that words, which ought to be conformed to things, should be so too; I mean in their signification: but yet we find the quite contrary. The far greatest part of words, that make all languages, are general terms; which has not been the effect of neglect or chance, but of reason and necessity.

First, It is impossible that every particular thing should have a distinct peculiar name. For the signification and use of words, depending on that connexion which the mind makes between its ideas and the sounds it uses as signs of them, it is necessary, in the application of names to things that the mind should have distinct ideas of the things, and retain also the particular name that belongs to every one, with its peculiar appropriation to that idea. But it is beyond the power of human capacity to frame and retain distinct ideas of all the particular things we meet with: every bird and beast men saw, every tree and plant that affected the senses, could not find a place in the most capacious understanding. If it be looked on as an instance of a prodigious memory, that some generals have been able to call every soldier in their army by his proper name, we may easily find a reason, why men have never attempted to give names to each sheep in their flock, or crow that flies over their heads; much less to call every leaf of plants, or grain of sand that came in their way, by a peculiar name.

Secondly, If it were possible, it would yet be useless; because it would not serve to the chief end of language. Men would in vain heap up names of particular things, that would not serve them to communicate their thoughts. Men learn names, and use them in talk with others, only that they may be understood: which is then only done, when by use or consent the sound I make by the organs of speech, excites in another man's mind, who hears it, the idea I apply it to in mine, when I speak it. This cannot be done by names applied to particular things, whereof I alone having the ideas in my mind, the names of them could not be significant or intelligible to another, who was not acquainted with all those very particular things which had fallen under my notice.

Thirdly, But yet granting this also feasible (which I think is not) yet a distinct name for every particular thing would not be of any great use for the improvement of knowledge: which, though founded in particular things, enlarges itself by general views: to which things reduced into sorts under general names, are properly subservient. These, with the names belonging to them, come within some compass, and do not multiply every moment, beyond what either the mind can contain, or use requires: and therefore, in these, men have for the most part stopped; but yet not so as to hinder themselves from distinguishing particular things, by appropriated names, where convenience demands it. And therefore in their own species, which they have most to do with, and wherein they have often occasion to mention particular persons, they make use of proper names; and there distinct individuals have distinct denominations.

The next thing to be considered, is, how general words come to be made. For since all things that exist are only particulars, how come we by general terms, or where find we those general natures they are supposed to stand for? Words become general, by being made the signs of general ideas; and ideas become general, by separating from them the circumstances of time, and place, and any other ideas, that may determine them to this or that particular existence. By this way of abstraction they are made capable of representing more individuals than one; each of which having in it a conformity to that abstract idea, is (as we call it) of that sort.

He that thinks general natures or notions are any

thing else but such abstract and partial ideas of more complex ones, taken at first from particular existences, will, I fear, be at a loss where to find them. For let any one reflect, and then tell me, wherein does his idea of man differ from that of Peter and Paul, or his idea of horse from that of Bucephalus, but in the leaving out something that is peculiar to each individual, and retaining so much of those particular complex ideas of several particular existences, as they are found to agree in? Of the complex ideas signified by the names man and horse, leaving out but those particulars wherein they differ, and retaining only those wherein they agree, and of those making a new distinct complex idea, and giving the name animal to it; one has a more general term, that comprehends with man several other creatures. Leave out of the idea of animal, sense and spontaneous motion; and the remaining complex idea. made up of the remaining simple ones of body, life, and nourishment, becomes a more general one, under the more comprehensive term *vivens*. And not to dwell longer upon this particular, so evident in itself, by the same way the mind proceeds to body, substance, and at last to being, thing, and such universal terms which stand for any of our ideas whatsoever. To conclude, this whole mystery of genera and species, which make such a noise in the schools, and are with justice so little regarded out of them, is nothing else but abstract ideas, more or less comprehensive, with names annexed to them. In all which this is constant and unvariable, that every more general term stands for such an idea, and is but a part of any of those contained under it.

To return to general words, it is plain by what has been said, that general and universal belong not to the real existence of things; but are the inventions and creatures of the understanding, made by it for its own use, and concern only signs, whether words or ideas. Words are general, as has been said, when used for signs of general ideas, and so are applicable indifferently to many particular things: and ideas are general, when they are set up as the representatives of many particular things: but universality belongs not to things themselves, which are all of them particular in their existence; even those words and ideas, which in their signification are general. When therefore we quit particulars, the generals that rest are only creatures of our own making; their general nature being nothing but the capacity they are put into by the understanding, of signifying or representing many particulars. For the signification they have is nothing but a relation, that by the mind of man is added to them.

THE ABUSE OF WORDS

Besides the imperfection that is naturally in language, and the obscurity and confusion that is so hard to be avoided in the use of words, there are several wilful faults and neglects which men are guilty of in this way of communication, whereby they render these signs less clear and distinct in their signification, than naturally they need to be.

First, in this kind, the first and most palpable abuse is, the using of words without clear and distinct ideas; or, which is worse, signs without any thing signified. Of these there are two sorts:

I. One may observe, in all languages, certain words, that if they be examined, will be found, in their first original and their appropriated use, not to stand for any clear and distinct ideas. These, for the most part, the several sects of philosophy and religion have introduced. For their authors, or promoters, either affecting something singular and out of the way of common apprehensions, or to support some strange opinions, or cover some weakness of their hypothesis, seldom fail to coin new words, and such as, when they come to be examined, may justly be called insignificant terms. For having either had no determinate collection of ideas annexed to them, when they were first invented; or at least such as, if well examined, will be found inconsistent; it is no wonder if afterwards, in the vulgar use of the same party, they remain empty sounds, with little or no signification, amongst those who think it enough to have them often in their mouths, as the distinguishing characters of their church, or school, without much troubling their heads to examine what are the precise ideas they stand for. I shall not need here to heap up instances; every man's reading and conversation will sufficiently furnish him; or if he wants to be better stored, the great mint-masters of this kind of terms, I mean the school-men and metaphysicians (under which, I think, the disputing natural and moral philosophers of these latter ages may be comprehended) have wherewithal abundantly to content him.

II. Others there be, who extend this abuse yet farther, who take so little care to lay by words, which in their primary notation have scarce any clear and distinct ideas which they are annexed to, that by an unpardonable negligence they familiarly use words, which the propriety of language has affixed to very important ideas, without any distinct meaning at all. Wisdom, glory, grace, etc., are words frequent enough in every man's mouth; but if a great many of those who use them, should be asked what they mean by them, they would be at a stand, and not know what to answer: a plain proof, that though they have learned those sounds, and have them ready at their tongue's end, yet there are no determined ideas laid up in their minds, which are to be expressed to others by them.

Men having been accustomed from their cradles to learn words, which are easily got and retained, before they knew, or had framed the complex ideas, to which they were annexed, or which were to be found in the things they were thought to stand for; they usually continue to do so all their lives; and without taking the pains necessary to settle in their minds determined ideas, they use their words for such unsteady and confused notions as they have, contenting themselves with the same words other people use: as if their very sound necessarily carried with it constantly the same meaning. This, though men make a shift with, in the ordinary occurrences of life, where they find it necessary to be understood, and therefore they make signs till they are so; yet this insignificancy in their words, when they come to reason concerning either their tenets or interest, manifestly fills their discourse with abundance of empty unintelligible noise and jargon, especially in moral matters, where the words for the most part standing for arbitrary and numerous collections of ideas, not regularly and permanently united in nature, their bare sounds are often only thought on, or at least very obscure and uncertain notions annexed to them. Men take the words they find in use amongst their neighbours; and that they may not seem ignorant what they stand for, use them confidently, without much troubling their heads about a certain fixed meaning; whereby, besides the ease of it, they obtain this advantage, that as in such discourses they seldom are in the right, so they are as seldom to be convinced that they are in the wrong; it being all one to go about to draw those men out of their mistakes, who have no settled notions, as to dispossess a vagrant of his habitation, who has no settled abode.

This I guess to be so; and every one may observe in himself and others, whether it be or no.

Secondly, another great abuse of words is inconstancy in the use of them. It is hard to find a discourse written of any subject, especially of controversy, wherein one shall not observe, if he read with attention, the same words (and those commonly the most material in the discourse, and upon which the argument turns) used sometimes for one collection of simple ideas, and sometimes for another: which is a perfect abuse of language. Words being intended for signs of my ideas, to make them known to others, not by any natural signification, but by a voluntary imposition, it is plain cheat and abuse, when I make them stand sometimes for one thing, and sometimes for another; the wilful doing whereof, can be imputed to nothing but great folly, or greater dishonesty. If men should do so in their reckonings, I wonder who would have to do with them? One who would speak thus, in the affairs and business of the world, and call 8 sometimes seven, and sometimes nine, as best served his advantage, would presently have clapped upon him one of the two names men are commonly disgusted with. And yet in arguings and learned contests, the same sort of proceedings passes commonly for wit and learning: but to me it appears a greater dishonesty, than the misplacing of counters in the casting up a debt; and the cheat the greater, by how much truth is of greater concernment and value than money.

Thirdly, another abuse of language is an affected obscurity, by either applying old words to new and unusual significations, or introducing new and ambiguous terms, without defining either; or else putting them so together, as may confound their ordinary meaning.

Artificial ignorance, and learned gibberish, prevailed mightily in these last ages, by the interest and artifice of those who found no easier way to that pitch of authority and dominion they have attained, than by amusing the men of business and ignorant with hard words, or employing the ingenious and idle in intricate disputes about unintelligible terms, and holding them perpetually entangled in that endless labyrinth. Besides, there is no such way to gain admittance, or give defence to strange and absurd doctrines, as to guard them round about with legions of obscure, doubtful, and undefined words: which yet make these retreats more like the dens of robbers, or holes of foxes, than the fortresses of fair warriors; which if it be hard to get them out of, it is not for the strength that is in them, but the briars and thorns, and the obscurity of the thickets they are beset with. For untruth being unacceptable to the mind of man, there is no other defence left for absurdity, but obscurity.

Thus learned ignorance, and this art of keeping, even inquisitive men, from true knowledge, hath been propagated in the world, and hath much perplexed whilst it pretended to inform the understanding. For we see that other well-meaning and wise men, whose education and parts had not acquired that acuteness, could intelligibly express themselves to one another; and in its plain use make a benefit of language. But though unlearned men well enough understood the words white and black, etc., and had constant notions of the ideas signified by those words; yet there were philosophers found, who had learning and subtilty enough to prove, that snow was black; i. e. to prove, that white was black. Whereby they had the advantage to destroy the instruments and means of discourse, conversation, instruction, and society; whilst with great art and subtilty they did no more but perplex and confound the signification of words, and thereby render language less useful, than the real defects of it had made it; a gift, which the illiterate had not attained to.

Nor hath this mischief stopped in logical niceties, or curious empty speculations; it hath invaded the great concernments of human life and society, obscured and perplexed the material truths of law and divinity; brought confusion, disorder, and uncertainty into the affairs of mankind; and if not destroyed, yet in a great measure rendered useless, these two great rules, religion and justice. What have the greatest part of the comments and disputes upon the laws of God and man served for, but to make the meaning more doubtful, and perplex the sense? What have been the effect of those multiplied curious distinctions and acute niceties, but obscurity and uncertainty, leaving the words more unintelligible, and the reader more at a loss? How else comes it to pass that princes, speaking or writing to their servants, in their ordinary commands, are easily understood; speaking to their people, in their laws, are not so? And, as I remarked before, doth it not often happen, that a man of an ordinary capacity very well understands a text or a law that he reads, till he consults an expositor, or goes to counsel; who, by that time he hath done explaining them, makes the words signify either nothing at all, or what he pleases.

Fourthly, another great abuse of words is, the taking them for things. This though it in some degree concerns all names in general, yet more particularly affects those of substances. To this abuse those men are most subject, who most confine their thoughts to any one system, and give themselves up into a firm belief of the perfection of any received hypothesis; whereby they come to be persuaded, that the terms of that sect are so suited to the nature of things, that they perfectly correspond with their real existence. Who is there, that has been bred up in the Peripatetic philosophy, who does not think the ten names, under which are ranked the ten predicaments, to be exactly conformable to the nature of things? Who is there of that school, that is not persuaded, that substantial forms, vegetative souls, abhorrence of a vacuum, intentional species, etc., are something real? These words men have learned from their very entrance upon knowledge, and have found their masters and systems lay great stress upon them; and therefore they cannot quit the opinion, that they are conformable to nature, and are the representations of something that really exists. The Platonists have their soul of the world, and the Epicureans their endeavour towards motion in their atoms when at rest. There is scarce any sect in philosophy has not a distinct set of terms, that others understand not; but yet this gibberish, which, in the weakness of human understanding, serves so well to palliate men's ignorance, and cover their errors, comes, by familiar use amongst those of the same tribe, to seem the most important part of language, and of all other the terms the most significant. And should aerial and ætherial vehicles come once, by the prevalency of that doctrine, to be generally received any where, no doubt those terms would make impressions on men's minds, so as to establish them in the persuasion of the reality of such things, as much as Peripatetic forms and intentional species have heretofore done.

REMEDIES FOR THE ABUSE OF WORDS

To REMEDY the defects of speech before-mentioned to some degree, and to prevent the inconveniencies that follow from them, I imagine the observation of these following rules may be of use, till somebody better able shall judge it worth his while to think more maturely on this matter, and oblige the world with his thoughts on it.

First, a man shall take care to use no word without a signification, no name without an idea for which he makes it stand. This rule will not seem altogether needless, to any one who shall take the pains to recollect how often he has met with such words, as instinct, sympathy and antipathy, etc., in the discourse of others, so made use of, as he might easily conclude that those that used them had no ideas in their minds to which they applied them; but spoke them only as sounds, which usually served instead of reasons on the like occasions. Not but that these words, and the like, have very proper significations in which they may be used; but there being no natural connexion between any words and any ideas, these and any other, may be learned by rote, and pronounced or writ by men, who have no ideas in their minds, to which they have annexed them, and for which they make them stand; which is necessary they should, if men would speak intelligibly even to themselves alone.

Secondly, it is not enough a man uses his words as signs of some ideas: those ideas he annexes them to, if they be simple, must be clear and distinct; if complex, must be determinate, i.e. the precise collection of simple ideas settled in the mind, with that sound annexed to it, as the sign of that precise determined collection, and no other. This is very necessary in names of modes, and especially moral words, which having no settled objects in nature, from whence their ideas are taken, as from their originals, are apt to be very confused. Justice is a word in every man's mouth, but most commonly with a very undetermined loose signification: which will always be so, unless a man has in his mind a distinct comprehension of the component parts, that complex idea consists of: and if it be decompounded, must be able to resolve it still on, till he at last comes to the simple ideas that make it up: and unless this be done, a man makes an ill use of the word, let it be justice, for example, or any other. I do not say, a man need stand to recollect and make this analysis at large, every time the word justice comes in his way: but this at least is necessary, that he have so examined the signification of that name, and settled the idea of all its parts in his mind, that he can do it when he pleases. If one, who makes his complex idea of justice to be such a treatment of the person or goods of another, as is according to law, hath not a clear and distinct idea what law is, which makes a part of his complex idea of justice; it is plain his idea of justice itself will be confused and imperfect. This exactness will, perhaps, be judged very troublesome; and therefore most men will think they may be excused from settling the complex ideas of mixed modes so precisely in their minds. But yet I must say, till this be done, it must not be wondered that they have a great deal of obscurity and confusion in their own minds, and a great deal of wrangling in their discourse with others.

Thirdly, it is not enough that men have ideas, determined ideas, for which they make these signs stand; but they must also take care to apply their words as near as may be, to such ideas as common use has annexed them to. For words, especially of languages already framed, being no man's private possession, but the common measure of commerce and communication, it is not for any one, at pleasure, to change the stamp they are current in, nor alter the ideas they are affixed to; or at least, when there is a necessity to do so, he is bound to give notice of it. Men's intentions in speaking, are, or at least should be, to be understood; which cannot be without frequent explanations, demands, and other the like incommodious interruptions, where men do not follow common use.

THE SPIRIT OF TOLERATION

Absolute liberty, just and true liberty, equal and impartial liberty, is the thing that we stand in need of.

The toleration of those that differ from others in matters of religion is so agreeable to the gospel of Jesus Christ, and to the genuine reason of mankind, that it seems monstrous for men to be so blind, as not to perceive the necessity and advantage of it in so clear a light. I will not here tax the pride and ambition of some, the passion and uncharitable zeal of others. These are faults from which human affairs can perhaps scarce ever be perfectly freed; but yet such as nobody will bear the plain imputation of, without covering them with some specious color, and so pretend to commendation whilst they are carried away by their own irregular passions. But however, that some may not color their spirit of persecution and unchristian cruelty with a pretence of care of the public weal and observation of the laws; and that others, under pretence of religion, may not seek impunity for their libertinism and licentiousness; in a word, that none may impose either upon himself or others, by the pretences of loyalty and obedience to the prince or of tenderness and sincerity in the worship of God, I esteem it above all things necessary to distinguish exactly the business of civil government from that of religion, and to settle the just bounds that lie between the one and the other. If this be not done, there can be no end put to the controversies that will be always arising between those that have or at least pretend to have, on the one side, a concernment for the interest of men's souls, and, on the other side, a care of the commonwealth.

The commonwealth seems to me to be a society of men constituted only for the procuring, preserving, and advancing their own civil interests.

Civil interest I call life, liberty, health, and indolency of body; and the possession of outward things, such as money, lands, houses, furniture, and the like.

It is the duty of the civil magistrate, by the impartial execution of equal laws, to secure unto all the people in general, and to everyone of his subjects in particular, the just possession of these things belonging to this life. If any one presume to violate the laws of public justice and equity, established for the preservation of these things, his presumption is to be checked by the fear of punishment, consisting in the deprivation or diminution of those civil interests or goods which otherwise he might and ought to enjoy. But seeing no man does willingly suffer himself to be punished by the deprivation of any part of his goods, and much less of his liberty or life, therefore is the magistrate armed with the force and strength of all his subjects, in order to the punishment of those that violate any other man's rights.

Let us now consider what a church is. A church then I take to be a voluntary society of men, joining themselves together of their own accord, in order to the public worshipping of God, in such a manner as they judge acceptable to him, and effectual to the salvation of their souls.

I say, it is a free and voluntary society. Nobody is born a member of any church; otherwise the religion of parents would descend unto children, by the same right of inheritance as their temporal estates, and every one would hold his faith by the same tenure he does his lands; than which nothing can be imagined more absurd.

Thus therefore that matter stands. No man by nature is bound unto any particular church or sect, but every one joins himself voluntarily to that society in which he believes he has found that profession and worship which is truly acceptable to God. The hope of salvation, as it was the only cause of his entrance into that communion, so it can be the only reason of his stay there. For if afterwards he discover anything either erroneous in the doctrine, or incongruous in the worship of that society to which he has joined himself, why should it not be as free for him to go out as it was to enter? No member of a religious society can be tried with any other bonds but what proceed from the certain expectation of eternal life. A church then is a society of members voluntarily uniting to this end.

The end of a religious society, as has already been said, is the public worship of God, and by means thereof the acquisition of eternal life. All discipline ought therefore to tend to that end, and all ecclesiastical laws to be thereunto confined. Nothing ought, nor can be transacted in this society, relating to the possession of civil or worldly goods. No force is here to be made use of, upon any occasion whatsoever; for force belongs wholly to the civil magistrate, and the possession of all outward goods is subject to his jurisdiction.

These things being thus determined, let us inquire in the next place, how far the duty of toleration extends, and what is required from every one by it.

And first, I hold that no church is bound by the duty of toleration to retain any such person in her bosom, as after admonition continues obstinately to offend against the laws of the society. For these being the condition of communion and the bond of society, if the breach of them were permitted without any animadversion, the society would immediately be thereby dissolved. But nevertheless in all such cases care is to be taken that the sentence of excommunication and the execution thereof carry with it no rough usage of word or action, whereby the ejected person may any ways be damnified in body or estate. The whole force of excommunication consists only in this, that the resolution of the society in that respect being declared, the union that was between the body and some member, comes thereby to be dissolved; and that relation ceasing, the participation of some certain things which the society communicated to its members and unto which no man has any civil right, comes also to cease.

Secondly, no private person has any right in any manner to prejudice another person in his civil enjoyments, because he is of another church or religion. All the rights and franchises that belong to him as a man or as a denizen are inviolably to be preserved to him. These are not the business of religion. No violence nor injury is to be offered him, whether he be Christian or pagan. Nay, we must not content ourselves with the narrow measures of bare justice: charity, bounty, and liberality must be added to it. This the gospel enjoins, this reason directs, and this that natural fellowship we are born into requires of us. If any man err from the right way, it is his own misfortune, no injury to thee: nor therefore art thou to punish him in the things of this life, because thou supposest he will be miserable in that which is to come.

Nobody therefore in fine, neither single persons, nor churches, nay, nor even commonwealths, have any just title to invade the civil rights and worldly goods of each other, upon pretence of religion. Those that are of another opinion would do well to consider with themselves how pernicious a seed of discord and war, how powerful a provocation to endless hatreds, rapines, and slaughters, they thereby furnish unto mankind. No peace and security, no not so much as common friendship, can ever be established or preserved amongst men, so long as this opinion prevails that dominion is founded in grace and that religion is to be propagated by force of arms.

The articles of religion are some of them practical and some speculative. Now though both sorts consist in the knowledge of truth, yet these terminate simply in the understanding, those influence the will and manners. Speculative opinions, therefore, and articles of faith as they are called which are required only to be believed, cannot be imposed on any church by the law of the land. For it is absurd that things should be enjoined by laws which are not in men's power to perform; and to believe this or that to be true does not depend upon our will.

Further, the magistrate ought not to forbid the preaching or professing of any speculative opinions in any church, because they have no manner of relation to the civil rights of the subjects. If a Roman Catholic believe that to be really the body of Christ which another man calls bread, he does no injury thereby to his neighbor. If a Jew does not believe the New Testament to be the word of God, he does not thereby alter anything in men's civil rights. If a heathen doubt of both testaments, he is not therefore to be punished as a pernicious citizen. The power of the magistrate and the estates of the people may be equally secure, whether any man believe these things or no. I readily grant that these opinions are false and absurd. But the business of laws is not to provide for the truth of opinions, but for the safety and security of the commonwealth and of every particular man's goods and person. And so it ought to be; for truth certainly would do well enough if she were once made to shift for herself. She seldom has received, and I fear never will receive, much assistance from the power of great men, to whom she is but barely known, and more rarely welcome. She is not taught by laws, nor has she any need of force to procure her entrance into the minds of men. Errors indeed prevail by the assistance of foreign and borrowed succours. But if truth makes not her way into the understanding by her own light, she will be but the weaker for any borrowed force violence can add to her. Thus much for speculative opinions. Let us now proceed to the practical ones.

A good life, in which consists not the least part of religion and true piety, concerns also the civil government; and in it lies the safety both of men's souls and of the commonwealth. Moral actions belong therefore to the jurisdiction both of the outward and inward court, both of the civil and domestic governor, I mean, both of the magistrate and conscience. Here therefore is great danger, lest one of these jurisdictions intrench upon the other, and discord arise between the keeper of the public peace and the overseers of souls. But if what has been already said concerning the limits of both these governments be rightly considered, it will easily remove all difficulty in this matter.

It is easy to understand to what end the legislative power ought to be directed and by what measures regulated; and that is the temporal good and outward prosperity of the society, which is the sole reason of men's entering into society and the only thing they seek and aim at in it. And it is also evident what liberty remains to men in reference to their eternal salvation, and that is that every one should do what he in his conscience is persuaded to be acceptable to the Almighty on whose good pleasure and acceptance depends his eternal happiness; for obedience is due in the first place to God and afterwards to the laws.

But to come to particulars. I say, first, no opinions contrary to human society or to those moral rules which are necessary to the preservation of civil society are to be tolerated by the magistrate. But of those indeed examples in any church are rare. For no sect can easily arrive to such a degree of madness, as that it should think fit to teach, for doctrines of religion, such things as manifestly undermine the foundations of society, and are therefore condemned by the judgment of all mankind; because their own interest, peace, reputation, everything would be thereby endangered.

Another more secret evil, but more dangerous to the commonwealth, is when men arrogate to themselves, and to those of their own sect, some peculiar prerogative covered over with a specious show of deceitful words, but in effect opposite to the civil rights of the community. These who attribute unto the faithful, religious, and orthodox, that is, in plain terms, unto themselves, any peculiar privilege or power above other mortals in civil concernments; or who, upon pretence of religion, do challenge any manner of authority over such as are not associated with them in their ecclesiastical communion; I say these have no right to be tolerated by the magistrate, as neither those that will not own and teach the duty of tolerating all men in matters of mere religion. For what do all these and the like doctrines signify, but that they may, and are ready upon any occasion to seize the government, and possess themselves of the estates and fortunes of their fellow-subjects; and that they only ask leave to be tolerated by the magistrates so long, until they find themselves strong enough to effect it?

Again, that church can have no right to be tolerated by the magistrate which is constituted upon such a bottom, that all those who enter into it do thereby *ipso facto* deliver themselves up to the protection and service of another prince. For by this means the magistrate would give way to the settling of a foreign jurisdiction in his own country and suffer his own people to be listed, as it were, for soldiers against his own government.

Lastly, those are not at all to be tolerated who deny the being of God. Promises, covenants, and oaths, which are the bonds of human society, can have no hold upon an atheist. The taking away of God, though but even in thought, dissolves all. Besides also, those that by their atheism undermine and destroy all religion, can have no pretence of religion whereupon to challenge the privilege of a toleration. As for other practical opinions, though not absolutely free from all error, yet if they do not tend to establish domination over others or civil impunity to the church in which they are taught, there can be no reason why they should not be tolerated.

Just and moderate governments are everywhere quiet, everywhere safe. But oppression raises ferments and makes men struggle to cast off an uneasy and tyrannical yoke. I know that seditions are very frequently raised upon pretence of religion. But it is as true that, for religion, subjects are frequently ill treated and live miserably. Believe me, the stirs that are made proceed not from any peculiar temper of this or that church or religious society, but from the common disposition of all mankind, who, when they groan under any heavy burden, endeavor naturally to shake off the yoke that galls their necks. Suppose this business of religion were let alone, and that there were some other distinction made between men and men, upon account of their different complexions, shapes, and features, so that those who have black hair, for example, or grey eyes, should not enjoy the same privileges as other citizens; that they should not be permitted either to buy or sell or live by their callings; that parents should not have the government and education of their own children; that they should either be excluded from the benefit of the laws, or meet with partial judges; can it be doubted but these persons, thus distinguished from others by the color of their hair and eyes, and united together by one common persecution, would be as dangerous to the magistrate, as any others that had associated themselves merely upon the account of religion? Some enter into company for trace and profit: others for want of business, have their clubs for claret. But there is one thing only which gathers people into seditious commotions, and that is oppression.

LIBERALISM IN RELIGION

Though the works of nature in every part of them sufficiently evidence a Deity, yet the world made so little use of their reason, that they saw him not, where, even by the impressions of himself, he was easy to be found. Sense and lust blinded their minds in some, and a careless inadvertancy in others, and fearful apprehensions in most, (who either believed there were, or could not but suspect there might be, superior unknown beings,) gave them up into the hands of their priests, to fill their heads with false notions of the Deity, and their worship with foolish rites, as they pleased. And what dread or craft once began, devotion soon made sacred and religion immutable. In this state of darkness and ignorance of the true God, vice and superstition held the world. Nor could any help be had or hoped for from reason; which could not be heard, and was judged to have nothing to do in the case; the priests everywhere, to secure their empire, having excluded reason from having anything to do in religion. And in the crowd of wrong notions and invented rites, the world had almost lost the sight of the one only true God. The rational and thinking part of mankind, it is true, when they sought after him, they found the one supreme, invisible God. But if they acknowledged and worshiped him, it was only in their own minds. They kept this truth locked up in their own breasts as a secret, nor ever durst venture it amongst the people, much less amongst the priests, those wary guardians of their own creeds and profitable inventions. Hence we see that reason, speaking ever so clearly to the wise and virtuous, had never authority enough to prevail on the multitude, and to persuade the societies of men that there was but one God that alone was to be owned and worshiped.

Next to the knowledge of one God, maker of all things, a clear knowledge of their duty was wanting to mankind. This part of knowledge, though cultivated with some care by some of the heathen philosophers, yet got little footing among the people. All men indeed, under pain of displeasing the gods, were to frequent the temples; every one went to their sacrifices and services; but the priests made it not their business to teach them virtue. If they were diligent in their observations and ceremonies, punctual in their feasts and solemnities and the tricks of religion, the holy tribe assured them the gods were pleased, and they looked no farther. Few went to the schools of the philosophers to be instructed in their duties, and to know what was good and evil in their actions. The priests sold the better pennyworths, and therefore had all the custom. Lustrations and processions were much easier than a clean conscience and a steady course of virtue; and an expiatory sacrifice that atoned for the want of it was much more convenient than a strict and holy life. No wonder then that religion was everywhere distinguished from and preferred to virtue, and that it was dangerous heresy and profaneness to think the contrary. So much virtue as was necessary to hold societies together and to contribute to the quiet of governments, the civil laws of commonwealths taught and forced upon men that lived under magistrates. But these laws, being for the most part made by such who had no other aims but their own power, reached no farther than those things that would serve to tie men together in subjection, or at most were directly to conduce to the prosperity and temporal happiness of any people. But natural religion in its full extent was nowhere that I know taken care of by the force of natural reason. It should seem, by the little that has hitherto been done in it, that it is too hard a task for unassisted reason to establish morality in all its parts upon its true foundation with a clear and convincing light. And it is at least a surer and shorter way to the apprehensions of the vulgar and mass of mankind, that one manifestly sent from God and coming with visible authority from him should, as a king and lawmaker, tell them their duties and require their obedience, than leave it to the long and sometimes intricate deductions of reason, to be made out to them. Such trains of reasoning the greatest part of mankind have neither leisure to weigh, nor, for want of education and use, skill to judge of. Experience shows that the knowledge of morality, by mere natural light, (how agreeable soever it be to it,) makes but a slow progress and little advance in the world. And the reason of it is not hard to be found in men's necessities, passions, vices, and mistaken interests, which turn their thoughts another way. And the designing leaders, as well as following herd, find it not to their purpose to employ much of their meditations this way. Or whatever else was the cause, it is plain in fact, that human reason unassisted failed men in its great and proper business of morality. It never from unquestionable principles, by clear deductions, made out an entire body of the law of nature.

In this state of darkness and error, our Saviour found the world. But the clear revelation he brought with him dissipated this darkness, made the one invisible true God known to the world, and that with such evidence and energy that polytheism and idolatry have nowhere been able to withstand it. But wherever the preaching of the truth he delivered and the light of the gospel hath come, those mists have been dispelled. And in effect we see that since our Saviour's time the belief of one God has prevailed and spread itself over the face of the earth. This light the world needed and this light is received from him: that there is but one God and he eternal, invisible, not like to visible objects, nor to be represented by them.

God therefore, out of his mercy to mankind and for the erecting of the kingdom of his Son and furnishing it with subjects out of every kindred and tongue and people and nation, proposed to the children of men, that as many of them as would believe Jesus his Son (whom he sent into the world) to be the Messiah, the promised Deliverer, and would receive him for their King and Ruler, should have all their past sins, disobedience, and rebellion forgiven them. And if for the future they lived in a sincere obedience to his law, to the utmost of their power, the sins of human frailty for the time to come, as well as all those of their past lives, should, for his Son's sake, because they gave themselves up to him, to be his subjects, be forgiven them. And so their faith, which made them be baptized into his name, (i.e. enrol themselves in the kingdom of Jesus the Messiah, and profess themselves his subjects, and consequently live by the laws of his kingdom,) should be accounted to them for righteousness, i.e. should supply the defects of a scanty obedience in the sight of God, who, counting faith to them for righteousness or complete obedience, did thus justify, or make them just, and thereby capable of eternal life.

This is the faith for which God of his free grace justifies sinful man. We shall show now that, besides believing him to be the Messiah their King, it was farther required that those who would have the privilege, advantage, and deliverance of his kingdom should enter themselves into it, and, by baptism being made denizens and solemnly incorporated into that kingdom, live as became subjects obedient to the laws of it. For if they believed him to be the Messiah their King, but would not obey his laws, and would not have him to reign over them, they were but the greater rebels. And God would not justify them for a faith that did but increase their guilt and oppose diametrically the kingdom and design of the Messiah. Faith without works, i.e. the works of sincere obedience to the laws and will of Christ, is not sufficient for our justification.

Neither indeed could it be otherwise. For life, eternal life, being the reward of justice or righteousness only, appointed by the righteous God (who is of purer eyes than to behold iniquity) to those who only had no taint or infection of sin upon them, it is impossible that he should justify those who had no regard to justice at all whatever he believed. This would have been to encourage iniquity, contrary to the purity of his nature, and to have condemned that eternal law of right which is holy, just, and good, of which no one precept or rule is abrogated or repealed, nor indeed can be, whilst God is an holy, just, and righteous God and man a rational creature. The duties of that law, arising from the constitution of his very nature, are of eternal obligation; nor can it be taken away or dispensed with, without changing the nature of things, overturning the measures of right and wrong, and thereby introducing and authorising irregularity, confusion, and disorder in the world. Christ's coming into the world was not for such an end as that; but on the contrary, to reform the corrupt state of degenerate men, and out of those who would mend their lives and bring forth fruit meet for repentance, erect a new kingdom.

This is the law of that kingdom, as well as of all mankind; and that law, by which all men shall be judged at the last day. Only those who have believed Jesus to be the Messiah and have taken him to be their King, with a sincere endeavor after righteousness in obeying his law, shall have their past sins not imputed to them, and shall have that faith taken instead of obedience, where frailty and weakness made them transgress and sin prevailed after conversion.

He did not expect, it is true, a perfect obedience, void of slips and falls. He knew our make and the weakness of our constitution too well, and was sent with a supply for that defect. Besides, perfect obedience was the righteousness of the law of works; and then the reward would be of debt and not of grace; and to such there was no need of faith to be imputed to them for righteousness. They stood upon their own legs, were just already, and needed no allowance to be made them for believing Jesus to be the Messiah, taking him for their king, and becoming his subjects. But that Christ does require obedience, sincere obedience, is evident from the law he himself delivers (unless he can be supposed to give and inculcate laws, only to have them disobeyed) and from the sentence he will pass when he comes to judge.

These two, faith and repentance, i.e. believing Jesus to be the Messiah, and a good life, are the indispensable conditions of the new covenant, to be performed by all those who would obtain eternal life.

To this, it is likely, it will be objected by some, that to believe only that Jesus of Nazareth is the Messiah is only an historical, and not a justifying or saving faith.

To which I answer, that I allow to the makers of

systems and their followers to invent and use what distinctions they please, and to call things by what names they think fit. But I cannot allow to them or to any man an authority to make a religion for me, or to alter that which God has revealed. And if they please to call the believing that which our Saviour and his apostles preached and proposed alone to be believed, an historical faith, they have their liberty. But they must have a care how they deny it to be a justifying or saving faith, when our Saviour and his apostles have declared it so to be, and taught no other which men should receive and whereby they should be made believers unto eternal life; unless they can so far make bold with our Saviour, for the sake of their beloved systems, as to say that he forgot what he came into the world for, and that he and his apostles did not instruct people right in the way and mysteries of salvation. For that this is the sole doctrine pressed and required to be believed in the whole tenor of our Saviour's and his apostles' preaching, we have showed. And I challenge them to show that there was any other doctrine upon their assent to which, or disbelief of it, men were pronounced believers or unbelievers, and accordingly received into the church of Christ as members of his body, as far as mere believing could make them so, or else kept out of it.

The other parts of divine revelation are objects of faith and are so to be received. They are truths whereof no one can be rejected. None that is once known to be such may or ought to be disbelieved. For to acknowledge any proposition to be of divine revelation and authority, and yet to deny or disbelieve it, is to offend against this fundamental article and ground of faith, that God is true. But yet a great many of the truths revealed in the gospel, everyone does and must confess a man may be ignorant of, nay, disbelieve, without danger to his salvation; as is evident in those who, allowing the authority, differ in the interpretation and meaning of several texts of Scripture, not thought fundamental. In all which, it is plain, the contending parties on one side or the other are ignorant of, nay, disbelieve the truths delivered in holy writ; unless contrarieties and contradictions can be contained in the same words, and divine revelation can mean contrary to itself.

Though all divine revelation requires the obedience of faith, yet every truth of inspired Scriptures is not one of those that by the law of faith is required to be explicitly believed to justification. What those are, we have seen by what our Saviour and his apostles proposed to and required in those whom they converted to the faith. Those are fundamentals, which it is not enough not to disbelieve; every one is required actually to assent to them. But any other proposition contained in the Scripture which God has not thus made a necessary part of the law of faith, (without an actual assent to which he will not allow any one to be a believer,) a man may be ignorant of, without hazarding his salvation by a defect in his faith. He believes all that God has made necessary for him to believe and assent to. And as for the rest of divine truths, there is nothing more required of him, but that he receive all the parts of divine revelation with a docility and disposition prepared to embrace and assent to all truths coming from God; and to submit his mind to whatsoever shall appear to him to bear that character.

The greatest part of mankind have not leisure for learning and logic and superfine distinctions of the schools. Where the hand is used to the plough and the spade, the head is seldom elevated to sublime notions, or exercised in mysterious reasoning. It is well if men of that rank (to say nothing of the other sex) can comprehend plain propositions, and a short reasoning about things familiar to their minds, and nearly allied to their daily experience. Go beyond this, and you amaze the greatest part of mankind, and may as well talk Arabic to a poor day-laborer as the notions and languages that the books and disputes of religion are filled with; and as soon you will be understood. Had God intended that none but the learned scribe, disputer, or wise of this world should be Christians or be saved, thus religion should have been prepared for them, filled with speculations and niceties, obscure terms, and abstract notions. But men of that expectation, men furnished with such acquisitions, the apostle tells us, are rather shut out from the simplicity of the gospel, to make way for those poor, ignorant, illiterate, who heard and believed promises of a Deliverer and believed Jesus to be him, who could conceive a man dead and made alive again, and believe that he should at the end of the world come again and pass sentence on all men, according to their deeds.

He that considers this will not be so hot to contend for a number of fundamental articles, all necessary, every one of them, to be explicitly believed by every one for salvation, without knowing them himself, or being able to enumerate them to another. Can there be anything more absurd than to say, there are several fundamental articles, each of which every man must explicitly believe, upon pain of damnation, and yet not be able to say which they be? This, as great an absurdity as it is, cannot be otherwise, whilst men will take upon them to alter the terms of the gospel. When you would know of them what then is enough, they cannot tell you. The reason whereof is visible, *viz.* because they being able to produce no other reason for their collection of fundamental articles, to prove them necessary to be believed, but because they are of divine authority, and contained in the Holy Scriptures, they know not where to stop, when they have once begun; those texts that they leave out or from which they deduce none of their fundamentals being of the same divine authority, and so upon that account equally fundamental with what they culled out, though not so well suited to their particular systems.

Hence come those endless and unreasonable contentions about fundamentals, whilst each censures the defect, redundancy, or falsehood of what others require as necessary to be believed. And yet he gives himself not a catalogue of his own fundamentals, which he will say is sufficient and complete. Nor is it to be wondered; since in this way it is impossible to stop short of putting every proposition, divinely revealed, into the list of fundamentals; all of them being of divine and so of equal authority; and upon that account, equally necessary to be believed by every one that is a Christian, though they are not all necessary to be believed to make any one a Christian. It is no wonder, therefore, there have been such fierce contests and such cruel havock made amongst Christians about fundamentals; whilst every one would set up his system, upon pain of fire and faggot in this and hell-fire in the other world.

LIBERALISM IN POLITICS

Political power I take to be a right of making laws with penalties of death, and consequently all less penalties, for the regulating and preserving of property, and of employing the force of the community, in the execution of such laws, and in the defence of the commonwealth from foreign injury; and all this only for the public good.

To understand political power aright, and derive it from its original, we must consider what state all men are naturally in, and that is a state of perfect freedom to order their actions and dispose of their possessions and persons as they think fit, within the bounds of the law of nature, without asking leave or depending upon the will of any other man. A state also of equality, wherein all the power and jurisdiction is reciprocal, no one having more than another; there being nothing more evident than that creatures of the same species and rank, promiscuously born to all the same advantages of nature and the use of the same faculties, should also be equal one amongst another without subordination or subjection; unless the lord and master of them all should, by manifest declaration of his will, set one above another, and confer on him, by an evident and clear appointment, an undoubted right to dominion and sovereignty.

But though this be a state of liberty, yet it is not a state of licence. Though man in that state have an uncontrollable liberty to dispose of his person or possessions, yet he has not liberty to destroy himself, or so much as any creature in his possession, but where some nobler use than its bare preservation calls for it. The state of nature has a law of nature to govern it, which obliges everyone; and reason, which is that law, teaches all mankind who will but consult it that, being all equal and independent, no one ought to harm another in his life, health, liberty or possessions. For men being all the workmanship of one omnipotent and infininitely wise Maker, all the servants of one sovereign master, sent into the world by his order and about his business, they are his property whose workmanship they are, made to last during his, not another's pleasure, and being furnished with like faculties, sharing all in one community of nature, there cannot be supposed any such subordination among us that may authorize us to destroy another, as if we were made for one another's uses, as the inferior ranks of creatures are for ours. Every one, as he is bound to preserve himself and not to quit his station wilfully, so by the like reason, when his own preservation comes not in competition, ought he as much as he can to preserve the rest of mankind, and may not, unless it be to do justice to an offender, take away or impair the life, or what tends to the preservation of life, the liberty, health, limb, or goods of another.

And that all men may be restrained from invading others' rights and from doing hurt to one another, and the law of nature be observed, which willeth the peace and preservation of all mankind, the execution of the law of nature is, in that state, put into every man's hands, whereby every one has a right to punish the transgressors of that law to such a degree as may hinder its violation. For the law of nature would, as all other laws that concern men in this world, be in vain, if there were nobody that in the state of nature had a power to execute that law, and thereby preserve the innocent and restrain offenders. And if any one in the state of nature may punish another for any evil he has done, every one may do so; for in that state of perfect equality, where naturally there is no superiority of jurisdiction of one over another, what any may do in prosecution of that law, every one must needs have a right to do.

I doubt not that it will be objected that it is unreasonable for men to be judges in their own cases, that self love will make men partial to themselves and their friends, and on the other side that ill-nature, passion and revenge will carry them too far in punishing others, and hence nothing but confusion and disorder will follow, and that therefore God hath certainly appointed government to restrain the partiality and violence of men. I easily grant that civil government is the proper remedy for the inconveniences of the state of nature, which must certainly be great where men may be judges in their own case, since it is easy to be imagined that he who was so unjust as to do his brother an injury will scarce be so just as to condemn himself for it. But I shall desire those who make this objection to remember that absolute monarchs are but men. And if government is to be the remedy of those evils which necessarily follow from men's being judges in their own cases, and the state of nature is therefore not to be endured, I desire to know what kind of government that is, and how much better it is than the state of nature, where one man commanding a multitude has the liberty to be judge in his own case, and may do to all his subjects whatever he pleases, without the least liberty to any one to question or control those who execute his pleasure? and in whatsoever he doth, whether led by reason, mistake, or passion, must be submitted to? Much better it is in the state of nature, wherein men are not bound to submit to the unjust will of another; and if he that judges, judges amiss in his own or any other case, he is answerable for it to the rest of mankind.

Whether we consider natural reason which tells us that men, being once born, have a right to their preservation, and consequently to meat and drink and such other things as nature affords for their subsistence; or revelation which gives us an account of those grants God made of the world to Adam and to Noah and his sons; it is very clear that God, as King David says (Psalm cxv, 16) "has given the earth to the children of men"; given it to mankind in common. I shall endeavor to show how men might come to have a property in several parts of that which God gave to mankind in common, and that without any express compact of all the commoners.

Though the earth and all inferior creatures be common to all men, yet every man has a property in his own person: this nobody has any right to but himself. The labor of his body and the work of his hands, we may say, are properly his. Whatsoever then he removes out of the state that nature has provided and left it in, he hath mixed his labor with, and joined to it something that is his own, and thereby makes it his property. It being by him removed from the common state nature hath placed it in, it hath by this labor something annexed to it that excludes the common right of other men. For this labor being the unquestionable property of the laborer, no man but he can have a right to what that is once joined to, at least where there is enough and as good left in common for others. He that is nourished by the acorns he picked up under an oak, or the apples he gathered from the trees in the wood, has certainly appropriated them to himself. Nobody can deny but the nourishment is his. I ask then, when did they begin to be his? when he digested? or when he eat? or when he boiled? or when he brought them home? or when he picked them up? And it is plain, if the first gathering made them not his, nothing else could. That labor put a distinction between them and common; that added something to them more than nature, the common mother of all, had done; and so they became his private right. And will any one say, he had no right to those acorns or apples he thus appropriated, because he had not the consent of all mankind to make them his? Was it a robbery thus to assume to himself what belonged to all in common? If such a consent as that was necessary, man had starved, notwithstanding the plenty God had given him. We see in commons, which remain so by compact, that it is the taking any part of what is common and removing it out of the state nature leaves it in, which begins the property; without which the common is of no use.

But the chief matter of property being now not the fruits of the earth and the beasts that subsist on it, but the earth itself, as that which takes in and carries with it all the rest, I think it is plain that property in that too is acquired as the former. As much land as a man tills, plants, improves, cultivates, and can use the product of, so much is his property. He by his labor does, as it were, enclose it from the common. Nor will it invalidate his right to say everybody else has an equal title to it, and therefore he cannot appropriate, he cannot enclose, without the consent of all his fellow-commoners, all mankind. God, when he gave the world in common to all mankind, commanded man also to labor, and the penury of his condition required it of him. God and his reason commanded him to subdue the earth, i.e. improve it for the benefit of life, and therein lay out something upon it that was his own, his labor. He that, in obedience to this command of God, subdued, tilled, and sowed any part of it, thereby annexed to it something that was his property, which another had no title to, nor could without injury take from him.

The measure of property nature has well set by the extent of men's labor and the conveniences of life. No man's labor could subdue or appropriate all. Nor could his enjoyment consume more than a small part. So it was impossible for any man, this way, to intrench upon the right of another, or acquire to himself a property to the prejudice of his neighbor, who would still have room for as good and as large a possession (after the other had taken out his) as before it was appropriated.

The greatest part of things really useful to the life of man, and such as the necessity of subsisting made the first commoners of the world look after, as it doth the Americans[1] now, are generally things of short duration; such as, if they are not consumed by use, will decay and perish of themselves. Gold, silver, and diamonds are things that fancy or agreement hath put the value on, more than real use and the necessary support of life. Now of those good things which nature hath provided in common, everyone had a right, (as hath been said) to as much as he could use, and property in all that he could effect with his labor. All that his industry could extend to, to alter from the state nature had put it in, was his. He that gathered a hundred bushels of acorns or apples had thereby a property in them. They were his goods as soon as gathered. He was only to look that he used them before they spoiled, else he took more than his share, and robbed others. And indeed it was a foolish thing, as well as dishonest, to hoard up more

[1] The reference is of course to the American Indians, whom Locke supposed to be living in a state of nature and without any kind of political organization.

than he could make use of. If he gave away a part to anybody else, so that it perished not uselessly in his possession, these he also made use of. And if he also bartered away plums that would have rotted in a week for nuts that would last good for his eating a whole year, he did no injury. He wasted not the common stock, destroyed no part of the portion of the goods that belonged to others, so long as nothing perished uselessly in his hands. Again, if he would give or exchange his sheep for shells, or wool for a sparkling pebble or a diamond, and keep those by him all his life, he invaded not the right of others. He might heap as much of these durable things as he pleased; the exceeding of the bounds of his just property not lying in the largeness of his possession, but the perishing of any thing uselessly in it.

And thus came in the use of money, some lasting thing that men might keep without spoiling, and that by mutual consent men would take in exchange for the truly useful, but perishable, supports of life.

And as different degrees of industry were apt to give men possessions in different proportions, so this invention of money gave them the opportunity to continue and enlarge them. Since gold and silver, being little useful to the life of man in proportion to food, raiment, and carriage, has its value only from the consent of men, whereof labor yet makes in great part the measure, it is plain that men have agreed to a disproportionate and unequal possession of the earth, they having, by a tacit and voluntary consent, found out a way how a man may fairly possess more land than he himself can use the product of, by receiving in exchange for the overplus, gold and silver, which may be hoarded up without injury to any one, these metals not spoiling or decaying in the hands of the possessor. This partage of things in an inequality of private possessions, men have made practicable out of the bounds of society and without compact, only by putting a value on gold and silver and tacitly agreeing in the use of money. For in governments the laws regulate the right of property, and the possession of land is determined by positive constitutions.

God having made man such a creature that, in his own judgment, it was not good for him to be alone, put him under strong obligations of necessity, convenience, and inclination to drive him into society, as well as fitted him with understanding and language to continue and enjoy it. The first society was between man and wife, which gave beginning to that between parents and children; to which, in time, that between master and servant came to be added. And though all these might and commonly did meet together and make up but one family, wherein the master or mistress of it had some sort of rule proper to a family; each of these or all together came short of political society, as we shall see, if we consider the different ends, ties, and bounds of each of these.

Man being born, as has been proved, with a title to perfect freedom and uncontrolled enjoyment of all the rights and privileges of the law of nature, equally with any other man or number of men in the world, hath by nature a power, not only to preserve his property, that is, his life, liberty, and estate, against the injuries and attempts of other men, but to judge of and punish the breaches of that law in others, as he is persuaded the offence deserves, even with death itself, in crimes where the heinousness of the fact in his opinion requires it. But because no political society can be nor subsist without having in itself the power to preserve the property, and, in order thereunto, punish the offences of all those of that society, there and there only is political society where every one of the members hath quitted his natural power, resigned it up into the hands of the community in all cases that exclude him not from appealing for protection to the law established by it. And thus all private judgment of every particular member being excluded, the community comes to be umpire by settled standing rules, indifferent and the same to all parties; and by men having authority from the community for the execution of those rules, decides all the differences that may happen between any members of that society concerning any matter of right, and punishes those offences which any member hath committed against the society, with such penalties as the law has established, whereby it is easy to discern who are and who are not in political society together. Those who are united into one body and have a common established law and judicature to appeal to, with authority to decide controversies between them, and punish offenders, are in civil society one with another; but those who have no such common appeal, I mean on earth, are still in the state of nature, each being, where there is no other, judge for himself and executioner, which is, as I have before showed, the perfect state of nature.

Men being, as has been said, by nature, all free, equal, and independent, no one can be put out of this estate and subjected to the political power of another, without his own consent. The only way whereby any one divests himself of his natural liberty and puts on the bonds of civil society is by agreeing with other men to join and unite into a community, for their comfortable, safe, and peaceable living one amongst another, in a secure enjoyment of their properties, and a greater security against any that are not of it. This any number of men may do, because it injures not the freedom of the rest: they are left as they were in the state of nature. When any number of men have so consented to make one community or government, they are thereby presently incorporated and make one body politic, wherein the majority have a right to act and conclude the rest.

For when any number of men have, by the consent of every individual, made a community, they have thereby made that community one body, with a power to act as one body, which is only by the will and determination of the majority. For that which acts any community, being only the consent of the individuals of it, and it being necessary to that which is one body to move one way, it is necessary the body should move that way whither the greater force carries it, which is the consent of the majority. Or else it is impossible it should act or continue one body, one community, which the consent of every individual that united into it agreed that it should. And so every one is bound by that consent to be concluded by the majority. And therefore we see that in assemblies, impowered to act by positive laws, where no number is set by that positive law which impowers them, the act of the majority passes for the act of the whole and of course determines, as having by the law of nature and reason the power of the whole.

And thus every man, by consenting with others to make one body politic under one government, puts himself under an obligation to every one of that society, to submit to the determination of the majority and to be concluded by it. Or else this original compact, whereby he with others incorporate into one society, would signify nothing and be no compact, if he be left free and under no other ties than he was in before, in the state of nature. For what appearance would there be of any compact? What new engagement if he were no farther tied by any decrees of the society, than he himself thought fit and did actually consent to? This would be still as great a liberty as he himself had before his compact, or any one else in the state of nature hath, who may submit himself and consent to any acts of it if he thinks fit.

For if the consent of the majority shall not in reason be received as the act of the whole and conclude every individual, nothing but the consent of every individual can make anything to be the act of the whole. But such a consent is next to impossible ever to be had, if we consider the infirmities of health, and avocations of business which in a number, though much less than that of a commonwealth, will necessarily keep many away from the public assembly.

Whosoever therefore out of a state of nature unite into a community, must be understood to give up all the power necessary to the ends for which they unite into society, to the majority of the community, unless they expressly agreed in any number greater than the majority. And this is done by barely agreeing to unite into one political society, which is all the compact that is or needs be between the individuals that enter into or make up a commonwealth. And thus that which begins and actually constitutes any political society is nothing but a consent of any number of freemen capable of a majority, to unite and incorporate into such a society. And this is that and that only, which did or could give beginning to any lawful government in the world.

If man in the state of nature be so free as has been said, if he be absolute lord of his own person and possessions, equal to the greatest and subject to nobody, why will he part with his freedom? why will he give up his empire and subject himself to the dominion and control of any other power? To which it is obvious to answer, that, though in the state of nature he hath such a right, yet the enjoyment of it is very uncertain and constantly exposed to the invasion of others. For all being kings as much as he, every man his equal, and the greater part no strict observers of equity and justice, the enjoyment of the property he has in this state is very unsafe, very unsecure. This makes him willing to quit a condition which, however free, is full of fears and continual dangers. And it is not without reason that he seeks out and is willing to join in society with others, who are already united or have a mind to unite, for the mutual preservation of their lives, liberties, and estates, which I call by the general name property.

The great and chief end therefore of men's uniting into commonwealths and putting themselves under government is the preservation of their property. To which in the state of nature there are many things wanting.

First, there wants an established, settled, known law, received and allowed by common consent to be the standard of right and wrong, and the common measure to decide all controversies between them. For though the law of nature be plain and intelligible to all rational creatures, yet men being biassed by their interest, as well as ignorant for want of studying it, are not apt to allow of it as a law binding to them in the application of it to their particular cases.

Secondly, in the state of nature there wants a known and indifferent judge, with authority to determine all differences according to the established law. For every one in that state being both judge and executioner of the law of nature, men being partial to themselves, passion and revenge is very apt to carry them too far, and with too much heat, in their own cases, as well as negligence and unconcernedness to make them too remiss in other men's.

Thirdly, in the state of nature there often wants power to back and support the sentence when right and to give it due execution. They who by any injustice offended will seldom fail, when they are able, by force to make good their injustice. Such resistance many times makes the punishments dangerous, and frequently destructive, to those who attempt it.

Thus mankind, notwithstanding all the privileges of the state of nature, being but in an ill condition, while they remain in it, are quickly driven into society. Hence it comes to pass that we seldom find any number of men live any time together in this state. The inconveniences that they are therein exposed to, by the irregular and uncertain exercise of the power every man has of punishing the transgressions of others, make them take sanctuary under the established laws of government, and therein seek the preservation of their property. It is this makes them so willingly give up every one his single power of punishing, to be exercised by such alone as shall be appointed to it amongst them, and by such rules as the community, or those authorized by them to that purpose, shall agree on. And in this we have the original right of both the legislative and executive power, as well as of the governments and societies themselves.

Political power is that power which every man having in the state of nature has given up into the hands of the society, and therein to the governors whom the society hath set over itself, with this express or tacit trust, that it shall be employed for their good and the preservation of their property. Now this power which every man has in the state of nature, and which he parts with to the society in all such cases where the society can secure him, is to use such means for the preserving of his own property as he thinks good and nature allows him, and to punish the breach of the law of nature in others, so as (according to the best of his reason) may most conduce to the preservation of himself and the rest of mankind. So that the end and measure of this power, when in every man's hands in the state of nature, being the preservation of all of his society, that is, all mankind in general, it can have no other end or measure when in the hands of the magistrate, but to preserve the members of that society in their lives, liberties, and possessions. And so it cannot be an absolute arbitrary power over their lives and fortunes, which are as much as possible to be preserved, but a power to make laws, and annex such penalties to them, as may tend to the preservation of the whole, by cutting off those parts and those only which are so corrupt that they threaten the sound and healthy, without which no severity is lawful. And this power has its original only from compact and agreement and the mutual consent of those who make up the community.

Wherever law ends, tyranny begins, if the law be transgressed to another's harm. And whosoever in authority exceeds the power given him by the law, and makes use of the force he has under his command, to compass that upon the subject which the law allows not, ceases in that to be a magistrate; and, acting without authority, may be opposed as any other man who by force invades the right of another. This is acknowledged in subordinate magistrates. He that hath authority to seize my person in the street may be opposed as a thief and a robber if he endeavors to break into my house to execute a writ, notwithstanding that I know he has such a warrant and such a legal authority as will impower him to arrest me abroad. And why this should not hold in the highest as well as in the most inferior magistrate, I would gladly be informed. Is it reasonable that the eldest brother, because he has the greatest part of his father's estate, should thereby have a right to take away any of his younger brother's portions? Or that a rich man, who possessed a whole country, should from thence have a right to seize when he pleased the cottage and garden of his poor neighbor? The being rightfully possessed of great power and riches, exceedingly beyond the greatest part of the sons of Adam, is so far from being an excuse, much less a reason, for rapine and oppression, which the endamaging another without authority is, that it is a great aggravation of it. For the exceeding the bounds of authority is no more a right in a great than in a petty officer, no more justifiable in a king than a constable; but is so much the worse in him, in that he has more trust put in him, has already a much greater share than the rest of his brethren, and is supposed from the advantages of his education, employment, and counsellors, to be more knowing in the measures of right and wrong.

"May the commands then of a prince be opposed? May he be resisted as often as any one shall find himself aggrieved, and but imagine he has not right done him? This will unhinge and overturn all policies and, instead of government and order, leave nothing but anarchy and confusion."

To this I answer that force is to be opposed to nothing but to unjust and unlawful force. Whoever makes any opposition in any other case draws on himself a just condemnation both from God and man. And so no such danger or confusion will follow, as is often suggested.

To this perhaps it will be said that the people being ignorant and always discontented, to lay the foundation of government in the unsteady opinion and uncertain humor of the people is to expose it to certain ruin; and no government will be able long to subsist, if the people may set up a new legislature, whenever they take offence at the old one. To this I answer, quite the contrary. People are not so easily got out of their old forms as some are apt to suggest. They are hardly to be prevailed with to amend the acknowledged faults in the frame they have been accustomed to. And if there be any original defects or adventitious ones introduced by time or corruption, it is not an easy thing to get them changed, even when all the world sees there is an opportunity for it.

But it will be said, this hypothesis lays a ferment for frequent rebellion. To which I answer:

First, no more than any other hypothesis. For when the people are made miserable, and find themselves exposed to the ill-usage of arbitrary power, cry up their governors as much as you will, for sons of Jupiter, let them be sacred or divine, descended or authorized from heaven, give them out for whom or what you please, the same will happen. The people, generally ill-treated and contrary to right, will be ready upon any occasion to ease themselves of a burden that sits heavy upon them. They will wish and seek for the opportunity which, in the change, weakness, and accidents of human affairs, seldom delays long to offer itself. He must have lived but a little while in the world who has not seen examples of this in his time. And he must have read very little who cannot produce examples of it in all sorts of governments in the world.

Secondly, I answer, such revolutions happen not upon every little mismanagement in public affairs. Great mistakes in the ruling part, many wrong and inconvenient laws, and all the slips of human frailty, will be borne by the people without mutiny or murmur. But if a long train of abuses, prevarications, and artifices, all tending the same way, make the design visible to the people, and they cannot but feel what they lie under and see whither they are going, it is not to be wondered that they should then arouse themselves, and endeavor to put the rule into such hands which may secure to them the ends for which government was at first erected, and without which ancient names and specious forms are so far from being better, that they are much worse, than the state of nature or pure anarchy; the inconveniences being all as great and as near, but the remedy farther off and more difficult.

Thirdly, I answer, that this doctrine of a power in the people of providing for their safety anew, by a new legislature, when their legislators have acted contrary to their trust, by invading their property, is the best fence against rebellion and the probablest means to hinder it. For rebellion being an opposition, not to persons but authority, which is founded only in the constitutions and laws of government, those, whoever they be, who by force break through and by force justify their violation of them, are truly and properly rebels. For when men, by entering into society and civil government, have excluded force and introduced laws for the preservation of property, peace, and unity amongst themselves, those who set up force again in opposition to the laws do *rebellare,* that is, bring back again the state of war, and are properly rebels; which they who are in power (by the pretence they have to authority, the temptation of force they have in their hands, and the flattery of those about them) being likeliest to do, the properest way to prevent the evil is to show them the danger and injustice of it, who are under the greatest temptation to run into it.

The end of government is the good of mankind. And which is best for mankind, that the people should be always exposed to the boundless will of tyranny, or that the rulers should be sometimes liable to be opposed, when they grow exorbitant in the use of their power and employ it for the destruction, and not the preservation, of the properties of their people?

Nor let any one say that mischief can arise from hence, as often as it shall please a busy head or turbulent spirit, to desire the alteration of the government. It is true, such men may stir, whenever they please. But it will be only to their own just ruin and perdition. For till the mischief be grown general and the ill designs of the rulers become visible, or their attempts sensible to the greater part, the people who are more disposed to suffer than right themselves by resistance, are not apt to stir. The examples of particular injustice or oppression, of here and there an unfortunate man, moves them not. But if they universally have a persuasion, grounded upon manifest evidence, that designs are carrying on against their liberties, and the general course and tendency of things cannot but give them strong suspicions of the evil intention of their governors, who is to be blamed for it? Who can help it, if they who might avoid it bring themselves into this suspicion? Are the people to be blamed, if they have the sense of rational creatures, and can think of things no otherwise than as they find and feel them? And is it not rather *their* fault, who put things into such a posture, that they would not have them thought to be as they are? I grant that the pride, ambition, and turbulency of private men have sometimes caused great disorders in commonwealths, and factions have been fatal to states and kingdoms. But whether the mischief hath oftener begun in the people's wantonness and a desire to cast off the lawful authority of their rulers, or in the rulers' insolence and endeavors to get and exercise an arbitrary power over their people; whether oppression or disobedience gave the first rise to the disorder; I leave it to impartial history to determine. This I am sure, whoever, either ruler or subject, by force goes about to invade the rights of either prince or people, and lays the foundation for overturning the constitution and frame of any just government, is highly guilty of the greatest crime, I think, a man is capable of; being to answer for all those mischiefs of blood, rapine, and desolation, which the breaking to pieces of governments brings on a country. And he who does it, is justly to be esteemed the common enemy and pest of mankind, and is to be treated accordingly.

LOCKE'S THEORY OF KNOWLEDGE, AS PRESENTED IN HIS ESSAY CONCERNING HUMAN UNDER-STANDING

INTRODUCTION

THE EPISTLE TO THE READER, SHOWING HOW THE ESSAY CAME TO BE WRITTEN

READER,

I HERE put into thy hands, what has been the diversion of some of my idle and heavy hours: if it has the good luck to prove so of any of thine, and thou hast but half so much pleasure in reading, as I had in writing it, thou wilt as little think thy money, as I do my pains, ill bestowed. Mistake not this, for a commendation of my work; nor conclude, because I was pleased with the doing of it, that therefore I am fondly taken with it now it is done. He that hawks at larks and sparrows, has no less sport, though a much less considerable quarry, than he that flies at nobler game: and he is little acquainted with the subject of this treatise, the UNDERSTANDING, who does not know, that as it is the most elevated faculty of the soul, so it is employed with a greater and more constant delight than any of the other. Its searches after truth, are a sort of hawking and hunting, wherein the very pursuit makes a great part of the pleasure. Every step the mind takes in its progress towards knowledge, makes some discovery, which is not only new, but the best too, for the time at least.

For the understanding, like the eye, judging of objects only by its own sight, cannot but be pleased with what it discovers, having less regret for what has escaped it, because it is unknown. Thus he who has raised himself above the alms-basket, and not content to live lazily on scraps of begged opinions, sets his own thoughts on work, to find and follow truth, will (whatever he lights on) not miss the hunter's satisfaction; every moment of his pursuit will reward his pains with some delight, and he will have reason to think his time not ill-spent, even when he cannot much boast of any great acquisition.

This, Reader, is the entertainment of those who let loose their own thoughts, and follow them in writing; which thou oughtest not to envy them, since they afford thee an opportunity of the like diversion, if thou wilt make use of thy own thoughts in reading. It is to them, if they are thy own, that I refer myself: but if they are taken upon trust from others, it is no great matter what they are, they not following truth, but some meaner consideration; and it is not worth while to be concerned, what he says or thinks, who says or thinks only as he is directed by another. If thou judgest for thyself, I know thou wilt judge candidly; and then I shall not be harmed or offended, whatever be thy censure. For though it be certain, that there is nothing in this treatise, of the truth whereof I am not fully persuaded; yet I consider myself as liable to mistakes, as I can think thee, and know that this book must stand or fall with thee, not by any opinion I have of it, but thy own. If thou findest little in it new or instructive to thee, thou art not to blame me for it. It was not meant for those that had already mastered this subject, and made a thorough acquaintance with their own understandings; but for my own information, and the satisfaction of a few friends, who acknowledged themselves not to have sufficiently considered it.

Were it fit to trouble thee with the history of this Essay, I should tell thee, that five or six friends meeting at my chamber, and discoursing on a subject very remote from this, found themselves quickly at a stand, by the difficulties that rose on every side. After we had a while puzzled ourselves, without coming any nearer a resolution of those doubts which perplexed us, it came into my thoughts, that we took a wrong course; and that before we set ourselves upon inquiries of that nature, it was necessary to examine our own abilities, and see what objects our understandings were, or were not, fitted to deal with. This I proposed to the company, who all readily assented; and thereupon it was agreed, that this should be our first inquiry. Some hasty and undigested thoughts on a subject I had never before considered, which I set down against our next meeting, gave the first entrance into this discourse; which having been thus begun by chance, was continued by intreaty; written by incoherent parcels; and after long intervals of neglect, resumed again, as my humour or occasions permitted; and at last, in a retirement, where an attendance on my health gave me leisure, it was brought into that order thou now seest it.

This discontinued way of writing may have occasioned, besides others, two contrary faults, *viz.* that too little and too much may be said in it. If thou findest any thing wanting, I shall be glad, that what I have writ gives thee any desire, that I should have gone farther: if it seems too much to thee, thou must blame the subject; for when I put pen to paper, I thought all I should have to say on this matter, would have been contained in one sheet of paper, but the farther I went, the larger prospect I had; new discoveries led me still on, and so it grew insensibly to the bulk it now appears in. I will not deny, but possibly it might be reduced to a narrower compass than it is; and that some parts of it might be contracted; the way it has been writ in, by catches, and many long intervals of interruption, being apt to cause some repetitions. But to confess the truth, I am now too lazy, or too busy to make it shorter.

I am not ignorant how little I herein consult my own reputation, when I knowingly let it go with a fault, so apt to disgust the most judicious, who are always the nicest readers. But they who know sloth is apt to content itself with any excuse, will pardon me, if mine has prevailed on me, where, I think, I have a very good one. I will not therefore allege in my defence, that the same notion, having different respects, may be convenient or necessary to prove or illustrate several parts of the same discourse; and that so it has happened in many parts of this: but waving that, I shall frankly avow, that I have sometimes dwelt long upon the same argument, and expressed it different ways, with a quite different design. I pretend not to publish this Essay for the information of men of large thoughts, and quick apprehensions; to such masters of knowledge, I profess myself a scholar, and therefore warn them beforehand not to expect any thing here, but what, being spun out of my own coarse thoughts, is fitted to men of my own size; to whom, perhaps, it will not be unacceptable, that I have taken some pains to make plain and familiar to their thoughts some truths, which established prejudice, or the abstractedness of the ideas themselves, might render difficult. Some objects had need be turned on every side: and when the notion is new, as I confess some of these are to me, or out of the ordinary road, as I suspect they will appear to others; it is not one simple view of it, that will gain it admittance into every understanding, or fix it there with a clear and lasting impression. There are few, I believe, who have not observed in themselves or others, that what in one way of proposing was very obscure, another way of expressing it has made very clear and intelligible; though afterward the mind found little difference in the phrases, and wondered why one failed to be understood more than the other. But every thing does not hit alike upon every man's imagination. We have our understandings no less different than our palates; and he that thinks the same truth shall be equally relished by every one in the same dress, may as well hope to feast every one with the same sort of cookery: the meat may be the same, and the nourishment good, yet every one not be able to receive it with that seasoning: and it must be dressed another way, if you will have it go down with some, even of strong constitutions. The truth is, those who advised me to publish it, advised me, for this reason, to publish it as it is; and since I have been brought to let it go abroad, I desire it should be understood by whoever gives himself the pains to read it; I have so little affection to be in print, that if I were not flattered this Essay might be of some use to others, as I think it has been to me, I should have confined it to the view of some friends, who gave the first occasion to it. My appearing therefore in print, being on purpose to be as useful as I may, I think it necessary to make what I have to say, as easy and intelligible to all sorts of readers, as I can. And I had much rather the speculative and quick-sighted should complain of my being in some parts tedious, than that any one, not accustomed to abstract speculations, or prepossessed with different notions, should mistake, or not comprehend my meaning.

It will possibly be censured as a great piece of vanity or insolence in me, to pretend to instruct this our knowing age; it amounting to little less, when I own, that I publish this Essay with hopes it may be useful to others. But if it may be permitted to speak freely of those, who with a feigned modesty condemn as useless, what they themselves write, methinks it savours much more of vanity or insolence, to publish a book for any other end; and he fails very much of that respect he owes the public, who prints, and consequently expects men should read that, wherein he intends not they should meet with any thing of use to themselves or others: and should nothing else be found allowable in this treatise, yet my design will not cease to be so; and the goodness of my intention ought to be some excuse for the worthlessness of my present. It is that chiefly which secures me from the fear of censure, which I expect not to escape more than better writers. Men's principles, notions, and relishes are so different, that it is hard to find a book which pleases or displeases all men. I acknowledge the age we live in is not the least knowing, and therefore not the most easy to be satisfied. If I have not the good luck to please, yet nobody ought to be offended with me. I plainly tell all my readers, except half a dozen, this treatise was not at first intended for them; and therefore they need not be at the trouble to be of that number. But yet if any one thinks fit to be angry, and rail at it, he may do it securely: for I shall find some better way of spending my time, than in such kind of conversation. I shall always have the satisfaction to have aimed sincerely at truth and usefulness, though in one of the meanest ways. The commonwealth of learning is not at this time without master-builders, whose mighty designs in advancing the sciences, will leave lasting monuments to the admiration of posterity; but every one must not hope to be a Boyle, or a Sydenham; and in an age that produces such masters, as the great Huygenius, and the incomparable Mr. Newton, with some others of that strain; it is ambition enough to be employed as an under-labourer in clearing the ground a little, and removing some of the rubbish that lies in the way to knowledge; which certainly had been very much more advanced in the world, if the endeavours of ingenious and industrious men had not been much cumbered with the learned but frivolous use of uncouth, affected, or unintelligible terms, introduced into the sciences, and there made an art of, to that degree, that philosophy, which is nothing but the true knowledge of things, was thought unfit, or uncapable to be brought into well-bred company, and polite conversation. Vague and insignificant forms of speech, and abuse of language, have so long passed for mysteries of science; and hard and misapplied words, with little or no meaning, have, by prescription, such a right to be mistaken for deep learning, and height of speculation, that it will not be easy to persuade, either those who speak, or those who hear them, that they are but the covers of ignorance, and hindrance of true knowledge. To break in upon the sanctuary of vanity and ignorance, will be, I suppose, some service to human understanding: though so few are apt to think they deceive or are deceived in the use of words; or that the language of the sect they are of, has any faults in it which ought to be examined or corrected; that I hope I shall be pardoned, if I have in the third book dwelt long on this subject, and endeavoured to make it so plain, that neither the inveterateness of the mischief, nor the prevalence of the fashion, shall be any excuse for those, who will not take care about the meaning of their own words, and will not suffer the significancy of their expressions to be inquired into.

THE GENERAL DESIGN AND PLAN OF THE ESSAY

SINCE it is the understanding, that sets man above the rest of sensible beings, and gives him all the advantage and dominion, which he has over them; it is certainly a subject, even for its nobleness, worth our labour to inquire into. The understanding, like the eye, whilst it makes us see and perceive all other things, takes no notice of itself; and it requires art and pains to set it at a distance, and make it its own object. But, whatever be the difficulties that lie in the way of this inquiry; whatever it be, that keeps us so much in the dark to ourselves; sure I am, that all the light we can let in upon our own minds, all the acquaintance we can make with our own understandings, will not only be very pleasant, but bring us great advantage, in directing our thoughts in the search of other things.

This, therefore, being my purpose, to inquire into the original, certainty, and extent of human knowledge; together with the grounds and degrees of belief, opinion, and assent; I shall not at present meddle with the physical consideration of the mind; or trouble myself to examine, wherein its essence consists, or by what motions of our spirits, or alterations of our bodies, we come to have any sensation by our organs, or any ideas in our understandings; and whether those ideas do in their formation, any, or all of them, depend on matter or no. These are speculations, which, however curious and entertaining, I shall decline, as lying out of my way in the design I am now upon. It shall suffice to my present purpose, to consider the discerning faculties of a man, as they are employed about the objects, which they have to do with. And I shall imagine I have not wholly misemployed myself in the thoughts I shall have on this occasion, if, in this historical, plain method, I can give any account of the ways, whereby our understandings come to attain those notions of things we have, and can set down any measures of the certainty of our knowledge, or the grounds of those persuasions, which are to be found amongst men, so various, different, and wholly contradictory; and yet asserted, somewhere or other, with such assurance and confidence, that he that shall take a view of the opinions of mankind, observe their opposition, and at the same time consider the fondness and devotion wherewith they are embraced, the resolution and eagerness wherewith they are maintained, may perhaps have reason to suspect, that either there is no such thing as truth at all; or that mankind hath no sufficient means to attain a certain knowledge of it.

It is, therefore, worth while to search out the bounds between opinion and knowledge; and examine by what measures, in things, whereof we have no certain knowledge, we ought to regulate our assent, and moderate our persuasions. In order whereunto, I shall pursue this following method.

First, I shall enquire into the origin of those ideas, notions, or whatever else you please to call them, which a man observes, and is conscious to himself he has in his mind; and the ways, whereby the understanding comes to be furnished with them.[1]

Secondly, I shall endeavour to shew what knowledge the understanding hath by those ideas; and the certainty, evidence, and extent of it.

Thirdly, I shall make some enquiry into the nature and grounds of faith, or opinion; whereby I mean that assent, which we give to any proposition as true, of whose truth yet we have no certain knowledge: and here we

[1] For further comments by Locke on the nature of ideas, cf. p. 321.

shall have occasion to examine the reasons and degrees of assent.

If, by this enquiry into the nature of the understanding, I can discover the powers thereof; how far they reach; to what things they are in any degree proportionate; and where they fail us: I suppose it may be of use to prevail with the busy mind of man, to be more cautious in meddling with things exceeding its comprehension; to stop when it is at the utmost extent of its tether; and to sit down in a quiet ignorance of those things, which, upon examination, are found to be beyond the reach of our capacities. We should not then perhaps be so forward, out of an affectation of an universal knowledge, to raise questions, and perplex ourselves and others with disputes about things, to which our understandings are not suited; and of which we cannot frame in our minds any clear or distinct perceptions, or whereof (as it has perhaps too often happened) we have not any notions at all. If we can find out how far the understanding can extend its view, how far it has faculties to attain certainty, and in what cases it can only judge and guess; we may learn to content ourselves with what is attainable by us in this state.

For, though the comprehension of our understandings comes exceeding short of the vast extent of things; yet we shall have cause enough to magnify the bountiful author of our being, for that proportion and degree of knowledge he has bestowed on us, so far above all the rest of the inhabitants of this our mansion. Men have reason to be well satisfied with what God hath thought fit for them, since he hath given them whatsoever is necessary for the conveniences of life, and information of virtue; and has put within the reach of their discovery the comfortable provision for this life, and the way that leads to a better. How short soever their knowledge may come of an universal or perfect comprehension of whatsoever is, it yet secures their great concernments, that they have light enough to lead them to the knowledge of their maker, and the sight of their own duties. Men may find matter sufficient to busy their heads, and employ their hands with variety, delight and satisfaction; if they will not boldly quarrel with their own constitution, and throw away the blessings their hands are filled with, because they are not big enough to grasp every thing. We shall not have much reason to complain of the narrowness of our minds, if we will but employ them about what may be of use to us; for of that they are very capable: and it will be an unpardonable, as well as childish peevishness, if we undervalue the advantages of our knowledge, and neglect to improve it to the ends for which it was given us, because there are some things that are set out of the reach of it. It will be no excuse to an idle and untoward servant, who would not attend his business by candle-light, to plead that he had not broad sun-shine. The candle, that is set up in us, shines bright enough for all our purposes. The discoveries we can make with this, ought to satisfy us; and we shall then use our understandings right, when we entertain all objects in that way and proportion that they are suited to our faculties, and upon those grounds they are capable of being proposed to us, and not peremptorily, or intemperately require demonstration, and demand certainty, where probability only is to be had, and which is sufficient to govern all our concernments. If we will disbelieve every thing, because we certainly cannot know all things; we shall do much-what as wisely as he, who would not use his legs, but sit still and perish, because he had no wings to fly.

When we know our own strength, we shall the better know what to undertake with hopes of success: and when we have well surveyed the powers of our own minds, and made some estimate what we may expect from them, we shall not be inclined either to sit still, and not set our thoughts on work at all, in despair of knowing any thing; or, on the other side, question every thing, and disclaim all knowledge, because some things are not to be understood. It is of great use to the sailor, to know the length of his line, though he cannot with it fathom all the depths of the ocean. It is well he knows, that it is long enough to reach the bottom, at such places as are necessary to direct his voyage, and caution him against running upon shoals that may ruin him. Our business here is not to know all things, but those which concern our conduct. If we can find out those measures, whereby a rational creature, put in that state in which man is in this world, may, and ought to govern his opinions, and actions depending thereon, we need not to be troubled that some other things escape our knowledge.

This was that which gave the first rise to this essay concerning the understanding. For I thought that the first step towards satisfying several enquiries, the mind of man was very apt to run into, was to take a survey of our own understandings, examine our own powers, and see to what things they were adapted. Till that was done, I suspected we began at the wrong end, and in vain sought for satisfaction in a quiet and sure possession of truths that most concerned us, whilst we let loose our thoughts into the vast ocean of being; as if all that boundless extent were the natural and undoubted possession of our understandings, wherein there was nothing exempt from its decisions, or that escaped its comprehension. Thus men extending their enquiries beyond their capacities, and letting their thoughts wander into those depths, where they can find no sure footing; it is no wonder, that they raise questions, and multiply disputes, which, never coming to any clear resolution, are proper only to continue and increase their doubts, and to confirm them at last in perfect scepticism. Whereas, were the capacities of our understandings well considered, the extent of our knowledge once discovered, and the horizon found, which sets the bounds between the enlightened and dark parts of things, between what is, and what is not comprehensible by us; men would perhaps with less scruple acquiesce in the avowed ignorance of the one, and employ their thoughts and discourse with more advantage and satisfaction in the other.

Thus much I thought necessary to say concerning the occasion of this enquiry into human understanding. But, before I proceed on to what I have thought on this subject, I must here in the entrance beg pardon of my reader for the frequent use of the word "idea," which he will find in the following treatise. It being that term, which, I think, serves best to stand for whatsoever is the object of the understanding when a man thinks; I have used it to express whatever is meant by phantasm, notion, species, or whatever it is which the mind can be employed about in thinking; and I could not avoid frequently using it.

I presume it will be easily granted me, that there are such ideas in men's minds; every one is conscious of them in himself, and men's words and actions will satisfy him that they are in others.

Our first enquiry then shall be, how they come into the mind.

ON IDEAS AS THE MATERIALS OF ALL OUR KNOWLEDGE

THE REJECTION OF INNATE IDEAS AND PRINCIPLES

It is an established opinion amongst some men, that there are in the understanding certain innate principles; some primary notions, Κοιναὶ ἔννοιαι, characters, as it were, stamped upon the mind of man, which the soul receives in its very first being; and brings into the world with it. It would be sufficient to convince unprejudiced readers of the falseness of this supposition, if I should only shew (as I hope I shall in the following parts of this discourse) how men, barely by the use of their natural faculties, may attain to all the knowledge they have, without the help of any innate impressions; and may arrive at certainty, without any such original notions or principles. For I imagine any one will easily grant, that it would be impertinent to suppose, the ideas of colours innate in a creature, to whom God hath given sight, and a power to receive them by the eyes, from external objects: and no less unreasonable would it be to attribute several truths to the impressions of nature, and innate characters, when we may observe in ourselves faculties, fit to attain as easy and certain knowledge of them, as if they were originally imprinted on the mind.

But because a man is not permitted without censure to follow his own thoughts in the search of truth, when they lead him ever so little out of the common road; I shall set down the reasons that made me doubt of the truth of that opinion, as an excuse for my mistake, if I be in one; which I leave to be considered by those, who, with me, dispose themselves to embrace truth, wherever they find it.

There is nothing more commonly taken for granted, than that there are certain principles, both speculative and practical (for they speak of both) universally agreed upon by all mankind: which therefore, they argue, must needs be constant impressions, which the souls of men receive in their first beings, and which they bring into the world with them, as necessarily and really as they do any of their inherent faculties.

This argument, drawn from universal consent, has this misfortune in it, that if it were true in matter of fact, that there were certain truths, wherein all mankind agreed, it would not prove them innate, if there can be any other way shewn, how men may come to that universal agreement, in the things they do consent in; which I presume may be done.

But, which is worse, this argument of universal consent, which is made use of to prove innate principles, seems to me a demonstration that there are none such; because there are none to which all mankind give an universal assent. I shall begin with the speculative, and instance in those magnified principles of demonstration; "whatsoever is, is;" and, "it is impossible for the same thing to be, and not to be;" which, of all others, I think have the most allowed title to innate. These have so settled a reputation of maxims universally received, that it will, no doubt, be thought strange, if any one should seem to question it. But yet I take liberty to say, that these propositions are so far from having an universal assent, that there are a great part of mankind to whom they are not so much as known.

For, first, it is evident, that all children and idiots

have not the least apprehension or thought of them; and the want of that is enough to destroy that universal assent, which must needs be the necessary concomitant of all innate truths: it seeming to me near a contradiction, to say, that there are truths imprinted on the soul, which it perceives or understands not; imprinting, if it signify any thing, being nothing else, but the making certain truths to be perceived. For to imprint any thing on the mind, without the mind's perceiving it, seems to me hardly intelligible. If therefore children and idiots have souls, have minds, with those impressions upon them, they must unavoidably perceive them, and necessarily know and assent to these truths: which since they do not, it is evident that there are no such impressions. For if they are not notions naturally imprinted, how can they be innate? and if they are notions imprinted, how can they be unknown? To say a notion is imprinted on the mind, and yet at the same time to say, that the mind is ignorant of it, and never yet took notice of it, is to make this impression nothing. No proposition can be said to be in the mind, which it never yet knew, which it was never yet conscious of. For if any one may, then, by the same reason, all propositions that are true, and the mind is capable of ever assenting to, may be said to be in the mind, and to be imprinted: since, if any one can be said to be in the mind, which it never yet knew, it must be only, because it is capable of knowing it, and so the mind is of all truths it ever shall know. Nay, thus truths may be imprinted on the mind, which it never did, nor ever shall know: for a man may live long, and die at last in ignorance of many truths, which his mind was capable of knowing, and that with certainty. So that if the capacity of knowing, be the natural impression contended for, all the truths a man ever comes to know, will, by this account, be every one of them innate; and this great point will amount to no more, but only to a very improper way of speaking; which, whilst it pretends to assert the contrary, says nothing different from those, who deny innate principles. For nobody, I think, ever denied that the mind was capable of knowing several truths. The capacity, they say, is innate, the knowledge acquired. But then to what end such contest for certain innate maxims? If truths can be imprinted on the understanding without being perceived, I can see no difference there can be, between any truths the mind is capable of knowing, in respect of their original: they must all be innate, or all adventitious: in vain shall a man go about to distinguish them. He therefore, that talks of innate notions in the understanding, cannot (if he intend thereby any distinct sort of truths) mean such truths to be in the understanding, as it never perceived, and is yet wholly ignorant of. For if these words (to be in the understanding) have any propriety, they signify to be understood: so that, to be in the understanding, and not to be understood; to be in the mind, and never to be perceived; is all one, as to say, any thing is, and is not, in the mind or understanding.

The senses at first let in particular ideas, and furnish the yet empty cabinet; and the mind by degrees growing familiar with some of them, they are lodged in the memory, and names got to them. Afterwards the mind, proceeding farther, abstracts them, and by degrees learns the use of general names. In this manner the mind comes to be furnished with ideas and language, the materials about which to exercise its discursive faculty: and the use of reason becomes daily more visible, as these materials, that give it employment, increase. But though the having of general ideas, and the use of general words and reason, usually grow together; yet, I see not, how this any way proves them innate. The knowledge of some truths, I confess, is very early in the mind; but in a way that shows them not to be innate. For, if we will observe, we shall find it still to be about ideas, not innate, but acquired: it being about those first which are imprinted by external things, with which infants have earliest to do, which make the most frequent impressions on their senses. In ideas thus got, the mind discovers that some agree, and others differ, probably as soon as it has any use of memory; as soon as it is able to retain and perceive distinct ideas. But whether it be then, or no, this is certain, it does so, long before it has the use of words, or comes to that, which we commonly call "the use of reason." For a child knows as certainly, before it can speak, the difference between the ideas of sweet and bitter (i. e. that sweet is not bitter) as it knows afterwards (when it comes to speak) that wormwood and sugar-plums are not the same thing.

A child knows not that three and four are equal to seven, till he comes to be able to count seven, and has got the name and idea of equality: and then, upon explaining those words, he presently assents to, or rather perceives the truth of that proposition. But neither does he then readily assent, because it is an innate truth, nor was his assent wanting till then, because he wanted the use of reason; but the truth of it appears to him, as soon as he has settled in his mind the clear and distinct ideas, that these names stand for: and then he knows the truth of that proposition, upon the same grounds, and by the same means, that he knew before, that a rod and a cherry are not the same thing; and upon the same grounds also, that he may come to know afterwards, "that it is impossible for the same thing to be, and not to be." So that the later it is before any one comes to have those general ideas, about which those maxims are; or to know the signification of those general terms that stand for them; or to put together in his mind the ideas they stand for; the later also will it be before he comes to assent to those maxims, whose terms, with the ideas they stand for, being no more innate than those of a cat or a weasel, he must stay till time and observation have acquainted him with them; and then he will be in a capacity to know the truth of these maxims, upon the first occasion that shall make him put together those ideas in his mind, and observe whether they agree or disagree, according as is expressed in those propositions. And therefore it is, that a man knows that eighteen and nineteen are equal to thirty-seven, by the same self-evidence, that he knows one and two to be equal to three: yet a child knows this not so soon as the other; not for want of the use of reason, but because the ideas the words eighteen, nineteen, and thirty-seven stand for, are not so soon got, as those which are signified by one, two, and three.

Nor is this the prerogative of numbers alone, and propositions made about several of them; but even natural philosophy, and all the other sciences, afford propositions, which are sure to meet with assent as soon as they are understood. That two bodies cannot be in the same place, is a truth, that nobody any more sticks at, than at these maxims, "that it is impossible for the same thing to be, and not to be; that white is not black; that a square is not a circle; that yellowness is not sweetness:" these and a million of such other propositions, as many at least as we have distinct ideas of, every man in his wits, at first hearing, and knowing what the names stand for, must necessarily assent to. If these men will be true to their own rule, and have assent at first hearing and understanding the terms, to be a mark of innate, they must allow, not only as many innate propositions as men have distinct ideas; but as many as men can make propositions wherein different ideas are denied one of another. Since every proposition, wherein one different idea is denied of another, will as certainly find assent at first hearing and understanding the terms, as this general one "it is impossible for the same thing to be, and not to be;" or that which is the foundation of it, and is the easier understood of the two, "the same is not different:" by which account they will have legions of innate propositions of this one sort, without mentioning any other. But since no proposition can be innate, unless the ideas about which it is, be innate; this will be, to suppose all our ideas of colours, sounds, tastes, figure, &c. innate; than which there cannot be any thing more opposite to reason and experience. Universal and ready assent upon hearing and understanding the terms is (I grant) a mark of self-evidence: but self-evidence, depending not on innate impressions, but on something else (as we shall shew hereafter) belongs to several propositions, which nobody was yet so extravagant as to pretend to be innate.

If those speculative maxims, whereof we discoursed in the foregoing chapter, have not an actual universal assent from all mankind, as we there proved, it is much more visible concerning practical principles, that they come short of an universal reception: and I think it will be hard to instance any one moral rule, which can pretend to so general and ready an assent as, "what is, is;" or to be so manifest a truth as this, "that it is impossible for the same thing to be, and not to be." Whereby it is evident, that they are farther removed from a title to be innate; and the doubt of their being native impressions on the mind, is stronger against those moral principles than the other. Not that it brings their truth at all in question: they are equally true, though not equally evident. Those speculative maxims carry their own evidence with them; but moral principles require reasoning and discourse, and some exercise of the mind, to discover the certainty of their truth.[1] They lie not open as natural characters engraven on the mind; which, if any such were, they must needs be visible by themselves, and by their own light be certain and known to every body. But this is no derogation to their truth and certainty, no more than it is to the truth or certainty of the three angles of a triangle being equal to two right ones; because it is not so evident, as "the whole is bigger than a part;" nor so apt to be assented to at first hearing. It may suffice, that these moral rules are capable of demonstration; and therefore it is our own fault, if we come not to a certain knowledge of them. But the ignorance wherein many men are of them, and the slowness of assent wherewith others receive them, are manifest proofs that they are not innate, and such as offer themselves to their view without searching.

Whether there be any such moral principles, wherein all men do agree, I appeal to any, who have been but moderately conversant in the history of mankind, and looked abroad beyond the smoke of their own chimneys. Where is that practical truth, that is universally received without doubt or question, as it must be, if innate? Justice, and keeping of contracts, is that which most men seem to agree in. This is a principle, which is thought to extend itself to the dens of thieves, and the confederacies of the greatest villains; and they who

[1] This distinction between truths which "carry their own evidence with them" and those which "require reasoning and discourse" is further discussed on p. 229. Locke tells us that the former may be said to be known intuitively and the latter through demonstration.

have gone farthest towards the putting off of humanity itself, keep faith and rules of justice one with another. I grant that out-laws themselves do this one amongst another; but it is without receiving these as the innate laws of nature. They practise them as rules of convenience within their own communities: but it is impossible to conceive, that he embraces justice as a practical principle, who acts fairly with his fellow highwayman, and at the same time plunders or kills the next honest man he meets with. Justice and truth are the common ties of society; and therefore, even out-laws and robbers, who break with all the world besides, must keep faith and rules of equity amongst themselves, or else they cannot hold together. But will any one say, that those that live by fraud or rapine, have innate principles of truth and justice which they allow and assent to?

Perhaps it will be urged, that the tacit assent of their minds agrees to what their practice contradicts. I answer, first, I have always thought the actions of men the best interpreters of their thoughts. But since it is certain, that most men's practices, and some men's open professions, have either questioned or denied these principles, it is impossible to establish an universal consent, (though we should look for it only amongst grown men) without which it is impossible to conclude them innate. Secondly, it is very strange and unreasonable to suppose innate practical principles, that terminate only in contemplation. Practical principles derived from nature are there for operation, and must produce conformity of action, not barely speculative assent to their truth, or else they are in vain distinguished from speculative maxims. Nature, I confess, has put into man a desire of happiness, and an aversion to misery: these indeed are innate practical principles, which (as practical principles ought) do continue constantly to operate and influence all our actions without ceasing: these may be observed in all persons and all ages, steady and universal; but these are inclinations of the appetite to good, not impressions of truth on the understanding. I deny not, that there are natural tendencies imprinted on the minds of men; and that, from the very first instances of sense and perception, there are some things that are grateful, and others unwelcome to them; some things, that they incline to, and others that they fly: but this makes nothing for innate characters on the mind, which are to be the principles of knowledge, regulating our practice. Such natural impressions on the understanding are so far from being confirmed hereby, that this is an argument against them; since, if there were certain characters imprinted by nature on the understanding, as the principles of knowledge, we could not but perceive them constantly operate in us and influence our knowledge, as we do those others on the will and appetite; which never cease to be the constant springs and motives of all our actions, to which we perpetually feel them strongly impelling us.

Another reason that makes me doubt of any innate practical principles, is, that I think there cannot any one moral rule be proposed, whereof a man may not justly demand a reason: which would be perfectly ridiculous and absurd, if they were innate, or so much as self-evident; which every innate principle must needs be, and not need any proof to ascertain its truth, nor want any reason to gain it approbation. He would be thought void of common sense, who asked on the one side, or on the other side went to give, a reason, why it is impossible for the same thing to be, and not to be. It carries its own light and evidence with it, and needs no other proof: he that understands the terms, assents to it for its own sake, or else nothing will ever be able to prevail with him to do it. But should that most unshaken rule of morality, and foundation of all social virtue, "that one should do as he would be done unto," be proposed to one who never heard it before, but yet is of capacity to understand its meaning, might he not without any absurdity ask a reason why? and were not he that proposed it bound to make out the truth and reasonableness of it to him? which plainly shows it not to be innate; for if it were, it could neither want nor receive any proof; but must needs (at least, as soon as heard and understood) be received and assented to, as an unquestionable truth, which a man can by no means doubt of. So that the truth of all these moral rules plainly depends upon some other antecedent to them, and from which they must be deduced; which could not be, if either they were innate, or so much as self-evident.

Principles of actions indeed there are lodged in men's appetites, but these are so far from being innate moral principles, that if they were left to their full swing, they would carry men to the overturning of all morality. Moral laws are set as a curb and restraint to these exorbitant desires, which they cannot be but by rewards and punishments, that will overbalance the satisfaction any one shall propose to himself in the breach of the law. If therefore any thing be imprinted on the minds of all men as a law, all men must have a certain and unavoidable knowledge, that certain and unavoidable punishment will attend the breach of it. For, if men can be ignorant or doubtful of what is innate, innate principles are insisted on, and urged to no purpose; truth and certainty (the things pretended) are not at all secured by them: but men are in the same uncertain, floating estate with, as without them. An evident indubitable knowledge of unavoidable punishment, great enough to make the transgression very uneligible, must accompany an innate law; unless, with an innate law, they can suppose an innate gospel too. I would not here be mistaken, as if, because I deny an innate law, I thought there were none but positive laws. There is a great deal of difference between an innate law, and a law of nature; between something imprinted on our minds in their very original, and something that we being ignorant of may attain to the knowledge of, by the use and due application of our natural faculties. And I think they equally forsake the truth, who, running into the contrary extremes, either affirm an innate law, or deny that there is a law knowable by the light of nature, i. e. without the help of positive revelation.

If any idea can be imagined innate, the idea of God may, of all others, for many reasons be thought so; since it is hard to conceive, how there should be innate moral principles, without an innate idea of a Deity: without a notion of a law-maker, it is impossible to have a notion of a law, and an obligation to observe it. Besides the atheists, taken notice of amongst the ancients, and left branded upon the records of history, hath not navigation discovered, in these later ages, whole nations at the bay of Soladania, in Brazil, in Boranday, and in the Caribbee islands, &c. amongst whom there was to be found no notion of a God, no religion? These are instances of nations where uncultivated nature has been left to itself, without the help of letters, and discipline, and the improvements of arts and sciences. But there are others to be found, who have enjoyed these in a very great measure; who yet, for want of a due application of their thoughts this way, want the idea and knowledge of God. It will, I doubt not, be a surprise to others, as it was to me, to find the Siamites of this number. But for this, let them consult the king of France's late envoy thither, who gives no better account of the Chinese themselves. And if we will not believe La Loubère, the missionaries of China, even the Jesuits themselves, the great encomiasts of the Chinese, do all to a man agree, and will convince us that the sect of the literati, or learned, keeping to the old religion of China, and the ruling party there, are all of them atheists. And perhaps if we should, with attention, mind the lives and discourses of people not so far off, we should have too much reason to fear, that many in more civilised countries have no very strong and clear impressions of a Deity upon their minds; and that the complaints of atheism, made from the pulpit, are not without reason. And though only some profligate wretches own it too bare-facedly now; yet perhaps we should hear more than we do of it from others, did not the fear of the magistrate's sword, or their neighbour's censure, tie up people's tongues: which, were the apprehensions of punishment or shame taken away, would as openly proclaim their atheism, as their lives do.

But had all mankind, every where, a notion of a God (whereof yet history tells us the contrary) it would not from thence follow, that the idea of him was innate. For though no nation were to be found without a name, and some few dark notions of him: yet that would not prove them to be natural impressions on the mind, any more than the names of fire, or the sun, heat, or number, do prove the ideas they stand for to be innate: because the names of those things, and the ideas of them, are so universally received and known amongst mankind. Nor, on the contrary, is the want of such a name, or the absence of such a notion out of men's minds, any argument against the being of a God; any more than it would be a proof that there was no load-stone in the world, because a great part of mankind had neither a notion of any such thing, nor a name for it; or be any show of argument to prove, that there are no distinct and various species of angels, or intelligent beings above us, because we have no ideas of such distinct species, or names for them: for men being furnished with words, by the common language of their own countries, can scarce avoid having some kind of ideas of those things, whose names, those they converse with, have occasion frequently to mention to them. And if they carry with it the notion of excellency, greatness, or something extraordinary: if apprehension and concernment accompany it; if the fear of absolute and irresistible power set it on upon the mind, the idea is likely to sink the deeper, and spread the farther; especially if it be such an idea as is agreeable to the common light of reason, and naturally deducible from every part of our knowledge, as that of a God is. For the visible marks of extraordinary wisdom and power appear so plainly in all the works of the creation, that a rational creature, who will but seriously reflect on them, cannot miss the discovery of a Deity.[1] And the influence that the discovery of such a being must necessarily have on the minds of all, that have but once heard of it, is so great, and carries such a weight of thought and communication with it, that it seems stranger to me, that a whole nation of men should be any where found so brutish, as to want the notion of a God; than that they should be without any notion of numbers, or fire.

The name of God being once mentioned in any part of the world, to express a superior, powerful, wise, invisible being, the suitableness of such a notion to the principles of common reason, and the interest men will

[1] For Locke's proofs for the existence of God, cf. pp. 258, 340.

always have to mention it often, must necessarily spread it far and wide, and continue it down to all generations; though yet the general reception of this name, and some imperfect and unsteady notions conveyed thereby to the unthinking part of mankind, prove not the idea to be innate; but only that they, who made the discovery, had made a right use of their reason, thought maturely of the causes of things, and traced them to their original; from whom other less considering people having once received so important a notion, it could not easily be lost again.

This is all could be inferred from the notion of a God, were it to be found universally in all the tribes of mankind, and generally acknowledged by men grown to maturity in all countries.

THE ORIGIN OF ALL OUR IDEAS IN EXPERIENCE

Every man being conscious to himself that he thinks, and that which his mind is applied about, whilst thinking, being the ideas that are there, it is past doubt, that men have in their minds several ideas, such as are those expressed by the words, Whiteness, Hardness, Sweetness, Thinking, Motion, Man, Elephant, Army, Drunkenness, and others. It is in the first place then to be inquired, how he comes by them. I know it is a received doctrine, that men have native ideas, and original characters, stamped upon their minds, in their very first being. This opinion I have, at large, examined already; and, I suppose, what I have said, in the foregoing book, will be much more easily admitted, when I have shewn, whence the understanding may get all the ideas it has, and by what ways and degrees they may come into the mind; for which I shall appeal to every one's own observation and experience.

Let us then suppose the mind to be, as we say, white paper, void of all characters, without any ideas; how comes it to be furnished? Whence comes it by that vast store which the busy and boundless fancy of man has painted on it, with an almost endless variety? Whence has it all the materials of reason [1] and knowledge? To this I answer, in one word, from experience; in all that our knowledge is founded, and from that it ultimately derives itself. Our observation employed either about external sensible objects, or about the internal

[1] For the relation between ideas as "the materials of reason" and knowledge as the product which reason makes out of these materials, cf. two groups of selections from Locke's later writings, pp. 322-328.

operations of our minds, perceived and reflected on by ourselves, is that which supplies our understandings with all the materials of thinking. These two are the fountains of knowledge, from whence all the ideas we have, or can naturally have, do spring.

First, Our senses, conversant about particular sensible objects, do convey into the mind several distinct perceptions of things, according to those various ways wherein those objects do affect them: and thus we come by those ideas we have, of Yellow, White, Heat, Cold, Soft, Hard, Bitter, Sweet, and all those which we call sensible qualities; which when I say the senses convey into the mind, I mean, they from external objects convey into the mind what produces there those perceptions. This great source of most of the ideas we have, depending wholly upon our senses, and derived by them to the understanding, I call SENSATION.

Secondly, The other fountain, from which experience furnisheth the understanding with ideas, is the perception of the operations of our own mind within us, as it is employed about the ideas it has got; which operations, when the soul comes to reflect on and consider, do furnish the understanding with another set of ideas, which could not be had from things without; and such are Perception, Thinking, Doubting, Believing, Reasoning, Knowing, Willing, and all the different actings of our own minds; which we being conscious of and observing in ourselves, do from these receive into our understandings as distinct ideas, as we do from bodies affecting our senses. This source of ideas every man has wholly in himself; and though it be not sense, as having nothing to do with external objects, yet it is very like it, and might properly enough be called internal sense. But as I call the other sensation, so I call this REFLECTION, the ideas it affords being such only as the mind gets by reflecting on its own operations within itself. By reflection then, in the following part of this discourse, I would be understood to mean that notice which the mind takes of its own operations, and the manner of them; by reason whereof there come to be ideas of these operations in the understanding. These two, I say, *viz.* external material things, as the objects of sensation; and the operations of our own minds within, as the objects of reflection; are to me the only originals from whence all our ideas take their beginnings. The term operations here I use in a large sense, as comprehending not barely the actions of the mind about its ideas, but some sort of passions arising sometimes from them, such as is the satisfaction or uneasiness arising from any thought.

The understanding seems to me not to have the least glimmering of any ideas, which it doth not receive from one of these two. External objects furnish the mind with the ideas of sensible qualities, which are all those different perceptions they produce in us: and the mind furnishes the understanding with ideas of its own operations.

These, when we have taken a full survey of them and their several modes, combinations, and relations, we shall find to contain all our whole stock of ideas; and that we have nothing in our minds which did not come in one of these two ways. Let any one examine his own thoughts, and thoroughly search into his understanding; and then let him tell me, whether all the original ideas he has there, are any other than of the objects of his senses, or of the operations of his mind, considered as objects of his reflection; and how great a mass of knowledge soever he imagines to be lodged there, he will, upon taking a strict view, see that he has not any idea in his mind, but what one of these two have imprinted; though perhaps, with infinite variety compounded and enlarged by the understanding, as we shall see hereafter.

To ask at what time a man has first any ideas, is to ask when he begins to perceive; having ideas, and perception, being the same thing. I know it is an opinion, that the soul always thinks, and that it has the actual perception of ideas in itself constantly as long as it exists; and that actual thinking is as inseparable from the soul, as actual extension is from the body: which if true, to inquire after the beginning of a man's ideas is the same as to inquire after the beginning of his soul. For by this account soul and its ideas, as body and its extension, will begin to exist both at the same time.

I see no reason therefore to believe, that the soul thinks before the senses have furnished it with ideas to think on; and as those are increased and retained, so it comes, by exercise, to improve its faculty of thinking, in the several parts of it, as well as afterwards, by compounding those ideas, and reflecting on its own operations; it increases its stock, as well as facility, in remembering, imagining, reasoning, and other modes of thinking.

Follow a child from its birth, and observe the alterations that time makes, and you shall find, as the mind by the senses comes more and more to be furnished with ideas, it comes to be more and more awake; thinks more, the more it has matter to think on. After some time it begins to know the objects, which, being most familiar with it, have made lasting impressions. Thus it comes by degrees to know the persons it daily converses with, and distinguish them from strangers; which are instances and effects of its coming to retain and distinguish the ideas the senses convey to it. And so we may observe how the mind, by degrees, improves in these, and advances to the exercise of those other faculties of enlarging, compounding, and abstracting its ideas, and of reasoning about them, and reflecting upon all these; of which I shall have occasion to speak more hereafter.

Thus the first capacity of human intellect is, that the mind is fitted to receive the impressions made on it; either through the senses by outward objects; or by its own operations when it reflects on them. This is the first step a man makes towards the discovery of any thing, and the ground-work whereon to build all those notions which ever he shall have naturally in this world. All those sublime thoughts which tower above the clouds, and reach as high as heaven itself, take their rise and footing here: in all that good extent wherein the mind wanders, in those remote speculations, it may seem to be elevated with, it stirs not one jot beyond those ideas which sense or reflection have offered for its contemplation.

In this part the understanding is merely passive; and whether or no it will have these beginnings, and as it were materials of knowledge, is not in its own power. For the objects of our senses do, many of them, obtrude their particular ideas upon our minds whether we will or no; and the operations of our minds will not let us be without, at least, some obscure notions of them. No man can be wholly ignorant of what he does when he thinks. These simple ideas, when offered to the mind, the understanding can no more refuse to have, nor alter, when they are imprinted, nor blot them out, and make new ones itself, than a mirror can refuse, alter, or obliterate the images or ideas which the objects set before it do therein produce. As the bodies that surround us do diversely affect our organs, the mind is forced to receive the impressions, and cannot avoid the perception of those ideas that are annexed to them.

A CLASSIFICATION OF OUR IDEAS

THE better to understand the nature, manner, and extent of our knowledge, one thing is carefully to be observed concerning the ideas we have; and that is, that some of them are simple, and some complex.

Though the qualities that affect our senses are, in the things themselves, so united and blended, that there is no separation, no distance between them; yet it is plain, the ideas they produce in the mind enter by the senses simple and unmixed. For though the sight and touch often take in from the same object, at the same time, different ideas; as a man sees at once motion and colour; the hand feels softness and warmth in the same piece of wax: yet the simple ideas, thus united in the same subject, are as perfectly distinct as those that come in by different senses: the coldness and hardness which a man feels in a piece of ice being as distinct ideas in the mind, as the smell and whiteness of a lily; or as the taste of sugar, and smell of a rose. And there is nothing can be plainer to a man, than the clear and distinct perception he has of those simple ideas; which, being each in itself uncompounded, contains in it nothing but one uniform appearance, or conception in the mind, and is not distinguishable into different ideas.

These simple ideas, the materials of all our knowledge, are suggested and furnished to the mind only by those two ways above-mentioned, *viz.* sensation and reflection. When the understanding is once stored with these simple ideas, it has the power to repeat, compare, and unite them, even to an almost infinite variety; and so can make at pleasure new complex ideas. But it is not in the power of the most exalted wit, or enlarged understanding, by any quickness or variety of thought, to invent or frame one new simple idea in the mind, not taken in by the ways aforementioned: nor can any force of the understanding destroy those that are there. The dominion of man, in this little world of his own understanding, being much-what the same as it is in the great world of visible things; wherein his power, however managed by art and skill, reaches no farther than to compound and divide the materials that are made to his hand; but can do nothing towards the making the least particle of new matter, or destroying one atom of what is already in being. The same inability will every one find in himself, who shall go about to fashion in his understanding any simple idea, not received in by his senses from external objects, or by reflection from the operations of his own mind about them. I would have any one try to fancy any taste, which had never affected his palate; or frame the idea of a scent he had never smelt: and when he can do this, I will also conclude that a blind man hath ideas of colours, and a deaf man true distinct notions of sounds.

This is the reason why, though we cannot believe it impossible to God to make a creature with other organs, and more ways to convey into the understanding the notice of corporeal things than those five, as they are usually counted, which he has given to man: yet I think, it is not possible for any one to imagine any other qualities in bodies, howsoever constituted, whereby they can be taken notice of, besides sounds, tastes, smells, visible and tangible qualities. And had mankind been made but with four senses, the qualities then, which are the object of the fifth sense, had been as far from our notice, imagination, and conception, as now any belonging to a sixth, seventh, or eighth sense, can possibly be: which, whether yet some other creatures, in some other parts of this vast and stupendous universe, may not have, will be a greater presumption to deny. He that will not set himself proudly at the top of all things, but will consider the immensity of this fabric, and the great variety that is to be found in this little and inconsiderable part of it which he has to do with, may be apt to think, that in other mansions of it there may be other and different intelligent beings, of whose faculties he has as little knowledge or apprehension, as a worm shut up in one drawer of a cabinet hath of the senses or understanding of a man: such variety and excellency being suitable to the wisdom and power of the maker.

SIMPLE IDEAS

THE better to conceive the ideas we receive from sensation, it may not be amiss for us to consider them, in reference to the different ways whereby they make their approaches to our minds, and make themselves perceivable by us.

First, Then, there are some which come into our minds by one sense only.

Secondly, There are others that convey themselves into the mind by more senses than one.

Thirdly, Others that are had from reflection only.

Fourthly, There are some that make themselves way, and are suggested to the mind by all the ways of sensation and reflection.

We shall consider them apart under their several heads.

There are some ideas which have admittance only through one sense, which is peculiarly adapted to receive them. Thus light and colours, as white, red, yellow, blue, with their several degrees or shades and mixtures, as green, scarlet, purple, sea-green, and the rest, come in only by the eyes: all kinds of noises, sounds, and tones, only by the ears: and several tastes and smells, by the nose and palate. And if these organs, or the nerves, which are the conduits to convey them from without to their audience in the brain, the mind's presence-room (as I may so call it) are any of them so disordered, as not to perform their functions, they have no postern to be admitted by; no other way to bring themselves into view, and be perceived by the understanding.

The most considerable of those belonging to the touch are heat and cold, and solidity: all the rest, consisting almost wholly in the sensible configuration, as smooth and rough, or else more or less firm adhesion of the parts, as hard and soft, tough and brittle, are obvious enough.

I think, it will be needless to enumerate all the particular simple ideas, belonging to each sense. Nor indeed is it possible, if we would; there being a great many more of them belonging to most of the senses, than we have names for. The variety of smells, which are as many almost, if not more, than species of bodies in the world, do most of them want names. Sweet and stinking commonly serve our turn for these ideas, which in effect is little more than to call them pleasing or displeasing; though the smell of a rose and violet, both sweet, are certainly very distinct ideas. Nor are the different tastes, that by our palates we receive ideas of, much better provided with names. Sweet, bitter, sour, harsh, and salt, are almost all the epithets we have to denominate that numberless variety of relishes, which are to be found distinct, not only in almost every sort of creatures, but in the different parts of the same plant, fruit, or animal. The same may be said of colours and sounds. I shall therefore, in the account of simple ideas I am here giving, content myself to set down only such, as are most material to our present purpose, or are in themselves less apt to be taken notice of, though they are very frequently the ingredients of our complex ideas, amongst which, I think, I may well account solidity; which therefore I shall treat of in the next chapter.

1. The Idea of Solidity

The idea of solidity we receive by our touch; and it arises from the resistance which we find in body, to the entrance of any other body into the place it possesses, till it has left it. There is no idea which we receive more constantly from sensation, than solidity. Whether we move or rest, in what posture soever we are, we always feel something under us that supports us, and hinders our farther sinking downwards; and the bodies which we daily handle make us perceive, that, whilst they remain between them, they do by an insurmountable force hinder the approach of the parts of our hands that press them. That which thus hinders the approach of two bodies, when they are moved one towards another, I call solidity.

This is the idea which belongs to body, whereby we conceive it to fill space. The idea of which filling of space is, that, where we imagine any space taken up by a solid substance, we conceive it so to possess it, that it excludes all other solid substances; and will for ever hinder any other two bodies, that move towards one another in a straight line, from coming to touch one another, unless it removes from between them, in a line not parallel to that which they move in. This idea of it the bodies which we ordinarily handle sufficiently furnish us with.

This resistance, whereby it keeps other bodies out of the space which it possesses, is so great, that no force, how great soever, can surmount it. All the bodies in the world, pressing a drop of water on all sides, will never be able to overcome the resistance which it will make, soft as it is, to their approaching one another, till it be removed out of their way: whereby our idea of solidity is distinguished both from pure space, which is capable neither of resistance nor motion; and from the ordinary idea of hardness.

By this idea of solidity, is the extension of body distinguished from the extension of space; the extension of body being nothing but the cohesion or continuity of solid, separable, moveable parts; and the extension of space, the continuity of unsolid, inseparable, and immoveable parts. Upon the solidity of bodies also depend their mutual impulse, resistance, and protrusion. Of pure space then, and solidity, there are several (amongst which I confess myself one) who persuade themselves they have clear and distinct ideas; and that they can think on space, without any thing in it that resists or is protruded by body. This is the idea of pure space, which they think they have as clear, as any idea they can have of the extension of body; the idea of the distance between the opposite parts of a concave superficies being equally as clear without as with the idea of any solid parts between: and on the other side they persuade themselves, that they have, distinct from that of pure space, the idea of something that fills space, that can be protruded by the impulse of other bodies, or resist their motion. If there be others that have not these two ideas distinct, but confound them, and make but one of them; I know not how men, who have the same idea under different names, or different ideas under the same name, can in that case talk with one another; any more than a man, who, not being blind or deaf, has distinct ideas of the colour of scarlet, and the sound of a trumpet, could discourse concerning scarlet colour with the blind man I mention in another place, who fancied that the idea of scarlet was like the sound of a trumpet.

If any one ask me, what this solidity is, I send him to his senses to inform him: let him put a flint or a football between his hands, and then endeavour to join them, and he will know. If he thinks this not a sufficient explication of solidity, what it is, and wherein it consists; I promise to tell him what it is, and wherein it consists, when he tells me what thinking is, or wherein it consists; or explains to me what extension or motion is, which perhaps seems much easier. The simple ideas we have are such as experience teaches them us, but if, beyond that, we endeavour by words to make them clearer in the mind, we shall succeed no better, than if we went about to clear up the darkness of a blind man's mind by talking; and to discourse into him the ideas of light and colours.

2. The Ideas of Space, Motion, etc.

The ideas we get by more than one sense are of space, or extension, figure, rest, and motion; for these make perceivable impressions, both on the eyes and touch: and we can receive and convey into our minds the ideas of the extension, figure, motion, and rest of bodies, both by seeing and feeling.

3. The Ideas of Reflection

The mind, receiving the ideas, mentioned in the foregoing chapters, from without, when it turns its view inward upon itself, and observes its own actions about those ideas it has, takes from thence other ideas, which are as capable to be the objects of its contemplation as any of those it received from foreign things.

The two great and principal actions of the mind, which are most frequently considered, and which are so frequent, that every one that pleases may take notice of them in himself, are these two: Perception or Thinking; and Volition, or Willing. The power of thinking is called the understanding, and the power of volition is called the will; and these two powers or abilities in the mind are denominated faculties. Of some of the modes of these simple ideas of reflection, such as are Remembrance, Discerning, Reasoning, Judging, Knowledge, Faith, &c. I shall have occasion to speak hereafter.

4. The Ideas of Pleasure and Pain, Existence, Unity, etc.

There be other simple ideas which convey themselves into the mind by all the ways of sensation and reflection, *viz.* Pleasure or Delight, and its opposite, Pain or Uneasiness, Power, Existence, Unity.

Delight or uneasiness, one or other of them, join themselves to almost all our ideas, both of sensation and reflection; and there is scarce any affection of our senses from without, any retired thought of our mind within, which is not able to produce in us pleasure or pain. By pleasure and pain I would be understood to signify whatsoever delights or molests us most; whether it arises from the thoughts of our minds, or any thing operating on our bodies. For whether we call it satisfaction, delight, pleasure, happiness, &c. on the one side; or uneasiness, trouble, pain, torment, anguish, misery, &c. on the other; they are still but different degrees of the same thing, and belong to the ideas of pleasure and pain, delight or uneasiness; which are the names I shall most commonly use for those two sorts of ideas.

The infinitely wise author of our being having given us the power over several parts of our bodies, to move or keep them at rest as we think fit; and also, by the motion of them, to move ourselves and other contiguous bodies, in which consist all the actions of our body; having also given a power to our minds in several instances, to choose, amongst its ideas, which it will think on, and to pursue the inquiry of this or that subject with consideration and attention, to excite us to these actions of thinking and motion that we are capable of; has been pleased to join to several thoughts, and several sensations, a perception of delight. If this were wholly separated from all our outward sensations and inward thoughts, we should have no reason to prefer one thought or action to another; negligence to attention; or motion to rest. And so we should neither stir our bodies nor employ our minds, but let our thoughts (if I may so call it) run a-drift, without any direction or design; and suffer the ideas of our minds, like unregarded shadows, to make their appearances there, as it happened, without attending to them. In which state man, however furnished with the faculties of understanding and will, would be a very idle unactive creature, and pass his time only in a lazy, lethargic dream. It has therefore pleased our wise Creator to annex to several objects, and the ideas which we receive from them, as also to several of our thoughts, a concomitant pleasure, and that in several objects, to several degrees; that those faculties which he had endowed us with might not remain wholly idle and unemployed by us.

Existence and unity are two other ideas that are suggested to the understanding by every object without, and every idea within. When ideas are in our minds, we consider them as being actually there, as well as we consider things to be actually without us; which is, that they exist, or have existence: and whatever we can consider as one thing, whether a real being or idea, suggests to the understanding the idea of unity.

Power also is another of those simple ideas which we receive from sensation and reflection. For observing in ourselves, that we can at pleasure move several parts of our bodies which were at rest; the effects also, that natural bodies are able to produce in one another, occurring every moment to our senses; we both these ways get the idea of power.

These, if they are not all, are at least (as I think) the most considerable of those simple ideas which the mind has, and out of which is made all its other knowledge: all which it receives only by the two forementioned ways of sensation and reflection.

Nor let any one think these too narrow bounds for the capacious mind of man to expatiate in, which takes its flight farther than the stars, and cannot be confined by the limits of the world; that extends its thoughts often even beyond the utmost expansion of matter, and makes excursions into that incomprehensible inane. I grant all this, but desire any one to assign any simple idea which is not received from one of those inlets beforementioned, or any complex idea not made out of those simple ones. Nor will it be so strange to think these few simple ideas sufficient to employ the quickest thought, or largest capacity; and to furnish the materials of all that various knowledge, and more various fancies and opinions of all mankind; if we consider how many words may be made out of the various composition of twenty-four letters; or if, going one step farther, we will but reflect on the variety of combinations may be made, with barely one of the above-mentioned ideas, *viz.* number, whose stock is inexhaustible and truly infinite; and what a large and immense field doth extension alone afford the mathematicians?

5. The Ideas of the Chief Functions of the Mind

Perception, as it is the first faculty of the mind, exercised about our ideas; so it is the first and simplest idea we have from reflection, and is by some called thinking in general. Though thinking, in the propriety of the English tongue, signifies that sort of operation in the mind about its ideas, wherein the mind is active; where it, with some degree of voluntary attention, considers any thing. For in bare naked perception, the mind is, for the most part, only passive: and what it perceives, it cannot avoid perceiving.

What perception is, every one will know better by reflecting on what he does himself, what he sees, hears, feels, &c. or thinks, than by any discourse of mine. Whoever reflects on what passes in his own mind, can not miss it: and if he does not reflect, all the words in the world cannot make him have any notion of it.

This is certain, that whatever alterations are made in the body, if they reach not the mind; whatever impressions are made on the outward parts, if they are not taken notice of within; there is no perception. Fire may burn our bodies, with no other effect, than it does a billet, unless the motion be continued to the brain, and there the sense of heat, or idea of pain, be produced in the mind, wherein consists actual perception.

This faculty of perception seems to me to be that, which puts the distinction betwixt the animal kingdom and the inferior parts of nature. For however vegetables have, many of them, some degrees of motion, and upon the different application of other bodies to them, do very briskly alter their figures and motions, and so have obtained the name of sensitive plants, from a motion which has some resemblance to that which in animals follows upon sensation: yet, I suppose, it is all bare mechanism; and no otherwise produced, than the turning of a wild oat-beard, by the insinuation of the particles of moisture; or the shortening of a rope, by the effusion of water. All which is done without any sensation in the subject, or the having or receiving any ideas.

Perception then being the first step and degree towards knowledge, and the inlet of all the materials of it; the fewer senses any man, as well as any other creature, hath, and the fewer and duller the impressions are that are made by them, and the duller the faculties are that are employed about them; the more remote are they from that knowledge, which is to be found in some men. But this being in great variety of degrees (as may be perceived amongst men) cannot certainly be discovered in the several species of animals, much less in their particular individuals. It suffices me only to have remarked here, that perception is the first operation of all our intellectual faculties, and the inlet of all knowledge in our minds. And I am apt too to imagine, that it is perception in the lowest degree of it, which puts the boundaries between animals and the inferior ranks of creatures. But this I mention only as my conjecture by the by; it being indifferent to the matter in hand, which way the learned shall determine of it.

The next faculty of the mind, whereby it makes a farther progress towards knowledge, is that which I call retention, or the keeping of those simple ideas, which from sensation or reflection it hath received. This is done two ways; first, by keeping the idea, which is brought into it, for some time actually in view; which is called contemplation.

The other way of retention, is the power to revive again in our minds those ideas, which after imprinting have disappeared, or have been as it were laid aside out of sight; and thus we do, when we conceive heat or light, yellow or sweet, the object being removed. This is memory, which is as it were the store-house of our ideas. For the narrow mind of man not being capable of having many ideas under view and consideration at once, it was necessary to have a repository to lay up those ideas, which at another time it might have use of. But our ideas being nothing but actual perceptions in the mind, which cease to be any thing, when there is no perception of them, this laying up of our ideas in the repository of the memory, signifies no more but this, that the mind has a power in many cases to revive perceptions, which it has once had, with this additional perception annexed to them, that it has had them before. And in this sense it is, that our ideas are said to be in our memories, when indeed they are actually no-where, but only there is an ability in the mind when it will to revive them again, and as it were paint them a-new on itself, though some with more, some with less difficulty; some more lively, and others more obscurely. And thus it is by the assistance of this faculty, that we are to have all those ideas in our understandings, which though we do not actually contemplate, yet we can bring in sight, and make appear again, and be the objects of our thoughts, without the help of those sensible qualities which first imprinted them there.

Attention and repetition help much to the fixing any

ideas in the memory; but those which naturally at first make the deepest and most lasting impression, are those which are accompanied with pleasure or pain. The great business of the senses being to make us take notice of what hurts or advantages the body, it is wisely ordered by nature (as has been shown) that pain should accompany the reception of several ideas; which supplying the place of consideration and reasoning in children, and acting quicker than consideration in grown men, makes both the old and young avoid painful objects, with that haste which is necessary for their preservation; and, in both, settles in the memory a caution for the future.

In this secondary perception, as I may so call it, or viewing again the ideas that are lodged in the memory, the mind is oftentimes more than barely passive; the appearance of those dormant pictures depending sometimes on the will. The mind very often sets itself on work in search of some hidden idea, and turns as it were the eye of the soul upon it; though sometimes too they start up in our minds of their own accord, and offer themselves to the understanding; and very often are roused and tumbled out of their dark cells into open day-light, by turbulent and tempestuous passions: our affections bringing ideas to our memory, which had otherwise lain quiet and unregarded. This farther is to be observed, concerning ideas lodged in the memory, and upon occasion revived by the mind, that they are not only (as the word revive imports) none of them new ones; but also that the mind takes notice of them, as of a former impression, and renews its acquaintance with them, as with ideas it had known before. So that though ideas formerly imprinted are not all constantly in view, yet in remembrance they are constantly known to be such as have been formerly imprinted; i. e. in view, and taken notice of before by the understanding.

Memory, in an intellectual creature, is necessary in the next degree to perception. It is of so great moment, that where it is wanting, all the rest of our faculties are in a great measure useless: and we in our thoughts, reasonings, and knowledge, could not proceed beyond present objects, were it not for the assistance of our memories, wherein there may be two defects.

First, That it loses the idea quite, and so far it produces perfect ignorance. For since we can know nothing farther than we have the idea of it, when that is gone, we are in perfect ignorance.

Secondly, That it moves slowly, and retrieves not the ideas that it has, and are laid up in store, quick enough to serve the mind upon occasion. This, if it be to a great degree, is stupidity; and he, who, through this default in his memory, has not the ideas that are really preserved there, ready at hand when need and occasion calls for them, were almost as good be without them quite, since they serve him to little purpose. The dull man who loses the opportunity whilst he is seeking in his mind for those ideas that should serve his turn, is not much more happy in his knowledge than one that is perfectly ignorant. It is the business therefore of the memory to furnish the mind with those dormant ideas which it has present occasion for; in the having them ready at hand on all occasions, consists that which we call invention, fancy, and quickness of parts.

Another faculty we may take notice of in our minds, is that of discerning and distinguishing between the several ideas it has. It is not enough to have a confused perception of something in general: unless the mind had a distinct perception of different objects and their qualities, it would be capable of very little knowledge; though the bodies that affect us were as busy about us as they are now, and the mind were continually employed in thinking. On this faculty of distinguishing one thing from another, depends the evidence and certainty of several, even very general propositions, which have passed for innate truths; because men, overlooking the true cause why those propositions find universal assent, impute it wholly to native uniform impressions: whereas it in truth depends upon this clear discerning faculty of the mind, whereby it perceives two ideas to be the same, or different. But of this more hereafter.

How much the imperfection of accurately discriminating ideas one from another lies either in the dulness or faults of the organs of sense; or want of acuteness, exercise, or attention, in the understanding; or hastiness and precipitancy, natural to some tempers, I will not here examine; it suffices to take notice, that this is one of the operations, that the mind may reflect on and observe in itself. It is of that consequence to its other knowledge, that so far as this faculty is in itself dull, or not rightly made use of, for the distinguishing one thing from another; so far our notions are confused, and our reason and judgment disturbed or misled. If in having our ideas in the memory ready at hand consists quickness of parts; in this of having them unconfused, and being able nicely to distinguish one thing from another, where there is but the least difference, consists, in a great measure, the exactness of judgment, and clearness of reason, which is to be observed in one man above another. And hence perhaps may be given some reason of that common observation, that men, who have a great deal of wit, and prompt memories, have not always the clearest judgment, or deepest reason: for wit lying most in the assemblage of ideas, and putting those together with quickness and variety, wherein can be found any resemblance or congruity, thereby to make up pleasant pictures, and agreeable visions in the fancy; judgment, on the contrary, lies quite on the other side, in separating carefully, one from another, ideas, wherein can be found the least difference; thereby to avoid being misled by similitude, and by affinity to take one thing for another. This is a way of proceeding quite contrary to metaphor and allusion, wherein for the most part lies that entertainment and pleasantry of wit, which strikes so lively on the fancy, and therefore is so acceptable to all people; because its beauty appears at first sight, and there is required no labour of thought to examine what truth or reason there is in it. The mind, without looking any farther, rests satisfied with the agreeableness of the picture, and the gaiety of the fancy; and it is a kind of an affront to go about to examine it by the severe rules of truth and good reason; whereby it appears, that it consists in something that is not perfectly conformable to them.

The comparing them one with another, in respect of extent, degrees, time, place, or any other circumstances, is another operation of the mind about its ideas, and is that upon which depends all that large tribe of ideas, comprehended under relations; which of how vast an extent it is, I shall have occasion to consider hereafter.

How far brutes partake in this faculty, is not easy to determine; I imagine they have it not in any great degree: for though they probably have several ideas distinct enough, yet it seems to me to be the prerogative of human understanding, when it has sufficiently distinguished any ideas, so as to perceive them to be perfectly different, and so consequently two, to cast about and consider in what circumstances they are capable to be compared: and therefore, I think, beasts compare not their ideas farther than some sensible circumstances annexed to the objects themselves. The other power of comparing, which may be observed in men, belonging to general ideas, and useful only to abstract reasonings, we may probably conjecture beasts have not.

The next operation we may observe in the mind about its ideas, is composition; whereby it puts together several of those simple ones it has received from sensation and reflection, and combines them into complex ones. Under this of composition may be reckoned also that of enlarging; wherein though the composition does not so much appear as in more complex ones, yet it is nevertheless a putting several ideas together, though of the same kind. Thus by adding several units together, we make the idea of a dozen; and putting together the repeated ideas of several perches, we frame that of a furlong.

When children have, by repeated sensations, got ideas fixed in their memories, they begin by degrees to learn the use of signs. And when they have got the skill to apply the organs of speech to the framing of articulate sounds, they begin to make use of words, to signify their ideas to others. These verbal signs they sometimes borrow from others, and sometimes make themselves, as one may observe among the new and unusual names children often give to things in the first use of language.

The use of words then being to stand as outward marks of our internal ideas, and those ideas being taken from particular things, if every particular idea that we take in should have a distinct name, names must be endless. To prevent this, the mind makes the particular ideas, received from particular objects, to become general; which is done by considering them as they are in the mind, such appearances, separate from all other existences, and the circumstances of real existence, as time, place, or any other concomitant ideas. This is called abstraction, whereby ideas, taken from particular beings, become general representatives of all of the same kind, and their names general names, applicable to whatever exists conformable to such abstract ideas. Such precise naked appearances in the mind, without considering how, whence, or with what others they came there, the understanding lays up (with names commonly annexed to them) as the standard to rank real existences into sorts, as they agree with these patterns, and to denominate them accordingly. Thus the same colour being observed to-day in chalk or snow, which the mind yesterday received from milk, it considers that appearance alone, makes it a representative of all of that kind; and having given it the name whiteness, it by that sound signifies the same quality, wheresoever to be imagined or met with: and thus universals, whether ideas or terms, are made.

And thus I have given a short, and, I think, true history of the first beginnings of human knowledge, whence the mind has its first objects, and by what steps it makes its progress to the laying in and storing up those ideas, out of which is to be framed all the knowledge it is capable of; wherein I must appeal to experience and observation, whether I am in the right: the best way to come to truth, being to examine things as really they are, and not to conclude they are, as we fancy of ourselves, or have been taught by others to imagine.

To deal truly, this is the only way that I can discover, whereby the ideas of things are brought into the understanding: if other men have either innate ideas, or infused principles, they have reason to enjoy them; and if they are sure of it, it is impossible for others to deny them the privilege that they have above their neighbours. I can speak but of what I find in myself, and is agreeable to those notions; which, if we will examine the whole course of men in their several ages, countries, and educations, seem to depend on those foundations which I have laid, and to correspond with this method in all the parts and degrees thereof.

I pretend not to teach, but to inquire, and therefore cannot but confess here again, that external and internal sensation are the only passages that I can find of knowledge to the understanding. These alone, as far as I can discover, are the windows by which light is let into this dark room: for methinks the understanding is not much unlike a closet wholly shut from light, with only some little opening left, to let in external visible resemblances, or ideas of things without: would the pictures coming into such a dark room but stay there, and lie so orderly as to be found upon occasion, it would very much resemble the understanding of a man, in reference to all objects of sight, and the ideas of them.

COMPLEX IDEAS

We have hitherto considered those ideas, in the reception whereof the mind is only passive, which are those simple ones received from sensation and reflection before mentioned, whereof the mind cannot make one to itself, nor have any idea which does not wholly consist of them. But as the mind is wholly passive in the reception of all its simple ideas, so it exerts several acts of its own, whereby out of its simple ideas as the materials and foundations of the rest, the other are framed. The acts of the mind, wherein it exerts its power over its simple ideas, are chiefly these three: 1. Combining several simple ideas into one compound one, and thus all complex ideas are made. 2. The second is bringing two ideas, whether simple or complex, together, and setting them by one another, so as to take a view of them at once, without uniting them into one; by which way it gets all its ideas of relations. 3. The third is separating them from all other ideas that accompany them in their real existence; this is called abstraction: and thus all its general ideas are made. This shows man's power, and its ways of operation, to be much-what the same in the material and intellectual world. For the materials in both being such as he has no power over, either to make or destroy, all that man can do is either to unite them together, or to set them by one another, or wholly separate them. I shall here begin with the first of these in the consideration of complex ideas, and come to the other two in their due places. As simple ideas are observed to exist in several combinations united together, so the mind has a power to consider several of them united together as one idea; and that not only as they are united in external objects, but as itself has joined them. Ideas thus made up of several simple ones put together, I call complex; such as are beauty, gratitude, a man, an army, the universe; which though complicated of various simple ideas, or complex ideas made up of simple ones, yet are, when the mind pleases, considered each by itself as one entire thing, and signified by one name.

In this faculty of repeating and joining together its ideas, the mind has great power in varying and multiplying the objects of its thoughts, infinitely beyond what sensation or reflection furnishes it with; but all this still confined to those simple ideas which it received from those two sources, and which are the ultimate materials of all its compositions: for simple ideas are all from things themselves, and of these the mind can have no more, nor other than what are suggested to it. It can have no other ideas of sensible qualities than what come from without by the senses; nor any ideas of other kind of operations of a thinking substance than what it finds in itself; but when it has once got these simple ideas, it is not confined barely to observation, and what offers itself from without: it can, by its own power, put together those ideas it has, and make new complex ones, which it never received so united.

Complex ideas, however compounded and decompounded, though their number be infinite, and the variety endless, wherewith they fill and entertain the thoughts of men; yet, I think, they may be all reduced under these three heads: 1. Modes. 2. Substances. 3. Relations.

First, Modes I call such complex ideas, which, however compounded, contain not in them the supposition of subsisting by themselves, but are considered as dependencies on or affections of substances; such as are ideas signified by the words triangle, gratitude, murder, &c. And if in this I use the word mode in somewhat a different sense from its ordinary signification, I beg pardon; it being unavoidable in discourses, differing from the ordinary received notions, either to make new words, or to use old words in somewhat a new signification: the latter whereof, in our present case, is perhaps the more tolerable of the two.

Of these modes, there are two sorts which deserve distinct consideration. First, there are some which are only variations, or different combinations of the same simple idea, without the mixture of any other; as a dozen or score; which are nothing but the ideas of so many distinct units added together: and these I call simple modes, as being contained within the bounds of one simple idea. Secondly, there are others compounded of simple ideas of several kinds, put together to make one complex one; v. g. beauty, consisting of a certain composition of colour and figure, causing delight in the beholder; theft, which being the concealed change of the possession of any thing, without the consent of the proprietor, contains, as is visible, a combination of several ideas of several kinds: and these I call mixed modes.

Secondly, the ideas of substances are such combinations of simple ideas, as are taken to represent distinct particular things subsisting by themselves; in which the supposed or confused idea of substance, such as it is, is always the first and chief. Thus if to substance be joined the simple idea of a certain dull whitish colour, with certain degrees of weight, hardness, ductility, and fusibility, we have the idea of lead, and a combination of the ideas of a certain sort of figure, with the powers of motion. Thought and reasoning, joined to substance, make the ordinary idea of a man. Now of substances also, there are two sorts of ideas; one of single substances, as they exist separately, as of a man or a sheep; the other of several of those put together, as an army of men, or flock of sheep: which collective ideas of several substances thus put together, are as much each of them one single idea, as that of a man, or an unit.

Thirdly, the last sort of complex ideas, is that we call relation, which consists in the consideration and comparing one idea with another. Of these several kinds we shall treat in their order.

If we trace the progress of our minds, and with attention observe how it repeats, adds together, and unites its simple ideas received from sensation or reflection, it will lead us farther than at first perhaps we should have imagined. And I believe we shall find, if we warily observe the originals of our notions, that even the most abstruse ideas, how remote soever they may seem from sense, or from any operations of our own minds, are yet only such as the understanding frames to itself, by repeating and joining together ideas, that it had either from objects of sense, or from its own operations about them: so that those even large and abstract ideas are derived from sensation or reflection, being no other than what the mind, by the ordinary use of its own faculties, employed about ideas received from objects of sense, or from the operations it observes in itself about them, may and does attain unto. This I shall endeavour to show in the ideas we have of space, time, and infinity, and some few others, that seem the most remote from those originals.

SIMPLE MODES

1. Simple Modes of Idea of Space

Though in the foregoing part I have often mentioned simple ideas, which are truly the materials of all our knowledge; yet having treated of them there, rather in the way that they come into the mind, than as distinguished from others more compounded, it will not be perhaps amiss to take a view of some of them again under this consideration, and examine those different modifications of the same idea: which the mind either finds in things existing, or is able to make within itself, without the help of any extrinsical object, or any foreign suggestion.

Those modifications of any one simple idea (which, as has been said, I call simple modes) are as perfectly different and distinct ideas in the mind, as those of the greatest distance or contrariety. For the idea of two is as distinct from that of one, as blueness from heat, or either of them from any number: and yet it is made up only of that simple idea of an unit repeated; and repetitions of this kind joined together, make those distinct simple modes, of a dozen, a gross, a million.

I shall begin with the simple idea of space. I have showed above that we get the idea of space, both by our sight and touch; which, I think, is so evident, that it would be as needless to go to prove that men perceive, by their sight, a distance between bodies of different colours, or between the parts of the same body, as that they see colours themselves; nor is it less obvious, that they can do so in the dark by feeling and touch.

This space considered barely in length between any two beings, without considering any thing else between them, is called distance; if considered in length, breadth, and thickness, I think it may be called capacity. The term extension is usually applied to it in what manner soever considered.

Each different distance is a different modification of space; and each idea of any different distance, or space, is a simple mode of this idea. Men for the use, and by the custom of measuring, settle in their minds the ideas of certain stated lengths, such as are an inch, foot, yard, fathom, mile, diameter of the earth, &c. which are so many distinct ideas made up only of space. When any such stated lengths or measures of space are made familiar to men's thoughts, they can in their minds repeat them as often as they will without mixing or joining to them the idea of body, or any thing else; and frame to themselves the ideas of long, square, or cubic, feet, yards, or fathoms, here amongst the bodies of the universe, or else beyond the utmost bounds of all bodies; and by adding these still one to another, enlarge their ideas of space as much as they please. The power of repeating, or doubling any idea we have of any distance, and adding it to the former as often as we will, without being ever able to come to any stop or stint, let us enlarge it as much as we will, is that which gives us the idea of immensity.

There is another modification of this idea, which is nothing but the relation which the parts of the termination of extension, or circumscribed space, have amongst themselves. This the touch discovers in sensible bodies, whose extremities come within our reach; and the eye takes both from bodies and colours, whose boundaries are within its view; where observing how the extremities terminate either in straight lines, which meet at discernible angles; or in crooked lines, wherein no angles can be perceived; by considering these as they relate to one another, in all parts of the extremities of any body or space, it has that idea we call figure, which affords to the mind infinite variety. For besides the vast number of different figures, that do really exist in the coherent masses of matter, the stock that the mind has in its power, by varying the idea of space, and thereby making still new compositions, by repeating its own ideas, and joining them as it pleases, is perfectly inexhaustible; and so it can multiply figures *in infinitum.*

Another idea coming under this head, and belonging to this tribe, is that we call place. As in simple space, we consider the relation of distance between any two bodies or points; so in our idea of place, we consider the relation of distance betwixt any thing, and any two or more points, which are considered as keeping the same distance one with another, and so considered as at rest: for when we find any thing at the same distance now, which it was yesterday, from any two or more points, which have not since changed their distance one with another, and with which we then compared it, we say it hath kept the same place; but if it hath sensibly altered its distance with either of those points, we say it hath changed its place: though vulgarly speaking, in the common notion of place, we do not always exactly observe the distance from these precise points; but from larger portions of sensible objects, to which we consider the thing placed to bear relation, and its distance from which we have some reason to observe.

There are some that would persuade us, that body and extension are the same thing: who either change the signification of words, which I would not suspect them of, they having so severely condemned the philosophy of others, because it hath been too much placed in the uncertain meaning, or deceitful obscurity of doubtful or insignificant terms. If therefore they mean by body and extension the same that other people do, viz. by body, something that is solid and extended, whose parts are separable and moveable different ways; and by extension, only the space that lies between the extremities of those solid coherent parts, and which is possessed by them: they confound very different ideas one with another. For I appeal to every man's own thoughts, whether the idea of space be not as distinct from that of solidity, as it is from the idea of scarlet colour? It is true, solidity cannot exist without extension, neither can scarlet colour exist without extension: but this hinders not, but that they are distinct ideas. Many ideas require others as necessary to their existence or conception, which yet are very distinct ideas. Body then and extension, it is evident, are two distinct ideas. For,

First, Extension includes no solidity, nor resistance to the motion of body, as body does.

Secondly, The parts of pure space are inseparable one from the other; so that the continuity cannot be separated neither really, nor mentally. For I demand of any one to remove any part of it from another, with which it is continued, even so much as in thought. To divide and separate actually, is, as I think, by removing the parts one from another, to make two superficies, where before there was a continuity; and to divide mentally, is to make in the mind two superficies, where before there was a continuity, and consider them as removed one from the other; which can only be done in things considered by the mind as capable of being separated; and by separation, of acquiring new distinct superficies, which they then have not, but are capable of; but neither of these ways of separation, whether real or mental, is, as I think, compatible to pure space.

Thirdly, The parts of pure space are immoveable, which follows from their inseparability: motion being nothing but change of distance between any two things: but this cannot be between parts that are inseparable: which therefore must needs be at perpetual rest one amongst another.

Thus the determined idea of simple space distinguishes it plainly and sufficiently from body; since its parts are inseparable, immovable, and without resistance to the motion of body.

2. Simple Modes of Idea of Duration

There is another sort of distance or length, the idea whereof we get not from the permanent parts of space, but from the fleeting and perpetually perishing parts of succession. This we call duration, the simple modes whereof are any different lengths of it, whereof we have distinct ideas, as hours, days, years, &c. time and eternity.

To understand time and eternity aright, we ought with attention to consider what idea it is we have of duration, and how we came by it. It is evident to any one, who will but observe what passes in his own mind, that there is a train of ideas which constantly succeed one another in his understanding, as long as he is awake. Reflection on these appearances of several ideas, one after another, in our minds, is that which furnishes us with the idea of succession; and the distance between any parts of that succession, or between the appearance of any two ideas in our minds, is that we call duration. For whilst we are thinking, or whilst we receive successively several ideas in our minds, we know that we do exist; and so we call the existence, or the continuation of the existence of ourselves, or any thing else, commensurate to the succession of any ideas in our minds, the duration of ourselves, or any such other thing coexistent with our thinking.

That we have our notion of succession and duration from this original, viz. from reflection on the train of ideas which we find to appear one after another in our own minds, seems plain to me, in that we have no perception of duration, but by considering the train of ideas that take their turns in our understandings. When that succession of ideas ceases, our perception of duration ceases with it; which every one clearly experiments in himself, whilst he sleeps soundly, whether an hour or a day, a month or a year: of which duration of things, while he sleeps or thinks not, he has no perception at all, but it is quite lost to him; and the moment wherein he leaves off to think, till the moment he begins to think again, seems to him to have no distance. And so I doubt not it would be to a waking man, if it were possible for him to keep only one idea in his mind, without variation and the succession of others. And we see, that one who fixes his thoughts very intently on one thing, so as to take but little notice of the succession of ideas that pass in his mind, whilst he is taken up with that earnest contemplation, lets slip out of his account a good part of that duration, and thinks that time shorter than it is. But if sleep commonly unites the distant parts of duration, it is because during that time we have no succession of ideas in our minds. For if a man, during his sleep, dreams, and variety of ideas make themselves perceptible in his mind one after another; he hath then, during such dreaming, a sense of duration, and of the length of it. By which it is to me very clear, that men derive their ideas of duration from their reflections on the train of the ideas they observe to succeed one another in their own understandings; without which observation they can have no notion of duration, whatever may happen in the world.

Thus by reflecting on the appearing of various ideas one after another in our understandings, we get the notion of succession; which, if any one would think we did rather get from our observation of motion by our senses, he will perhaps be of my mind, when he considers that even motion produces in his mind an idea of succession, no otherwise than as it produces there a continued train of distinguishable ideas. For a man looking upon a body really moving, perceives yet no motion at all, unless that motion produces a constant train of successive ideas: v. g. a man becalmed at sea, out of sight of land, in a fair day, may look on the sun, or sea, or ship, a whole hour together, and perceive no motion at all in either; though it be certain that two, and perhaps all of them, have moved during that time a great way. But as soon as he perceives either of them to have changed distance with some other body, as soon as this motion produces any new idea in him, then he perceives that there has been motion. But wherever a man is, with all things at rest about him, without perceiving any motion at all; if during this hour of quiet he has been thinking, he will perceive the various ideas of his own thoughts in his own mind, appearing one after another, and thereby observe and find succession where he could observe no motion.

Having thus got the idea of duration, the next thing natural for the mind to do, is to get some measure of this common duration, whereby it might judge of its different lengths, and consider the distinct order wherein several things exist, without which a great part of our knowledge would be confused, and a great part of history be rendered very useless. This consideration of duration, as set out by certain periods, and marked by certain measures or epochs, is that, I think, which most properly we call time.

In the measuring of extension, there is nothing more required but the application of the standard or measure we make use of to the thing, of whose extension we would be informed. But in the measuring of duration, this cannot be done, because no two different parts of succession can be put together to measure one another: and nothing being a measure of duration but duration, as nothing is of extension but extension, we cannot keep by us any standing unvarying measure of duration, which consists in a constant fleeting succession, as we can of certain lengths of extension, as inches, feet, yards, &c. marked out in permanent parcels of matter. Nothing then could serve well for a convenient measure of time, but what has divided the whole length of its duration into apparently equal portions, by constantly repeated periods. What portions of duration are not distinguished, or considered as distinguished and measured by such periods, come not so properly under the notion of time, as appears by such phrases as these, viz. before all time, and when time shall be no more.

The diurnal and annual revolutions of the sun, as having been, from the beginning of nature, constant, regular, and universally observable by all mankind, and supposed equal to one another, have been with reason made use of for the measure of duration.

The mind having once got such a measure of time as the annual revolution of the sun, can apply that measure to duration, wherein that measure itself did not exist, and with which, in the reality of its being, it had nothing to do. The idea of duration equal to an annual revolution of the sun, is as easily applicable in our thoughts to duration, where no sun or motion was, as the idea of a foot or yard, taken from bodies here, can be applied in our thoughts to distances beyond the confines of the world, where are no bodies at all.

By the same means therefore, and from the same original that we come to have the idea of time, we have also that idea which we call eternity: viz. having got the idea of succession and duration, by reflecting on the train of our own ideas, caused in us either by the natural appearances of those ideas coming constantly of themselves into our waking thoughts, or else caused by external objects successively affecting our senses; and having from the revolutions of the sun got the ideas of certain lengths of duration, we can, in our thoughts, add such lengths of duration to one another, as often as we please, and apply them, so added, to durations past or to come: and this we can continue to do on, without bounds or limits, and proceed *in infinitum,* and apply thus the length of the annual motion of the sun to duration, supposed before the sun's, or any other motion had its being.

And thus I think it is plain, that from those two fountains of all knowledge before-mentioned, viz. reflection and sensation, we get ideas of duration, and the measures of it.

For, first, by observing what passes in our minds, how our ideas there in train constantly some vanish, and others begin to appear, we come by the idea of succession.

Secondly, by observing a distance in the parts of this succession, we get the idea of duration.

Thirdly, by sensation observing certain appearances, at certain regular and seeming equidistant periods, we get the ideas of certain lengths or measures of duration, as minutes, hours, days, years, &c.

Fourthly, by being able to repeat those measures of time, or ideas of stated length of duration in our minds, as often as we will, we can come to imagine duration, where nothing does really endure or exist; and thus we imagine to-morrow, next year, or seven years hence.

Fifthly, by being able to repeat ideas of any length of time as of a minute, a year, or an age, as often as we will in our own thoughts, and adding them one to another, without ever coming to the end of such addition any nearer than we can to the end of number, to which we can always add; we come by the idea of eternity, as the future eternal duration of our souls, as well as the eternity of that infinite Being, which must necessarily have always existed.

Sixthly, by considering any part of infinite duration, as set out by periodical measures, we come by the idea of what we call time in general.

3. Simple Modes of Idea of Number

Amongst all the ideas we have, as there is none suggested to the mind by more ways, so there is none more simple, than that of unity, or one. It has no shadow of variety or composition in it: every object our senses are employed about, every idea in our understandings, every thought of our minds, brings this idea along with it. And therefore it is the most intimate to our thoughts, as well as it is, in its agreement to all other things, the most universal idea we have. For number applies itself to men, angels, actions, thoughts, every thing that either doth exist, or can be imagined.

By repeating this idea in our minds, and adding the repetitions together, we come by the complex ideas of the modes of it. Thus by adding one to one, we have the complex idea of a couple; by putting twelve units together, we have the complex idea of a dozen; and so of a score, or a million, or any other number.

The simple modes of numbers are of all other the most distinct; every the least variation, which is an unit, making each combination as clearly different from that which approacheth nearest to it, as the most remote: two being as distinct from one, as two hundred; and the idea of two as distinct from the idea of three, as the magnitude of the whole earth is from that of a mite. This is not so in other simple modes, in which it is not so easy, nor perhaps possible for us to distinguish betwixt two approaching ideas, which yet are really different. For who will undertake to find a difference between the white of this paper, and that of the next degree to it; or can form distinct ideas of every the least excess in extension?

The clearness and distinctness of each mode of number from all others, even those that approach nearest, makes me apt to think that demonstrations in numbers, if they are not more evident and exact than in extension, yet they are more general in their use, and more determinate in their application.

4. The Idea of Infinity

He that would know what kind of idea it is to which we give the name of infinity, cannot do it better, than by considering to what infinity is by the mind more immediately attributed, and then how the mind comes to frame it.

Finite and infinite seem to me to be looked upon by the mind as the modes of quantity, and to be attributed primarily in their first designation only to those things which have parts, and are capable of increase or diminution, by the addition or subtraction of any the least part: and such are the ideas of space, duration, and number, which we have considered in the foregoing chapters. It is true, that we cannot but be assured, that the great God, of whom and from whom are all things, is incomprehensibly infinite: but yet when we apply to that first and supreme being our idea of infinite, in our weak and narrow thoughts, we do it primarily in respect to his duration and ubiquity; and, I think, more figuratively to his power, wisdom, and goodness, and other attributes, which are properly inexhaustible and incomprehensible, &c. For, when we call them infinite, we have no other idea of this infinity, but what carries with it some reflection on, and imitation of, that number or extent of the acts or objects of God's power, wisdom, and goodness, which can never be supposed so great or so many, which these attributes will not always surmount and exceed, let us multiply them in our thoughts as far as we can, with all the infinity of endless number. I do not pretend to say how these attributes are in God, who is infinitely beyond the reach of our narrow capacities. They do, without doubt, contain in them all possible perfection: but this, I say, is our way of conceiving them, and these our ideas of their infinity.

Finite then, and infinite, being by the mind looked on as modifications of expansion and duration, the next thing to be considered, is, how the mind comes by them. As for the idea of finite, there is no great difficulty. The obvious portions of extension that affect our senses, carry with them into the mind the idea of finite: and the ordinary periods of succession, whereby we measure time and duration, as hours, days, and years, are bounded lengths. The difficulty is, how we come by those boundless ideas of eternity and immensity, since the objects we converse with, come so much short of any approach or proportion to that largeness.

Every one that has any idea of any stated lengths of spàce, as a foot, finds that he can repeat that idea; and, joining it to the former, make the idea of two feet; and by the addition of a third, three feet; and so on, without ever coming to an end of his addition, whether of the same idea of a foot, or if he pleases of doubling it, or any other idea he has of any length, as a mile, or diameter of the earth, or of the *orbis magnus:* for whichsoever of these he takes, and how often soever he doubles, or any otherwise multiplies it, he finds that after he has continued his doubling in his thoughts, and enlarged his idea as much as he pleases, he has no more reason to stop, nor is one jot nearer the end of such addition, than he was at first setting out. The power of enlarging his idea of space by farther additions remaining still the same, he hence takes the idea of infinite space.

This, I think, is the way whereby the mind gets the idea of infinite space. It is a quite different consideration, to examine whether the mind has the idea of such a boundless space actually existing, since our ideas are not always proofs of the existence of things; but yet, since this comes here in our way, I suppose I may say, that we are apt to think that space in itself is actually boundless; to which imagination, the idea of space or expansion of itself naturally leads us. For it being considered by us, either as the extension of body, or as existing by itself, without any solid matter taking it up, it is impossible the mind should be ever able to find or suppose any end of it, or be stopped any where in its progress in this space, how far soever it extends its thoughts.

As by the power we find in ourselves of repeating, as often as we will, any idea of space, we get the idea of immensity; so, by being able to repeat the idea of any length of duration we have in our minds, with all the endless addition of number, we come by the idea of eternity. For we find in ourselves, we can no more come to an end of such repeated ideas, than we can come to the end of number, which every one perceives he cannot. But here again it is another question, quite different from our having an idea of eternity, to know whether there were any real being, whose duration has been eternal.

Though our idea of infinity arise from the contemplation of quantity, and the endless increase the mind is able to make in quantity, by the repeated additions of what portions thereof it pleases; yet I guess we cause great confusion in our thoughts, when we join infinity to any supposed idea of quantity the mind can be thought to have, and so discourse or reason about an infinite quantity, viz. an infinite space, or an infinite duration. For our idea of infinity being as I think, an endless growing idea, by the idea of any quantity the mind has, being at that time terminated in that idea, (for be it as great as it will, it can be no greater than it is) to join infinity to it, is to adjust a standing measure to a growing bulk; and therefore I think it is not an insignificant subtilty, if I say that we are carefully to distinguish between the idea of the infinity of space, and the idea of a space infinite: the first is nothing but a supposed endless progression of the mind, over what repeated ideas of space it pleases; but to have actually in the mind the idea of a space infinite, is to suppose the mind already passed over, and actually to have a view of all those repeated ideas of space, which an endless repetition can never totally represent to it; which carries in it a plain contradiction.

For let a man frame in his mind an idea of any space or number, as great as he will: it is plain the mind rests and terminates in that idea, which is contrary to the idea of infinity, which consists in a supposed endless progression. And therefore I think it is, that we are so easily confounded, when we come to argue and reason about infinite space or duration, &c. Because the parts of such an idea not being perceived to be, as they are, inconsistent, the one side or other always perplexes, whatever consequences we draw from the other; as an idea of motion not passing on would perplex any one, who should argue from such an idea, which is not better than an idea of motion at rest: and such another seems to me to be the idea of a space, or (which is the same thing) a number infinite, i. e. of a space or number which the mind actually has, and so views and terminates in; and of a space or number, which in a constant and endless enlarging and progression, it can in thought never attain to. For how large soever an idea of space I have in my mind, it is no larger than it is that instant that I have it, though I be capable the next instant to double it, and so on *in infinitum:* for that alone is infinite which has no bounds; and that the idea of infinity, in which our thoughts can find none.

Though it be hard, I think, to find any one so absurd as to say, he has the positive idea of an actual infinite number; the infinity whereof lies only in a power still of adding any combination of units to any former number, and that as long and as much as one will; the like also being in the infinity of space and duration, which power leaves always to the mind room for endless additions; yet there be those who imagine they have positive ideas of infinite duration and space. It would, I think, be enough to destroy any such positive idea of infinite, to ask him that has it, whether he could add to it or no; which would easily show the mistake of such a positive idea. We can, I think, have no positive idea of any space or duration which is not made up, and commensurate to repeated numbers of feet or yards, or days and years, which are the common measures, whereof we have the ideas in our minds, and whereby we judge of the greatness of this sort of quantities. And therefore, since an infinite idea of space or duration must needs be made up of infinite parts, it can have no other infinity than that of number, capable still of farther addition: but not an actual positive idea of a number infinite. For, I think, it is evident that the addition of finite things together (as are all lengths, whereof we have the positive ideas) can never otherwise produce the idea of infinite, than as number does; which consisting of additions of finite units one to another, suggests the idea of infinite, only by a power we find we have of still increasing the sum, and adding more of the same kind, without coming one jot nearer the end of such progression.

5. *Simple Modes of Thinking*

When the mind turns its view inwards upon itself, and contemplates its own actions, thinking is the first that occurs. In it the mind observes a great variety of modifications, and from thence receives distinct ideas. Thus the perception which actually accompanies, and is annexed to any impression on the body, made by an external object, being distinct from all other modifications of thinking, furnishes the mind with a distinct idea, which we call sensation; which is, as it were, the actual entrance of any idea into the understanding by the senses. The same idea, when it again recurs without the operation of the like object on the external sensory, is remembrance; if it be sought after by the mind, and with pain and endeavour found, and brought again in view, it is recollection; if it be held there long under attentive consideration, it is contemplation. When ideas float in our mind, without any reflection or regard of the understanding, it is that which the French call reverie, our language has scarce a name for it. When the ideas that offer themselves (for, as I have observed in another place, whilst we are awake, there will always be a train of ideas succeeding one another in our minds) are taken notice of, and, as it were, registered in the memory, it is attention. When the mind with great earnestness, and of choice, fixes its view on any idea, considers it on all sides, and will not be called off by the ordinary solicitation of other ideas, it is that we call intention, or study. Sleep, without dreaming, is rest from all these: and dreaming itself, is the having of ideas (whilst the outward senses are stopped, so that they receive not outward objects with their usual quickness) in the mind, not suggested by any external objects, or known occasion, nor under any choice or conduct of the understanding at all. And whether that, which we call ecstasy, be not dreaming with the eyes open, I leave to be examined.

These are some few instances of those various modes of thinking, which the mind may observe in itself, and so have as distinct ideas of, as it hath of white and red, a square or a circle. I do not pretend to enumerate them all, nor to treat at large of this set of ideas, which are got from reflection: that would be to make a volume. It suffices to my present purpose to have shown here, by some few examples, of what sort these ideas are, and how the mind comes by them; especially since I shall have occasion hereafter to treat more at large of reasoning, judging, volition, and knowledge, which are some of the most considerable operations of the mind, and modes of thinking.

6. Simple Modes of Pleasure and Pain

Amongst the simple ideas, which we receive both from sensation and reflection, pain and pleasure are two very considerable ones. For as in the body there is sensation barely in itself, or accompanied with pain or pleasure: so the thought or perception of the mind is simply so, or else accompanied also with pleasure or pain, delight or trouble, call it how you please. These, like other simple ideas, cannot be described, nor their names defined; the way of knowing them is, as of the simple ideas of the senses, only by experience.

Thus any one reflecting upon the thought he has of the delight, which any present or absent thing is apt to produce in him, has the idea we call love. For when a man declares in autumn, when he is eating them, or in spring, when there are none, that he loves grapes, it is no more but that the taste of grapes delights him; let an alteration of health or constitution destroy the delight of their taste, and he then can be said to love grapes no longer.

On the contrary, the thought of the pain, which any thing present or absent is apt to produce in us, is what we call hatred. Were it my business here to inquire any farther than into the bare ideas of our passions, as they depend on different modifications of pleasure and pain, I should remark, that our love and hatred of inanimate insensible beings, is commonly founded on that pleasure and pain which we receive from their use and application any way to our senses, though with their destruction: but hatred or love, to beings capable of happiness or misery, is often the uneasiness or delight, which we find in ourselves arising from a consideration of their very being or happiness. Thus the being and welfare of a man's children or friends, producing constant delight in him, he is said constantly to love them. But it suffices to note, that our ideas of love and hatred are but the dispositions of the mind, in respect of pleasure and pain in general, however caused in us.

The uneasiness a man finds in himself upon the absence of any thing, whose present enjoyment carries the idea of delight with it, is that we call desire; which is greater or less, as that uneasiness is more or less vehement.

Joy is a delight of the mind, from the consideration of the present or assured approaching possession of a good: and we are then possessed of any good when we have it so in our power, that we can use it when we please. Thus a man almost starved has joy at the arrival of relief, even before he has the pleasure of using it: and a father, in whom the very well-being of his children causes delight, is always, as long as his children are in such a state, in the possession of that good; for he needs but to reflect on it, to have that pleasure.

Sorrow is uneasiness in the mind, upon the thought of a good lost, which might have been enjoyed longer; or the sense of a present evil.

Hope is that pleasure in the mind, which every one finds in himself, upon the thought of a profitable future enjoyment of a thing, which is apt to delight him.

Fear is an uneasiness of the mind, upon the thought of future evil likely to befal us.

Despair is the thought of the unattainableness of any good, which works differently in men's minds, sometimes producing uneasiness or pain, sometimes rest and indolency.

Anger is uneasiness or discomposure of the mind, upon the receipt of any injury, with a present purpose of revenge.

Envy is an uneasiness of the mind, caused by the consideration of a good we desire, obtained by one we think should not have had it before us.

I would not be mistaken here, as if I meant this as a discourse of the passions; they are many more than those I have here named: and those I have taken notice of would each of them require a much larger, and more accurate discourse. I have only mentioned these here as so many instances of modes of pleasure and pain resulting in our minds from various considerations of good and evil. I might perhaps have instanced in other modes of pleasure and pain more simple than these, as the pain of hunger and thirst, and the pleasure of eating and drinking to remove them: the pain of tender eyes, and the pleasure of musick; pain from captious uninstructive wrangling, and the pleasure of rational conversation with a friend, or of well-directed study in the search and discovery of truth. But the passions being of much more concernment to us, I rather made choice to instance in them, and show how the ideas we have of them are derived from sensation and reflection.

7. The Idea of Power

The mind being every day informed, by the senses, of the alteration of those simple ideas it observes in things without, and taking notice how one comes to an end, and ceases to be, and another begins to exist which was not before; reflecting also on what passes within himself, and observing a constant change of its ideas, sometimes by the impression of outward objects on the senses, and sometimes by the determination of its own choice; and concluding from what it has so constantly observed to have been, that the like changes will for the future be made in the same things by like agents, and by the like ways; considers in one thing the possibility of having any of its simple ideas changed, and in another the possibility of making that change: and so comes by that idea which we call power. Thus we say, fire has a power to melt gold, i. e. to destroy the consistency of its insensible parts, and consequently its hardness, and make it fluid; and gold has a power to be melted: that the sun has a power to blanch wax, and wax a power to be blanched by the sun, whereby the yellowness is destroyed, and whiteness made to exist in its room. In which, and the like cases, the power we consider is in reference to the change of perceivable ideas: for we cannot observe any alteration to be made in, or operation upon, any thing, but by the observable change of its sensible ideas; nor conceive any alteration to be made, but by conceiving a change of some of its ideas.

Power, thus considered, is two-fold, viz. as able to make, or able to receive, any change: the one may be called active, and the other passive power. Whether matter be not wholly destitute of active power, as its author God is truly above all passive power; and whether the intermediate state of created spirits be not that alone which is capable of both active and passive power, may be worth consideration. I shall not now enter into that inquiry: my present business being not to search into the original of power, but how we come by the idea of it. But since active powers make so great a part of our complex ideas of natural substances (as we shall see hereafter) and I mention them as such according to common apprehension; yet they being not perhaps so truly active powers, as our hasty thoughts are apt to represent them, I judge it not amiss, by this intimation, to direct our minds to the consideration of God and spirits, for the clearest idea of active powers.

We are abundantly furnished with the idea of passive power by almost all sorts of sensible things. In most of them we cannot avoid observing their sensible qualities, nay, their very substances, to be in a continual flux: and therefore with reason we look on them as liable still to the same change. Nor have we of active power (which is the more proper signification of the word power) fewer instances: since whatever change is observed, the mind must collect a power somewhere able to make that change, as well as a possibility in the thing itself to receive it. But yet, if we will consider it attentively, bodies, by our senses, do not afford us so clear and distinct an idea of active power, as we have from reflection on the operations of our minds. For all power relating to action, and there being but two sorts of action, whereof we have any idea, viz. thinking and motion; let us consider whence we have the clearest ideas of the powers which produce these actions. 1. Of thinking body affords us no idea at all, it is only from reflection that we have that. 2. Neither have we from body any idea of the beginning of motion. A body at rest affords us no idea of any active power to move; and when it is set in motion itself, that motion is rather a passion, than an action in it. For when the ball obeys the motion of a billiard stick, it is not any action of the ball, but bare passion: also when by impulse it sets another ball in motion that lay in its way, it only communicates the motion it had received from another, and loses in itself so much as the other received: which gives us but a very obscure idea of an active power moving in body, whilst we observe it only to transfer, but not produce any motion. For it is but a very obscure idea of power, which reaches not the production of the action, but the continuation of the passion. For so is motion in a body impelled by another; the continuation of the alteration made in it from rest to motion being little more an action, than the continuation of the alteration of its figure by the same blow is an action. The idea of the beginning of motion we have only from reflection on what passes in ourselves, where we find by experience, that barely by willing it, barely by a thought of the mind, we can move the parts of our bodies, which were before at rest. So that it seems to me, we have from the observation of the operation of bodies by our senses but a very imperfect obscure idea of active power, since they afford us not any idea in themselves of the power to begin any action, either motion or thought. But if, from the impulse bodies are observed to make one upon another, any one thinks he has a clear idea of power, it serves as well to my purpose, sensation being one of those ways whereby the mind comes by its ideas: only I thought it worth while to consider here by the way, whether the mind doth not receive its idea of active power clearer from reflection on its own operations, than it doth from any external sensation.

This at least I think evident, that we find in ourselves a power to begin or forbear, continue or end several actions of our minds, and motions of our bodies, barely by a thought or preference of the mind ordering, or, as it were, commanding the doing or not doing such or such a particular action. This power which the mind has thus to order the consideration of any idea, or the forbearing to consider it; or to prefer the motion of any part of the body to its rest, and vice versa, in any particular instance: is that which we call the will. The actual exercise of that power, by directing any particular action, or its forbearance, is that which we call volition or willing. The forbearance, of that action, consequent to such order or command of the mind, is called voluntary. And whatsoever action is performed without such a thought of the mind, is called involuntary. The power of perception is that which we call the understanding. Perception, which we make the act of the understanding, is of three sorts: 1. The perception of ideas in our mind. 2. The perception of the signification of signs. 3. The perception of the connexion or repugnancy, agreement or disagreement, that there is between any of our ideas. All these are attributed to the understanding, or perceptive power, though it be the two latter only that use allows us to say we understand.

These powers of the mind, viz. of perceiving and of preferring, are usually called by another name: and the ordinary way of speaking, is, that the understanding and will are two faculties of the mind; a word proper enough, if it be used as all words should be, so as not to breed any confusion in men's thoughts, by being supposed (as I suspect it has been) to stand for some real beings in the soul that performed those actions of understanding and volition. For when we say the will is the commanding and superior faculty of the soul: that it is, or is not free; that it determines the inferior faculties; that it follows the dictates of the understanding, &c. though these, and the like expressions, by those that carefully attend to their own ideas, and conduct their thoughts more by the evidence of things, than the sound of words, may be understood in a clear and distinct sense; yet I suspect, I say, that this way of speaking of faculties has misled many into a confused notion of so many distinct agents in us, which had their several provinces and authorities, and did command, obey, and perform several actions, as so many distinct beings; which has been no small occasion of wrangling, obscurity, and uncertainty in questions relating to them.

Every one I think, finds in himself a power to begin or forbear, continue or put an end to several actions in himself. From the consideration of the extent of this power of the mind over the actions of the man, which every one finds in himself, arise the ideas of liberty and necessity.

All the actions that we have any idea of, reducing themselves, as has been said, to these two, viz. thinking and motion; so far as a man has power to think, or not to think; to move, or not to move, according to the preference or direction of his own mind; so far is a man free. Wherever any performance or forbearance are not equally in a man's power; wherever doing or not doing, will not equally follow upon the preference of his mind directing it: there he is not free, though perhaps the action may be voluntary. So that the idea of liberty is the idea of a power in any agent to do or forbear any particular action, according to the determination or thought of the mind, whereby either of them is preferred to the other; where either of them is not in the power of the agent to be produced by him according to his volition, there he is not at liberty; that agent is under necessity. So that liberty cannot be where there is no thought, no volition, no will; but there may be thought, there may be will, there may be volition, where there is no liberty. Voluntary then is not opposed to necessary, but to involuntary. For a man may prefer what he can do, to what he cannot do: the state he is in, to its absence or change, though necessity has made it in itself unalterable.

If this be so (as I imagine it is) I leave it to be considered whether it may not help to put an end to that long agitated, and I think, unreasonable, because unintelligible question, viz. Whether man's will be free, or no? For if I mistake not, it follows from what I have said, that the question itself is altogether improper; and it is as insignificant to ask whether man's will be free, as to ask whether his sleep be swift, or his virtue square; liberty being as little applicable to the will, as swiftness of motion is to sleep, or squareness to virtue. Every one would laugh at the absurdity of such a question, as either of these; because it is obvious, that the modifications of motion belong not to sleep, nor the difference of figure to virtue: and when any one well considers it, I think he will as plainly perceive, that liberty, which is but a power, belongs only to agents, and cannot be an attribute or modification of the will, which is also but a power.

However the name faculty, which men have given to this power called the will, and whereby they have been led into a way of talking of the will as acting, may, by an appropriation that disguises its true sense, serve a little to palliate the absurdity; yet the will in truth signifies nothing but a power, or ability, to prefer or choose: and when the will under the name of a faculty, is considered as it is, barely as an ability to do something, the absurdity in saying it is free, or not free, will easily discover itself. For if it be reasonable to suppose and talk of faculties, as distinct beings that can act (as we do, when we say the will orders, and the will is free) it is fit that we should make a speaking faculty, and a walking faculty, and a dancing faculty, by which those actions are produced, which are but several modes of motion; as well as we make the will and understanding to be faculties, by which the actions of choosing and perceiving are produced, which are but several modes of thinking; and we may as properly say, that it is the singing faculty sings, and the dancing faculty dances; as that the will chooses, or that the understanding conceives; or as is usual, that the will directs the understanding, or the understanding obeys, or obeys not the will: it being altogether as proper and intelligible to say, that the power of speaking directs the power of singing, or the power of singing obeys or disobeys the power of speaking.

I grant, that this or that actual thought may be the occasion of volition, or exercising the power a man has to choose: or the actual choice of the mind, the cause of actual thinking on this or that thing: as the actual singing of such a tune, may be the cause of dancing such a dance, and the actual dancing of such a dance the occasion of singing such a tune. But in all these it is not one power that operates on another: but it is the mind that operates and exerts these powers; it is the man that does the action, it is the agent that has power, or is able to do. For powers are relations, not agents: and that which has the power, or not the power to operate, is that alone which is or is not free, and not the power itself. For freedom, or not freedom, can belong to nothing, but what has or has not a power to act.

The attributing to faculties that which belonged not to them, has given occasion to this way of talking: but the introducing into discourses concerning the mind, with the name of faculties, a notion of their operating, has, I suppose, as little advanced our knowledge in that part of ourselves, as the great use and mention of the like invention of faculties, in the operations of the body, has helped us in the knowledge of physic. Not that I deny there are faculties, both in the body and mind: they both of them have their powers of operating, else neither the one nor the other could operate. For nothing can operate that is not able to operate; and that is not able to operate, that has no power to operate. Nor do I deny, that those words, and the like, are to have their place in the common use of languages, that have made them current. It looks like too much affectation wholly to lay them by: and philosophy itself, though it likes not a gaudy dress, yet when it appears in public, must have so much complacency, as to be clothed in the ordinary fashion and language of the country, so far as it can consist with truth and perspicuity. But the fault has been, that faculties have been spoken of and represented as so many distinct agents. For it being asked, what it was that digested the meat in our stomachs? it was a ready and very satisfactory answer, to say that it was the digestive faculty. What was it that made any thing come out of the body? the expulsive faculty. What moved? the motive faculty. And so in the mind, the intellectual faculty, or the understanding, understood; and the elective faculty, or the will, willed or commanded. This is in short to say, that the ability to digest, digested; and the ability to move, moved; and the ability to understand, understood. For faculty, ability, and power, I think, are but different names of the same things; which ways of speaking, when put into more intelligible words, will, I think, amount to thus much; that digestion is performed by something that is able to digest, motion by something able to move, and understanding by something able to understand. And in truth it would be very strange if it should be otherwise; as strange as it would be for a man to be free without being able to be free.

To return then to the inquiry about liberty, I think the question is not proper, whether the will be free, but whether a man be free. Thus, I think, that so far as any one can, by the direction or choice of his mind, preferring the existence of any action to the non-existence of that action, and vice versa, make it to exist or not exist; so far he is free. For if I can, by a thought directing the motion of my finger, make it move when it was at rest, or vice versa; it is evident, that in respect of that I am free: and if I can, by a like thought of my mind, preferring one to the other, produce either words or silence, I am at liberty to speak, or hold my peace; and as far as this power reaches, of acting, or not acting, by the determination of his own thought preferring either, so far is a man free. For how can we think any one freer, than to have the power to do what he will? And so far as any one can, by preferring any action to its not being, or rest to any action, produce that action or rest, so far can he do what he will. For such a preferring of action to its absence, is the willing of it; and we can scarce tell how to imagine any being freer, than to be able to do what he wills. So that in respect of actions within the reach of such a power in him, a man seems as free, as it is possible for freedom to make him.

But the inquisitive mind of man, willing to shift off from himself, as far as he can, all thoughts of guilt, though it be by putting himself into a worse state than that of fatal necessity, is not content with this; freedom, unless it reaches farther than this, will not serve the turn: and it passes for a good plea, that a man is not free at all, if he be not as free to will, as he is to act what he wills. Concerning a man's liberty, there yet therefore is raised this farther question, Whether a man be free to will? which I think is what is meant, when it is disputed whether the will be free. And as to that I imagine, that willing, or volition, being an action, and freedom consisting in a power of acting or not acting, a man in respect of willing or the act of volition, when any action in his power is once proposed to his thoughts, as presently to be done, cannot be free. The reason whereof is very manifest: for it being unavoidable that the action depending on his will should exist, or not exist: and its existence, or not existence, following perfectly the determination and preference of his will; he cannot avoid willing the existence, or not existence of that action; it is absolutely necessary that he will the one, or the other; i. e. prefer the one to the other; since one of them must necessarily follow; and that which does follow, follows by the choice and determination of his mind, that is, by his willing it; for if he did not will it, it would not be. So that in respect of the act of willing, a man in such a case is not free: liberty consisting in a power to act, or not to act; which, in regard of volition, a man, upon such a proposal, has not. For it is unavoidably necessary to prefer the doing or forbearance of an action in a man's power, which is once so proposed to his thoughts: a man must necessarily will the one or the other of them, upon which preference or volition, the action or its forbearance certainly follows, and is truly voluntary. But the act of volition, or preferring one of the two, being that which he cannot avoid, a man in respect of that act of willing is under a necessity, and so cannot be free; unless necessity and freedom can consist together, and a man can be free and bound at once.

This then is evident, that in all proposals of present action, a man is not at liberty to will or not to will, because he cannot forbear willing: liberty consisting in a power to act or to forbear acting, and in that only. Liberty is a power to act or not to act, according as the mind directs. A power to direct the operative faculties to motion or rest in particular instances, is that which we call the will. That which, in the train of our voluntary actions, determines the will to any change of operation, is some present uneasiness; which is, or at least is always accompanied with, that of desire. Desire is always moved by evil, to fly it: because a total freedom from pain always makes a necessary part of our happiness: but every good, nay every greater good, does not constantly move desire, because it may not make, or may not be taken to make any necessary part of our happiness. For all that we desire, is only to be happy. But though this general desire of happiness operates constantly and invariably, yet the satisfaction of any particular desire can be suspended from determining the will to any subservient action, till we have maturely examined, whether the particular apparent good, which we then desire, makes a part of our real happiness, or be consistent or inconsistent with it. The result of our judgment upon that examination is what ultimately determines the man, who could not be free if his will were determined by any thing but his own desire, guided by his own judgment. I know that liberty by some is placed in an indifferency of the man, antecedent to the determination of his will. I wish they, who lay so much stress on such an antecedent indifferency, as they call it, had told us plainly, whether this supposed indifferency be antecedent to the thought and judgment of the understanding, as well as to the decree of the will. For it is pretty hard to state it between them; i. e. immediately after the judgment of the understanding, and before the determination of the will, because the determination of the will immediately follows the judgment of the understanding: and to place liberty in an indifferency, antecedent to the thought and judgment of the understanding, seems to me to place liberty in a state of darkness, wherein we can neither see nor say any thing of it; at least it places it in a subject incapable of it, no agent being allowed capable of liberty, but in consequence of thought and judgment. I am not nice about phrases, and therefore consent to say, with those that love to speak so, that liberty is placed in indifferency; but it is an indifferency which remains after the judgment of the understanding; yea, even after the determination of the will: and that is an indifferency not of the man, (for after he has once judged which is best, viz. to do, or forbear, he is no longer indifferent) but an indifferency of the operative powers of the man, which remaining equally able to operate, or to forbear operating after, as before the decree of the will, are in a state, which, if one pleases, may be called indifferency; and as far as this indifferency reaches, a man is free, and no farther; v. g. I have the ability to move my hand, or to let it rest; that operative power is indifferent to move, or not to move my hand; I am then in that respect perfectly free. My will determines that operative power to rest; I am yet free; because the indifferency of that my operative power to act, or not to act, still remains; the power of moving my hand is not at all impaired by the determination of my will, which at present orders rest; the indifferency of that power to act, or not to act, is just as it was before, as will appear, if the will puts it to the trial, by ordering the contrary. But if during the rest of my hand, it be seized by a sudden palsy, the indifferency of that operative power is gone, and with it my liberty; I have no longer freedom in that respect, but am under a necessity of letting my hand rest. On the other side, if my hand be put into motion by a convulsion, the indifferency of that operative faculty is taken away by that motion, and my liberty in that case is lost; for I am under a necessity of having my hand move.

SUMMARY OF THE DISCUSSION OF IDEAS

And thus I have, in a short draught, given a view of our original ideas, from whence all the rest are derived, and of which they are made up; which if I would consider, as a philosopher, and examine on what causes they depend, and of what they are made, I believe they all might be reduced to these very few primary and original ones, viz. Extension, Solidity, Mobility, or the power of being moved; which by our senses we receive from body; Perceptivity, or the power of perception, or thinking; Motivity, or the power of moving; which by reflection we receive from our minds. I crave leave to make use of these two new words, to avoid the danger of being mistaken in the use of those which are equivocal. To which if we add Existence, Duration, Number; which belong both to the one and the other; we have, perhaps, all the original ideas, on which the rest depend. For by these, I imagine, might be explained the nature of colours, sounds, tastes, smells, and all other ideas we have, if we had but faculties acute enough to perceive the severally modified extensions and motions of these minute bodies, which produce those several sensations in us. But my present purpose being only to inquire into the knowledge the mind has of things, by those ideas and appearances, which God has fitted it to receive from them, and how the mind comes by that knowledge, rather than into their causes, or manner of production; I shall not, contrary to the design of this essay, set myself to inquire philosophically into the peculiar constitution of bodies, and the configuration of parts, whereby they have the power to produce in us the ideas of their sensible qualities: I shall not enter any farther into that disquisition, it sufficing to my purpose to observe, that gold or saffron has a power to produce in us the idea of yellow, and snow or milk the idea of white, which we can only have by our sight, without examining the texture of the parts of those bodies, or the particular figures or motion of the particles which rebound from them, to cause in us that particular sensation: though when we go beyond the bare ideas in our minds, and would inquire into their causes, we cannot conceive any thing else to be in any sensible object, whereby it produces different ideas in us, but the different bulk, figure, number, texture, and motion of its insensible parts.

MIXED MODES

Having treated of simple modes in the foregoing chapters, and given several instances of some of the most considerable of them, to show what they are, and how we come by them; we are now in the next place to consider those we call mixed modes: such are the complex ideas we mark by the names Obligation, Drunkenness, a Lye, &c. which consisting of several combinations of simple ideas of different kinds, I have called mixed modes, to distinguish them from the more simple modes, which consist only of simple ideas of the same kind. These mixed modes being also such combinations of simple ideas, as are not looked upon to be characteristical marks of any real beings that have a steady existence, but scattered and independent ideas put together by the mind, are thereby distinguished from the complex ideas of substances.

That the mind, in respect of its simple ideas, is wholly passive, and receives them all from the existence and operations of things, such as sensation or reflection offers them, without being able to make any one idea, experience shows us: but if we attentively consider these ideas I call mixed modes, we are now speaking of, we shall find their original quite different. The mind often exercises an active power in making these several combinations: for it being once furnished with simple ideas, it can put them together in several compositions, and so make variety of complex ideas, without examining whether they exist so together in nature. And hence I think it is that these ideas are called notions, as if they had their original and constant existence more in the thoughts of men, than in the reality of things; and to form such ideas, it sufficed, that the mind puts the parts of them together, and that they were consistent in the understanding, without considering whether they had any real being: though I do not deny, but several of them might be taken from observation, and the existence of several simple ideas so combined, as they are put together in the understanding. For the man who first framed the idea of hypocrisy, might have either taken it at first from the observation of one, who made show of good qualities which he had not, or else have framed that idea in his mind, without having any such pattern to fashion it by: for it is evident, that in the beginning of languages and societies of men, several of those complex ideas, which were consequent to the constitutions established amongst them, must needs have been in the minds of men, before they existed any where else: and that many names that stood for such complex ideas were in use, and so those ideas framed before the combinations they stood for ever existed.

Indeed now that languages are made, and abound with words standing for such combinations, an usual way of getting these complex ideas is by the explication of those terms that stand for them. For consisting of a company of simple ideas combined, they may by words, standing for those simple ideas, be represented to the mind of one who understands those words, though that complex combination of simple ideas were never offered to his mind by the real existence of things. Thus a man may come to have the idea of sacrilege or murder, by enumerating to him the simple ideas which these words stand for, without ever seeing either of them committed.

Every mixed mode consisting of many distinct simple ideas, it seems reasonable to inquire, "whence it has its unity, and how such a precise multitude comes to make but one idea, since that combination does not always exist together in nature?" To which I answer, it is plain it has its unity from an act of the mind combining those several simple ideas together, and considering them as one complex one, consisting of those parts; and the mark of this union, or that which is looked on generally to complete it, is one name given to that combination. For it is by their names that men commonly regulate their account of their distinct species of mixed modes, seldom allowing or considering any number of simple ideas to make one complex one, but such collections as there be names for. Thus, though the killing of an old man be as fit in nature to be united into one complex idea, as the killing a man's father; yet there being no name standing precisely for the one, as there is the name of parricide to mark the other, it is not taken for a particular complex idea, nor a distinct species of actions from that of killing a young man, or any other man.

There are therefore three ways whereby we get the complex ideas of mixed modes. 1. By experience and observation of things themselves. Thus by seeing two men wrestle or fence, we get the idea of wrestling or fencing. 2. By invention, or voluntary putting together of several simple ideas in our minds: so he that first invented printing, or etching, had an idea of it in his mind, before it ever existed. 3. Which is the most usual way, by explaining the names of actions we never saw, or notions we cannot see; and by enumerating, and thereby, as it were, setting before our imaginations all those ideas which go to the making them up, and are the constituent parts of them. For having by sensation and reflection stored our minds with simple ideas, and by use got the names that stand for them, we can by those means represent to another any complex idea we would have him conceive; so that it has in it no simple ideas, but what he knows, and has with us the same name for. For all our complex ideas are ultimately resolvable into simple ideas, of which they are compounded and originally made up, though perhaps their immediate ingredients, as I may so say, are also complex ideas. All our complex ideas may at last be resolved into simple ideas, which are all the materials of knowledge or thought we have, or can have. Nor shall we have reason to fear that the mind is hereby stinted to too scanty a number of ideas, if we consider what an inexhaustible stock of simple modes number and figure alone afford us. How far then mixed modes which admit of the various combinations of different simple ideas, and their infinite modes, are from being few and scanty, we may easily imagine. So that before we have done, we shall see that nobody need be afraid he shall not have scope and compass enough for his thoughts to range in, though they be, as I pretend, confined only to simple ideas received from sensation or reflection, and their several combinations.

To conclude: Let us examine any modes of action, v. g. consideration and assent, which are actions of the mind; running and speaking, which are actions of the body; revenge and murder, which are actions of both together: and we shall find them but so many collections of simple ideas, which together make up the complex ones signified by those names.

COMPLEX IDEAS OF SUBSTANCE

The mind being, as I have declared, furnished with a great number of the simple ideas, conveyed in by the senses, as they are found in exterior things, or by reflection on its own operations, takes notice also, that a certain number of these simple ideas go constantly together; which being presumed to belong to one thing, and words being suited to common apprehensions, and made use of for quick dispatch, are called, so united in one subject, by one name: which, by inadvertency, we are apt afterward to talk of, and consider as one simple idea, which indeed is a complication of many ideas together; because, as I have said, not imagining how these simple ideas can subsist by themselves, we accustom ourselves to suppose some substratum wherein they do subsist, and from which they do result; which therefore we call substance.

So that if any one will examine himself concerning his notion of pure substance in general, he will find he has no other idea of it at all, but only a supposition of he knows not what support of such qualities, which are capable of producing simple ideas in us; which qualities are commonly called accidents. If any one should be asked, what is the subject wherein colour or weight inheres, he would have nothing to say, but the solid extended parts: and if he were demanded, what is it that solidity and extension adhere in, he would not be in a much better case than the Indian, who, saying that the world was supported by a great elephant, was asked what the elephant rested on; to which his answer was, a great tortoise. But being again pressed to know what gave support to the broad-backed tortoise, replied, something he knew not what.[1] And thus here, as in all other cases where we use words without having clear and distinct ideas, we talk like children; who being questioned what such a thing is, which they know not, readily give this satisfactory answer, that it is something; which in truth signifies no more, when so used either by children or men, but that they know not what; and that the thing they pretend to know and talk of, is what they have no distinct idea of at all, and so are perfectly ignorant of it, and in the dark. The idea then we have, to which we give the general name substance, being nothing but the supposed, but unknown support of those qualities we find existing, which we imagine cannot subsist, *sine re substante,* without something to support them, we call that support *substantia;* which, according to the true import of the word, is in plain English, standing under or upholding.

An obscure and relative idea of substance in general being thus made, we come to have the ideas of particular sorts of substances, by collecting such combinations of simple ideas, as are by experience and observation of men's senses taken notice of to exist together, and are

[1] This paragraph, with its humor, led some of Locke's critics to suppose that he wished to deny the real existence of substance. That he intended nothing of the kind is further shown by passages quoted on p. 328.

therefore supposed to flow from the particular internal constitution, or unknown essence of that substance. Thus we come to have the ideas of a man, horse, gold, water, &c. of which substances, whether any one has any other clear idea, farther than of certain simple ideas co-existent together, I appeal to every man's own experience. It is the ordinary qualities observable in iron, or a diamond, put together, that make the true complex idea of those substances, which a smith or a jeweller commonly knows better than a philosopher; who, whatever substantial forms he may talk of, has no other idea of those substances, than what is framed by a collection of those simple ideas which are to be found in them; only we must take notice, that our complex ideas of substances, besides all those simple ideas they are made up of, have always the confused idea of something to which they belong, and in which they subsist. And therefore, when we speak of any sort of substance, we say it is a thing having such or such qualities: as body is a thing that is extended, figured, and capable of motion; spirit, a thing capable of thinking; and so hardness, friability, and power to draw iron, we say, are qualities to be found in a loadstone. These, and the like fashions of speaking, intimate, that the substance is supposed always something besides the extension, figure, solidity, motion, thinking, or other observable ideas, though we know not what it is.

Hence, when we talk or think of any particular sort of corporeal substances, as horse, stone, &c. though the idea we have of either of them be but the complication or collection of those several simple ideas of sensible qualities, which we used to find united in the thing called horse or stone; yet because we cannot conceive how they should subsist alone, or one in another, we suppose them existing in and supported by some common subject; which support we denote by the name substance, though it be certain we have no clear or distinct idea of that thing we suppose a support.

The same thing happens concerning the operations of the mind, viz. thinking, reasoning, fearing, &c. which we concluding not to subsist of themselves, nor apprehending how they can belong to any body, or be produced by it, we are apt to think these the actions of some other substance, which we call spirit; whereby yet it is evident, that having no other idea or notion of matter, but something wherein those many sensible qualities which affect our senses do subsist; by supposing a substance, wherein thinking, knowing, doubting, and a power of moving, &c. do subsist, we have as clear a notion of the substance of spirit, as we have of body: the one being supposed to be (without knowing what it is) the substratum to those simple ideas we have from without; and the other supposed (with a like ignorance of what it is) to be the substratum to those operations we experiment in ourselves within. It is plain then, that the idea of corporeal substance in matter is as remote from our conceptions and apprehensions, as that of spiritual substance or spirit; and therefore from our not having any notion of the substance of spirit, we can no more conclude its non-existence, than we can for the same reason deny the existence of body; it being as rational to affirm there is no body, because we have no clear and distinct idea of the substance of matter, as to say there is no spirit, because we have no clear and distinct idea of the substance of a spirit.

Whatever therefore be the secret, abstract nature of substance in general, all the ideas we have of particular distinct sorts of substances, are nothing but several combinations of simple ideas, co-existing in such, though unknown, cause of their union, as make the whole subsist of itself. It is by such combinations of simple ideas, and nothing else, that we represent particular sorts of substances to ourselves: such are the ideas we have of their several species in our minds; and such only do we, by their specific names, signify to others, v. g. man, horse, sun, water, iron: upon hearing which words, every one who understands the language, frames in his mind a combination of those several simple ideas, which he has usually observed, or fancied to exist together under that denomination; all which he supposes to rest in, and be as it were adherent to that unknown common subject, which inheres not in any thing else. Though in the mean time it be manifest, and every one upon inquiry into his own thoughts will find, that he has no other idea of any substance, v. g. let it be gold, horse, iron, man, vitriol, bread, but what he has barely of those sensible qualities, which he supposes to inhere, with a supposition of such a substratum, as gives, as it were, a support to those qualities or simple ideas, which he has observed to exist united together. Thus the idea of the sun, what is it but an aggregate of those several simple ideas, bright, hot, roundish, having a constant regular motion, at a certain distance from us, and perhaps some other? As he who thinks and discourses of the sun, has been more or less accurate in observing those sensible qualities, ideas, or properties, which are in that thing which he calls the sun.

For he has the perfectest idea of any of the particular sorts of substances, who has gathered and put together most of those simple ideas which do exist in it, among which are to be reckoned its active powers, and passive capacities; which though not simple ideas, yet in this respect, for brevity's sake, may conveniently enough be reckoned amongst them. Thus the power of drawing iron, is one of the ideas of the complex one of that substance we call a load-stone; and a power to be so drawn is a part of the complex one we call iron: which powers pass for inherent qualities in those subjects. Because every substance, being as apt, by the powers we observe in it, to change some sensible qualities in other subjects, as it is to produce in us those simple ideas which we receive immediately from it, does, by those new sensible qualities introduced into other subjects, discover to us those powers, which do thereby immediately affect our senses, as regularly as its sensible qualities do it immediately: v. g. we immediately by our senses perceive in fire its heat and colour; which are, if rightly considered, nothing but powers in it to produce those ideas in us: we also by our senses perceive the colour and brittleness of charcoal, whereby we come by the knowledge of another power in fire, which it has to change the colour and consistency of wood. By the former, fire immediately, by the latter it mediately discovers to us these several qualities, which therefore we look upon to be a part of the qualities of fire, and so make them a part of the complex idea of it. For all those powers that we take cognizance of, terminating only in the alteration of some sensible qualities in those subjects on which they operate, and so making them exhibit to us new sensible ideas; therefore it is that I have reckoned these powers amongst the simple ideas, which make the complex ones of the sorts of substances; though these powers, considered in themselves, are truly complex ideas. And in this looser sense I crave leave to be understood, when I name any of these potentialities among the simple ideas, which we recollect in our minds when we think of particular substances. For the powers that are severally in them are necessary to be considered, if we will have true distinct notions of the several sorts of substances.

Nor are we to wonder, that powers make a great part of our complex ideas of substances: since their secondary qualities are those, which in most of them serve principally to distinguish substances one from another, and commonly make a considerable part of the complex idea of the several sorts of them. For our senses failing us in the discovery of the bulk, texture, and figure of the minute parts of bodies, on which their real constitutions and differences depend, we are fain to make use of their secondary qualities, as the characteristical notes and marks, whereby to frame ideas of them in our minds, and distinguish them one from another. All which secondary qualities, as has been shown, are nothing but bare powers. For the colour and taste of opium are, as well as its soporific or anodyne virtues, mere powers depending on its primary qualities, whereby it is fitted to produce different operations on different parts of our bodies.

The ideas that make our complex ones of corporeal substances, are of these three sorts. First, the ideas of the primary qualities of things which are discovered by our senses, and are in them even when we perceive them not; such are the bulk, figure, number, situation, and motion of the parts of bodies, which are really in them, whether we take notice of them or no. Secondly, the sensible secondary qualities, which depending on these, are nothing but the powers those substances have to produce several ideas in us by our senses; which ideas are not in the things themselves, otherwise than as any thing is in its cause. Thirdly, the aptness we consider in any substance to give or receive such alterations of primary qualities, as that the substance so altered should produce in us different ideas from what it did before; these are called active and passive powers: all which powers, as far as we have any notice or notion of them, terminate only in sensible simple ideas. For whatever alteration a loadstone has the power to make in the minute particles of iron, we should have no notion of any power it had at all to operate on iron, did not its sensible motion discover it: and I doubt not, but there are a thousand changes, that bodies we daily handle have a power to cause in one another, which we never suspect, because they never appear in sensible effects.

Powers therefore justly make a great part of our complex ideas of substances. He that will examine his complex idea of gold, will find several of its ideas that make it up to be only powers: as the power of being melted, but of not spending itself in the fire; of being dissolved in aqua regia; are ideas as necessary to make up our complex idea of gold, as its colour and weight: which, if duly considered, are also nothing but different powers. For to speak truly, yellowness is not actually in gold; but is a power in gold to produce that idea in us by our eyes, when placed in a due light: and the heat, which we cannot leave out of our ideas of the sun, is no more really in the sun, than the white colour it introduces into wax. These are both equally powers in the sun, operating, by the motion and figure of its sensible parts, so on a man, as to make him have the idea of heat; and so on wax, as to make it capable to produce in a man the idea of white.

Had we senses acute enough to discern the minute particles of bodies, and the real constitution on which their sensible qualities depend, I doubt not but they would produce quite different ideas in us; and that which is now the yellow colour of gold, would then disappear, and instead of it we should see an admirable texture of parts of a certain size and figure. This microscopes plainly discover to us; for what to our naked eyes produces a certain colour, is, by thus augmenting the acuteness of our senses, discovered to be quite a different thing; and the thus altering, as it were, the proportion of the bulk of the minute parts of a coloured object to our usual sight, produces different ideas from what it did before. Thus sand or pounded glass, which is opaque, and white to the naked eye, is pellucid in a microscope; and a hair seen this way, loses its former colour, and is in a great measure pellucid, with a mixture of some bright sparkling colours, such as appear from the refraction of diamonds, and other pellucid bodies. Blood to the naked eye appears all red; but by a good microscope, wherein its lesser parts appear, shows only some few globules of red, swimming in a pellucid liquor: and how these red globules would appear, if glasses could be found that could yet magnify them a thousand or ten thousand times more, is uncertain.

The infinitely wise contriver of us, and all things about us, hath fitted our senses, faculties, and organs, to the conveniences of life, and the business we have to do here. We are able, by our senses, to know and distinguish things; and to examine them so far, as to apply them to our uses, and several ways to accommodate the exigencies of this life. We have insight enough into their admirable contrivances and wonderful effects, to admire and magnify the wisdom, power, and goodness of their author. Such a knowledge as this, which is suited to our present condition, we want not faculties to attain. But it appears not, that God intended we should have a perfect, clear, and adequate knowledge of them: that perhaps is not in the comprehension of any finite being. We are furnished with faculties (dull and weak as they are) to discover enough in the creatures, to lead us to the knowledge of the Creator, and the knowledge of our duty: and we are fitted well enough with abilities to provide for the conveniences of living: these are our business in this world. But were our senses altered, and made much quicker and acuter, the appearance and outward scheme of things would have quite another face to us; and, I am apt to think, would be inconsistent with our being, or at least well-being, in this part of the universe which we inhabit. He that considers how little our constitution is able to bear a remove into parts of this air, not much higher than that we commonly breathe in, will have reason to be satisfied, that in this globe of earth allotted for our mansion, the all-wise Architect has suited our organs, and the bodies that are to affect them, one to another. If our sense of hearing were but one thousand times quicker than it is, how would a perpetual noise distract us? And we should in the quietest retirement be less able to sleep or meditate, than in the middle of a sea-fight. Nay, if that most instructive of our senses, seeing, were in any man a thousand or a hundred thousand times more acute than it is by the best microscope, things several millions of times less than the smallest object of his sight now, would then be visible to his naked eyes, and so he would come nearer to the discovery of the texture and motion of the minute parts of corporeal things; and in many of them, probably get ideas of their internal constitutions. But then he would be in a quite different world from other people: nothing would appear the same to him, and others; the visible ideas of every thing would be different. So that I doubt, whether he and the rest of men could discourse concerning the objects of sight, or have any communication about colours, their appearances being so wholly different. And perhaps such a quickness and tenderness of sight could not endure bright sun-shine, or so much as open day-light; nor take in but a very small part of any object at once, and that too only at a very near distance. And if, by the help of such microscopical eyes (if I may so call them), a man could penetrate farther than ordinary into the secret composition and radical texture of bodies, he would not make any great advantage by the change, if such an acute sight would not serve to conduct him to the market and exchange; if he could not see things he was to avoid, at a convenient distance; nor distinguish things he had to do with, by those sensible qualities others do. He that was sharp-sighted enough to see the configuration of the minute particles of the spring of a clock, and observe upon what peculiar structure and impulse its elastic motion depends, would no doubt discover something very admirable: but if eyes so framed could not view at once the hand, and the characters of the hour-plate, and thereby at a distance see what o'clock it was, their owner could not be much benefited by that acuteness; which, whilst it discovered the secret contrivance of the parts of the machine, made him lose its use.

Besides the complex ideas we have of material sensible substances, of which I have last spoken, by the simple ideas we have taken from those operations of our own minds, which we experiment daily in ourselves, as thinking, understanding, willing, knowing, and power of beginning motion, &c. co-existing in some substance: we are able to frame the complex idea of an immaterial spirit. And thus by putting together the ideas of thinking, perceiving, liberty, and power of moving themselves, and other things, we have as clear a perception and notion of immaterial substances, as we have of material. For putting together the ideas of thinking and willing, or the power of moving or quieting corporeal motion, joined to substance of which we have no distinct idea, we have the idea of an immaterial spirit; and by putting together the ideas of coherent solid parts, and a power of being moved, joined with substance, of which likewise we have no positive idea, we have the idea of matter. The one is as clear and distinct an idea as the other: the idea of thinking, and moving a body, being as clear and distinct ideas, as the ideas of extension, solidity, and being moved. For our idea of substance is equally obscure, or none at all in both: it is but a supposed I know not what, to support those ideas we call accidents. It is for want of reflection that we are apt to think, that our senses show us nothing but material things. Every act of sensation, when duly considered, gives us an equal view of both parts of nature, the corporeal and spiritual. For whilst I know, by seeing or hearing, &c. that there is some corporeal being without me, the object of that sensation; I do more certainly know, that there is some spiritual being within me, that sees and hears. This, I must be convinced, cannot be the action of bare insensible matter; nor ever could be, without an immaterial thinking being.

The primary ideas we have peculiar to body, as contradistinguished to spirit, are the cohesion of solid, and consequently separable, parts, and a power of communicating motion by impulse. These, I think, are the original ideas proper and peculiar to body; for figure is but the consequence of finite extension.

The ideas we have belonging, and peculiar to spirit, are thinking and will, or a power of putting body into motion by thought, and which is consequent to it, liberty. For as body cannot but communicate its motion by impulse to another body, which it meets with at rest; so the mind can put bodies into motion, or forbear to do so, as it pleases. The ideas of existence, duration, and mobility, are common to them both.

To conclude; sensation convinces us, that there are solid extended substances; and reflection, that there are thinking ones: experience assures us of the existence of such beings; and that the one hath a power to move body by impulse, the other by thought; this we cannot doubt of. Experience, I say, every moment furnishes us with the clear ideas, both of the one and the other. But beyond these ideas, as received from their proper sources, our faculties will not reach. If we would inquire farther into their nature, causes, and manner, we perceive not the nature of extension clearer than we do of thinking. If we would explain them any farther, one is as easy as the other; and there is no more difficulty to conceive how a substance we know not should by thought set body into motion, than how a substance we know not should by impulse set body into motion. So that we are no more able to discover wherein the ideas belonging to body consist, than those belonging to spirit. From whence it seems probable to me, that the simple ideas we receive from sensation and reflection are the boundaries of our thoughts; beyond which the mind, whatever efforts it would make, is not able to advance one jot; nor can it make any discoveries, when it would pry into the nature and hidden causes of those ideas.

And thus we have seen, what kind of ideas we have of substances of all kinds, wherein they consist, and how we came by them. From whence, I think, it is very evident,

First, That all our ideas of the several sorts of substances are nothing but collections of simple ideas, with a supposition of something to which they belong, and in which they subsist; though of this supposed something we have no clear distinct idea at all.

Secondly, That all the simple ideas, that thus united in one common substratum make up our complex ideas of several sorts of substances, are no other but such as we have received from sensation or reflection. So that even in those which we think we are most intimately acquainted with, and that come nearest the comprehension of our most enlarged conceptions, we cannot go beyond those simple ideas. And even in those which seem most remote from all we have to do with, and do infinitely surpass any thing we can perceive in ourselves by reflection, or discover by sensation in other things, we can attain to nothing but those simple ideas, which we originally received from sensation or reflection; as is evident in the complex ideas we have of angels, and particularly of God himself.

Thirdly, That most of the simple ideas, that make up our complex ideas of substances, when truly considered, are only powers, however we are apt to take them for positive qualities; v. g. the greatest part of the ideas that make our complex idea of gold are yellowness, great weight, ductility, fusibility and solubility in aqua regia, &c. all united together in an unknown substratum: all which ideas are nothing else but so many relations to other substances, and are not really in the gold, considered barely in itself, though they depend on those real and primary qualities of its internal constitution, whereby it has a fitness differently to operate, and be operated on by several other substances.

IDEAS OF RELATIONS

Besides the ideas, whether simple or complex, that the mind has of things, as they are in themselves, there are others it gets from their comparison one with another. The understanding, in the consideration of any thing, is not confined to that precise object: it can carry any idea as it were beyond itself, or at least look beyond it, to see how it stands in conformity to any other. When the mind so considers one thing, that it does as it were bring it to and set it by another, and carry its view from one to the other: this is, as the words import, relation and respect; and the denominations given to positive things, intimating that respect, and serving as marks to lead the thoughts beyond the subject itself denominated to something distinct from it, are what we call relatives: and the things, so brought together, related.

The nature therefore of relation consists in the referring or comparing two things one to another; from which comparison, one or both comes to be denominated. And if either of those things be removed or cease to be, the relation ceases, and the denomination consequent to it, though the other receive in itself no alteration at all: v. g. Caius, whom I consider to-day as a father, ceases to be so to-morrow, only by the death of his son, without any alteration made in himself. Nay, barely by the mind's changing the object to which it compares any thing, the same thing is capable of having contrary denominations at the same time; v. g. Caius, compared to several persons, may truly be said to be older and younger, stronger and weaker, &c.

This farther may be considered concerning relation, that though it be not contained in the real existence of things, but something extraneous and superinduced; yet the ideas which relative words stand for, are often clearer and more distinct, than of those substances to which they do belong. The notion we have of a father, or brother, is a great deal clearer and more distinct, than that we have of a man; or, if you will, paternity is a thing whereof it is easier to have a clear idea, than of humanity: and I can much easier conceive what a friend is, than what God. Because the knowledge of one action, or one simple idea, is oftentimes sufficient to give me the notion of a relation: but to the knowing of any substantial being, an accurate collection of sundry ideas is necessary. A man, if he compares two things together, can hardly be supposed not to know what it is, wherein he compares them: so that when he compares any things together, he cannot but have a very clear idea of that relation. The ideas then of relations are capable at least of being more perfect and distinct in our minds than those of substances. Because it is commonly hard to know all the simple ideas which are really in any substance, but for the most part easy enough to know the simple ideas that make up any relation I think on, or have a name for: v. g. comparing two men, in reference to one common parent, it is very easy to frame the ideas of brothers, without having yet the perfect idea of a man. For significant relative words, as well as others, standing only for ideas; and those being all either simple, or made up of simple ones, it suffices, for the knowing the precise idea the relative term stands for, to have a clear conception of that which is the foundation of the relation: which may be done without having a perfect and clear idea of the thing it is attributed to.

Having laid down these premises concerning relation in general, I shall now proceed to show, in some instances, how all the ideas we have of relation are made up, as the others are, only of simple ideas; and that they all, how refined or remote from sense soever they seem, terminate at last in simple ideas. I shall begin with the most comprehensive relation, wherein all things that do or can exist are concerned; and that is the relation of cause and effect. The idea whereof, how derived from the two fountains of all our knowledge, sensation, and reflection, I shall in the next place consider.

1. The Idea of Cause and Effect

In the notice that our senses take of the constant vicissitude of things, we cannot but observe, that several particular, both qualities and substances, begin to exist; and that they receive this their existence from the due application and operation of some other being. From this observation we get our ideas of cause and effect. That which produces any simple or complex idea we denote by the general name cause; and that which is produced, effect. Thus finding that in that substance which we call wax fluidity, which is a simple idea that was not in it before, is constantly produced by the application of a certain degree of heat; we call the simple idea of heat, in relation to fluidity in wax, the cause of it, and fluidity the effect. So also finding that the substance of wood, which is a certain collection of simple ideas, so called, by the application of fire is turned into another substance, called ashes, i. e. another complex idea, consisting of a collection of simple ideas, quite different from that complex idea which we call wood; we consider fire, in relation to ashes, as cause, and the ashes as effect. So that whatever is considered by us to conduce or operate to the producing any particular simple idea, or collection of simple ideas, whether substance or mode, which did not before exist, hath thereby in our minds, the relation of a cause, and so is denominated by us.[1]

[1] For a further statement of the idea of causation, cf. p. 330.

2. *Of Identity and Diversity*

Another occasion the mind often takes of comparing, is the very being of things; when considering any thing as existing at any determined time and place, we compare it with itself existing at another time, and thereon form the ideas of identity and diversity. When we see any thing to be in any place in any instant of time, we are sure (be it what it will) that it is that very thing, and not another, which at that same time exists in another place, how like and undistinguishable soever it may be in all other respects: and in this consists identity, when the ideas it is attributed to vary not at all from what they were at that moment wherein we consider their former existence, and to which we compare the present. For we never finding, nor conceiving it possible, that two things of the same kind should exist in the same place at the same time, we rightly conclude, that whatever exists any where at any time, excludes all of the same kind, and is there itself alone. When therefore we demand, whether any thing be the same or no; it refers always to something that existed such a time in such a place, which it was certain at that instant was the same with itself, and no other. From whence it follows, that one thing cannot have two beginnings of existence, nor two things one beginning; it being impossible for two things of the same kind to be or exist in the same instant, in the very same place, or one and the same thing in different places. That therefore that had one beginning, is the same thing; and that which had a different beginning in time and place from that, is not the same, but diverse. That which has made the difficulty about this relation, has been the little care and attention used in having precise notions of the things to which it is attributed.

We have the ideas but of three sorts of substances; 1. God. 2. Finite intelligences. 3. Bodies. First, God is without beginning, eternal, unalterable, and every where; and therefore concerning his identity, there can be no doubt. Secondly, finite spirits having had each its determinate time and place of beginning to exist, the relation to that time and place will always determine to each of them its identity, as long as it exists. Thirdly, the same will hold of every particle of matter, to which no addition or subtraction of matter being made, it is the same. For though these three sorts of substances, as we term them, do not exclude one another out of the same place; yet we cannot conceive but that they must necessarily each of them exclude any of the same kind out of the same place: or else the notions and names of identity and diversity would be in vain, and there could be no such distinction of substances, or any thing else one from another. For example: could two bodies be in the same place at the same time, then those two parcels of matter must be one and the same, take them great or little: nay, all bodies must be one and the same. For by the same reason that two particles of matter may be in one place, all bodies may be in one place: which, when it can be supposed, takes away the distinction of identity and diversity of one and more, and renders it ridiculous. But it being a contradiction, that two or more should be one, identity and diversity are relations and ways of comparing well-founded, and of use to the understanding.

From what has been said, it is easy to discover what is so much inquired after, the *principium individuationis;* and that, it is plain, is existence itself, which determines a being of any sort to a particular time and place, incommunicable to two beings of the same kind. This, though it seems easier to conceive in simple substances or modes, yet when reflected on is not more difficult in compound ones, if care be taken to what it is applied: v. g. let us suppose an atom, i. e. a continued body under one immutable superficies, existing in a determined time and place; it is evident that, considered in any instant of its existence, it is in that instant the same with itself. For being at that instant what it is, and nothing else, it is the same, and so must continue as long as its existence is continued; for so long it will be the same, and no other. In like manner, if two or more atoms be joined together into the same mass, every one of those atoms will be the same, by the foregoing rule: and whilst they exist united together, the mass, consisting of the same atoms, must be the same mass, or the same body, let the parts be ever so differently jumbled. But if one of these atoms be taken away, or one new one added, it is no longer the same mass, or the same body. In the state of living creatures, their identity depends not on a mass of the same particles, but on something else. For in them the variation of great parcels of matter alters not the identity: an oak growing from a plant to a great tree, and then lopped, is still the same oak; and a colt grown up to a horse, sometimes fat, sometimes lean, is all the while the same horse: though in both these cases, there may be a manifest change of the parts; so that truly they are not either of them the same masses of matter, though they be truly one of them the same oak, and the other the same horse. The reason whereof is, that in these two cases, a mass of matter, and a living body, identity is not applied to the same thing.

We must therefore consider wherein an oak differs from a mass of matter, and that seems to me to be in this, that the one is only the cohesion of particles of matter any how united, the other such a disposition of them as constitutes the parts of an oak; and such an organization of those parts as is fit to receive and distribute nourishment, so as to continue and frame the wood, bark, and leaves, &c. of an oak, in which consists the vegetable life. That being then one plan which has such an organization of parts in one coherent body partaking of one common life, it continues to be the same plant as long as it partakes of the same life, though that life be communicated to new particles of matter vitally united to the living plant, in a like continued organization conformable to that sort of plants. For this organization being at any one instant in any one collection of matter, is in that particular concrete distinguished from all other, and is that individual life which existing constantly from that moment both forwards and backwards, in the same continuity of insensibly succeeding parts united to the living body of the plant, it has that identity, which makes the same plant, and all the parts of it parts of the same plant, during all the time that they exist united in that continued organization, which is fit to convey that common life to all the parts so united.

The case is not so much different in brutes, but that any one may hence see what makes an animal, and continues it the same.

This also shows wherein the identity of the same man consists: viz. in nothing but a participation of the same continued life, by constantly fleeting particles of matter, in succession vitally united to the same organized body. He that shall place the identity of man in any thing else, but like that of other animals in one fitly organized body, taken in any one instant, and from thence continued under one organization of life in several successively fleeting particles of matter united to it, will find it hard to make an embryo, one of years, mad and sober, the same man, by any supposition, that will not make it possible for Seth, Ismael, Socrates, Pilate, St. Austin, and Cæsar Borgia, to be the same man. For if the identity of soul alone makes the same man, and there be nothing in the nature of matter why the same individual spirit may not be united to different bodies, it will be possible that those men living in distant ages, and of different tempers, may have been the same man: which way of speaking must be, from a very strange use of the word man, applied to an idea, out of which body and shape are excluded. And that way of speaking would agree yet worse with the notions of those philosophers who allow of transmigration, and are of opinion that the souls of men may, for their miscarriages, be detruded into the bodies of beasts, as fit habitations, with organs suited to the satisfaction of their brutal inclinations. But yet I think nobody, could he be sure that the soul of Heliogabalus were in one of his hogs, would yet say that hog were a man or Heliogabalus.

It is not therefore unity of substance that comprehends all sorts of identity, or will determine it in every case: but to conceive and judge of it aright, we must consider what idea the word it is applied to stands for; it being one thing to be the same substance, another the same man, and a third the same person, if person, man, and substance, are three names standing for three different ideas; for such as is the idea belonging to that name, such must be the identity: which, if it had been a little more carefully attended to, would possibly have prevented a great deal of that confusion which often occurs about this matter, with no small seeming difficulties, especially concerning personal identity, which therefore we shall, in the next place, a little consider.

This being premised, to find wherein personal identity

consists, we must consider what person stands for; which, I think, is a thinking intelligent being, that has reason and reflection, and can consider itself as itself, the same thinking thing in different times and places; which it does only by that consciousness which is inseparable from thinking, and, as it seems to me, essential to it: it being impossible for any one to perceive, without perceiving that he does perceive. When we see, hear, smell, taste, feel, meditate, or will any thing, we know that we do so. Thus it is always as to our present sensations and perceptions: and by this every one is to himself that which he calls self; it not being considered in this case whether the same self be continued in the same or divers substances. For since consciousness always accompanies thinking, and it is that which makes every one to be what he calls self, and thereby distinguishes himself from all other thinking things; in this alone consists personal identity, i. e. the sameness of a rational being: and as far as this consciousness can be extended backwards to any past action or thought, so far reaches the identity of that person; it is the same self now it was then; and it is by the same self with this present one that now reflects on it, that that action was done.

But it is farther inquired, whether it be the same identical substance? This few would think they had reason to doubt of, if these perceptions, with their consciousness, always remained present in the mind, whereby the same thinking thing would be always consciously present, and, as would be thought, evidently the same to itself. But that which seems to make the difficulty is this, that this consciousness being interrupted always by forgetfulness, there being no moment of our lives wherein we have the whole train of all our past actions before our eyes in one view, but even the best memories losing the sight of one part whilst they are viewing another; and we sometimes, and that the greatest part of our lives, not reflecting on our past selves, being intent on our present thoughts, and in sound sleep having no thoughts at all, or at least none with that consciousness which remarks our waking thoughts: I say, in all these cases, our consciousness being interrupted, and we losing the sight of our past selves, doubts are raised whether we are the same thinking thing, i. e. the same substance or no. Which however reasonable or unreasonable, concerns not personal identity at all: the question being, what makes the same person, and not whether it be the same identical substance, which always thinks in the same person; which in this case matters not at all: different substances, by the same consciousness (where they do partake in it), being united into one person, as well as different bodies by the same life are united into one animal, whose identity is preserved, in that change of substances, by the unity of one continued life. For it being the same consciousness that makes a man be himself to himself, personal identity depends on that only, whether it be annexed solely to one individual substance, or can be continued in a succession of several substances. For as far as any intelligent being can repeat the idea of any past action with the same consciousness it had of it at first, and with the same consciousness it has of any present action; so far it is the same personal self. For it is by the consciousness it has of its present thoughts and actions, that it is self to itself now, and so will be the same self, as far as the same consciousness can extend to actions past or to come; and would be by distance of time, or change of substance, no more two persons, than a man be two men by wearing other clothes to-day than he did yesterday, with a long or a short sleep between: the same consciousness uniting those distant actions into the same person, whatever substances contributed to their production.

Self is that conscious thinking thing, whatever substance made up of (whether spiritual or material, simple or compounded, it matters not), which is sensible, or conscious of pleasure and pain, capable of happiness or misery, and so is concerned for itself, as far as that consciousness extends. Thus every one finds, that whilst comprehended under that consciousness, the little finger is as much a part of himself as what is most so. Upon separation of this little finger, should this consciousness go along with the little finger, and leave the rest of the body, it is evident the little finger would be the person, the same person; and self then would have nothing to do with the rest of the body. As in this case it is the consciousness that goes along with the substance, when one part is separate from another, which makes the same person, and constitutes this inseparable self; so it is in reference to substances remote in time. That with which the consciousness of this present thinking thing can join itself, makes the same person, and is one self with it, and with nothing else; and so attributes to itself, and owns all the actions of that thing, as its own, as far as that consciousness reaches, and no farther; as every one who reflects will perceive.

I agree, the more probable opinion is, that this consciousness is annexed to, and the affection of one individual immaterial substance.

But let men, according to their diverse hypotheses, resolve of that as they please, this every intelligent being, sensible of happiness or misery, must grant, that there is something that is himself that he is concerned for, and would have happy: that this self has existed in a continued duration more than one instant, and therefore it is possible may exist, as it has done, months and years to come, without any certain bounds to be set to its duration, and may be the same self, by the same consciousness continued on for the future. And thus, by this consciousness, he finds himself to be the same self which did such or such an action some years since, by which he comes to be happy or miserable now. In all which account of self, the same numerical substance is not considered as making the same self; but the same continued consciousness, in which several substances may have been united, and again separated from it; which, whilst they continued in a vital union with that, wherein this consciousness then resided, made a part of that same self. Thus any part of our bodies vitally united to that which is conscious in us, makes a part of ourselves: but upon separation from the vital union, by which that consciousness is communicated, that which a moment since was part of ourselves, is now no more so, than a part of another man's self is a part of me: and it is not impossible, but in a little time may become a real part of another person. And so we have the same numerical substance become a part of two different persons; and the same person preserved under the change of various substances. Could we suppose any spirit wholly stripped of all its memory or consciousness of past actions, as we find our minds always are of a great part of ours, and sometimes of them all; the union or separation of such a spiritual substance would make no variation of personal identity, any more than that of any particle of matter does. Any substance vitally united to the present thinking being, is a part of that very same self which now is: any thing united to it by a consciousness of former actions, makes also a part of the same self, which is the same both then and now.

3. *Ideas of Moral Relations*

There is another sort of relation, which is the conformity, or disagreement, men's voluntary actions have to a rule to which they are referred, and by which they are judged of; which, I think, may be called moral relation, as being that which denominates our moral actions, and deserves well to be examined; there being no part of knowledge wherein we should be more careful to get determined ideas, and avoid, as much as may be, obscurity and confusion. Human actions, when with their various ends, objects, manners, and circumstances, they are framed into distinct complex ideas, are, as has been shown, so many mixed modes, a great part whereof have names annexed to them. Thus, supposing gratitude to be a readiness to acknowledge and return kindness received, polygamy to be the having more wives than one at once; when we frame these notions thus in our minds, we have there so many determined ideas of mixed modes. But this is not all that concerns our actions; it is not enough to have determined ideas of them, and to know what names belong to such and such combinations of ideas. We have a farther and greater concernment, and that is, to know whether such actions so made up are morally good or bad.

The laws that men generally refer their actions to, to judge of their rectitude or obliquity, seem to me to be these three. 1. The divine law. 2. The civil law. 3. The law of opinion or reputation, if I may so call it. By the relation they bear to the first of these, men judge whether their actions are sins or duties; by the second, whether they be criminal or innocent; and by the third, whether they be virtues or vices.

First, the divine law, whereby I mean that law which God has set to the actions of men, whether promulgated to them by the light of nature, or the voice of revelation. That God has given a rule whereby men should govern themselves, I think there is nobody so brutish as to deny. He has a right to do it, we are his creatures: he has goodness and wisdom to direct our actions to that which is best; and he has power to enforce it by rewards and punishments, of infinite weight and duration in another life: for nobody can take us out of his hands. This is the only true touchstone of moral rectitude; and by comparing them to this law it is, that men judge of the most considerable moral good or evil of their actions: that is, whether as duties or sins, they are like to procure them happiness or misery from the hands of the Almighty.

Secondly, the civil law, the rule set by the commonwealth to the actions of those who belong to it, is another rule to which men refer their actions, to judge whether they be criminal or no. This law nobody overlooks, the rewards and punishments that enforce it being ready at hand, and suitable to the power that makes it; which is the force of the commonwealth, engaged to protect the lives, liberties, and possessions of those who live according to its law; and has power to take away life, liberty, or goods from him who disobeys: which is the punishment of offences committed against this law.

Thirdly, the law of opinion or reputation. Virtue and vice are names pretended and supposed every where to stand for actions in their own nature right and wrong; and as far as they really are so applied, they so far are co-incident with the divine law above-mentioned. But yet whatever is pretended, this is visible, that these names virtue and vice, in the particular instances of their application, through the several nations and societies of men in the world, are constantly attributed only to such actions as in each country and society are in reputation or discredit. Nor is it to be thought strange, that men every where should give the name of virtue to those actions, which amongst them are judged praise-worthy; and call that vice, which they account blameable; since otherwise they would condemn themselves, if they should think any thing right, to which they allowed not commendation: any thing wrong, which they let pass without blame. Thus the measure of what is every where called and esteemed virtue and vice, is the approbation or dislike, praise or blame, which by a secret and tacit consent establishes itself in the several societies, tribes, and clubs of men in the world; whereby several actions come to find credit or disgrace amongst them, according to the judgment, maxims, or fashion of that place. For though men uniting into politic societies have resigned up to the public the disposing of all their force, so that they cannot employ it against any fellow-citizens, any farther than the law of the country directs; yet they retain still the power of thinking well or ill, approving or disapproving of the actions of those whom they live amongst, and converse with: and by this approbation and dislike they establish amongst themselves what they will call virtue and vice.

THE RELATION OF OUR SIMPLE IDEAS TO THE QUALITIES OF OBJECTS

To DISCOVER the nature of our ideas the better, and to discourse of them intelligibly, it will be convenient to distinguish them as they are ideas or perceptions in our minds, and as they are modifications of matter in the bodies that cause such perceptions in us: that so we may not think (as perhaps usually is done) that they are exactly the images and resemblances of something inherent in the subject; most of those of sensation being in the mind no more the likeness of something existing without us, than the names that stand for them are the likeness of our ideas, which yet upon hearing they are apt to excite in us.

Whatsoever the mind perceives in itself, or is the immediate object of perception, thought, or understanding, that I call idea; and the power to produce any idea in our mind I call quality of the subject wherein that power is. Thus a snow-ball having the power to produce in us the ideas of white, cold, and round, the powers to produce those ideas in us, as they are in the snow-ball, I call qualities; and as they are sensations or perceptions in our understandings, I call them ideas: which ideas, if I speak of sometimes, as in the things themselves, I would be understood to mean those qualities in the objects which produce them in us.

Qualities thus considered in bodies are, first, such as are utterly inseparable from the body, in what estate soever it be; such as in all the alterations and changes it suffers, all the force can be used upon it, it constantly keeps; and such as sense constantly finds in every particle of matter which has bulk enough to be perceived, and the mind finds inseparable from every particle of matter, though less than to make itself singly be perceived by our senses, v. g. Take a grain of wheat, divide it into two parts, each part has still solidity, extension, figure, and mobility; divide it again, and it retains still the same qualities; and so divide it on till the parts become insensible, they must retain still each of them all those qualities. For division (which is all that a mill, or pestle, or any other body does upon another, in reducing it to insensible parts) can never take away either solidity, extension, figure, or mobility from any body, but only makes two or more distinct separate masses of matter, of that which was but one before: all which distinct masses, reckoned as so many distinct bodies, after division make a certain number. These I call original or primary qualities of body, which I think we may observe to produce simple ideas in us, viz. solidity, extension, figure, motion or rest, and number.

Secondly, such qualities which in truth are nothing in the objects themselves, but powers to produce various sensations in us by their primary qualities, i. e. by the bulk, figure, texture, and motion of their insensible parts, as colours, sounds, tastes, &c. these I call secondary qualities. To these might be added a third sort, which are allowed to be barely powers, though they are as much real qualities in the subject, as those which I, to comply with the common way of speaking, call qualities, but for distinction, secondary qualities. For the power in fire to produce a new colour, or consistency, in wax or clay, by its primary qualities, is as much a quality in fire, as the power it has to produce in me a new idea or sensation of warmth or burning, which I felt not before by the same primary qualities, viz. the bulk, texture, and motion of its insensible parts.

The ideas of primary qualities of bodies are resemblances of them, and their patterns do really exist in the bodies themselves; but the ideas, produced in us by these secondary qualities, have no resemblance of them at all. There is nothing like our ideas existing in the bodies themselves. They are in the bodies, we denominate from them, only a power to produce those sensations in us: and what is sweet, blue or warm in idea, is but the certain bulk, figure, and motion of the insensible parts in the bodies themselves, which we call so.

The particular bulk, number, figure, and motion of the parts of fire, or snow, are really in them, whether any one's senses perceive them or no; and therefore they may be called real qualities, because they really exist in those bodies: but light, heat, whiteness or coldness, are no more really in them, than sickness or pain is in manna. Take away the sensation of them; let not the eyes see light, or colours, nor the ears hear sounds; let the palate not taste, nor the nose smell; and all colours, tastes, odours, and sounds, as they are such particular ideas, vanish and cease, and are reduced to their causes, i. e. bulk, figure, and motion of parts.

Let us consider the red and white colours in porphyry: hinder light from striking on it, and its colours vanish, it no longer produces any such ideas in us; upon the return of light, it produces these appearances on us again. Can any one think any real alterations are made in the porphyry, by the presence or absence of light; and that those ideas of whiteness and redness are really in porphyry in the light, when it is plain it has no colour in the dark? It has, indeed, such a configuration of particles, both night and day, as are apt, by the rays of light rebounding from some parts of that hard stone, to produce in us the idea of redness, and from others the idea of whiteness; but whiteness or redness are not in it at any time, but such a texture, that hath the power to produce such a sensation in us.

Pound an almond, and the clear white colour will be altered into a dirty one, and the sweet taste into an oily one. What real alteration can the beating of the pestle make in any body, but an alteration of the texture of it?

I have in what just goes before been engaged in physical inquiries a little farther than perhaps I intended. But it being necessary to make the nature of sensation a little understood, and to make the difference between the qualities in bodies, and the ideas produced by them in the mind, to be distinctly conceived, without which it were impossible to discourse intelligibly of them; I hope I shall be pardoned this little excursion into natural philosophy, it being necessary in our present inquiry to distinguish the primary and real qualities of bodies, which are always in them (viz. solidity, extension, figure, number, and motion, or rest; and are sometimes perceived by us, viz. when the bodies they are in are big enough singly to be discerned) from those secondary and imputed qualities, which are but the powers of several combinations of those primary ones when they operate, without being distinctly discerned; whereby we may also come to know what ideas are, and what are not, resemblances of something really existing in the bodies we denominate from them.

The qualities then that are in bodies rightly considered, are of three sorts.

First, the bulk, figure, number, situation, and motion, or rest of their solid parts; those are in them, whether we perceive them or no; and when they are of that size, that we can discover them, we have by these an idea of the thing, as it is in itself, as is plain in artificial things. These I call primary qualities.

Secondly, the power that is in any body, by reason of its insensible primary qualities, to operate after a peculiar manner on any of our senses, and thereby produce in us the different ideas of several colours, sounds, smells, tastes, &c. These are usually called sensible qualities.

Thirdly, the power that is in any body, by reason of the particular constitution of its primary qualities, to make such a change in the bulk, figure, texture, and motion of another body, as to make it operate on our senses, differently from what it did before. Thus the sun has a power to make wax white, and fire to make lead fluid. These are usually called powers.

The first of these, as has been said, I think, may be properly called real, original, or primary qualities, because they are in the things themselves, whether they are perceived or no; and upon their different modifications it is, that the secondary qualities depend.

The other two are only powers to act differently upon other things, which powers result from the different modifications of those primary qualities.

To conclude, beside those before mentioned primary qualities in bodies, viz. bulk, figure, extension, number, and motion of their solid parts; all the rest whereby we take notice of bodies, and distinguish them one from another, are nothing else but several powers in them depending on those primary qualities; whereby they are fitted, either by immediately operating on our bodies, to produce several different ideas in us; or else by operating on other bodies, so to change their primary qualities, as to render them capable of producing ideas in us, different from what before they did. The former of these, I think, may be called secondary qualities, immediately perceivable: the latter, secondary qualities mediately perceivable.

THE RELATIVE VALUE OF OUR DIFFERENT IDEAS

HAVING shown the original of our ideas, and taken a view of their several sorts; considered the difference between the simple and the complex, and observed how the complex ones are divided into those of modes, substances, and relations; all which, I think, is necessary to be done by any one, who would acquaint himself thoroughly with the progress of the mind in its apprehension and knowledge of things: it will, perhaps, be thought I have dwelt long enough upon the examination of ideas. I must, nevertheless, crave leave to offer some few other considerations concerning them.

1. Of Clear and Obscure Ideas

The first is, that some are clear, and others obscure; the perception of the mind being most aptly explained by words relating to the sight, we shall best understand what is meant by clear and obscure in our ideas, by reflecting on what we call clear and obscure in the objects of sight. Light being that which discovers to us visible objects, we give the name of obscure to that which is not placed in a light sufficient to discover minutely to us the figure and colours, which are observable in it, and which, in a better light, would be discernible. In like manner our simple ideas are clear, when they are such as the objects themselves, from whence they were taken, did or might, in a well-ordered sensation or perception, present them. Whilst the memory retains them thus, and can produce them to the mind, whenever it has occasion to consider them, they are clear ideas. So far as they either want any thing of the original exactness, or have lost any of their first freshness, and are, as it were, faded or tarnished by time; so far are they obscure. Complex ideas, as they are made up of simple ones, so they are clear when the ideas that go to their composition are clear: and the number and order of those simple ideas, that are the ingredients of any complex one, is determinate and certain.

The causes of obscurity in simple ideas seem to be either dull organs, or very slight and transient impressions made by the objects, or else a weakness in the memory not able to retain them as received. For, to return again to visible objects to help us to apprehend this matter: if the organs or faculties of perception, like wax over-hardened with cold, will not receive the impression of the seal, from the usual impulse wont to imprint it; or, like wax of a temper too soft, will not hold it well when well imprinted; or else supposing the wax of a temper fit, but the seal not applied with a sufficient force to make a clear impression: in any of these cases the print left by the seal will be obscure. This, I suppose, needs no application to make it plainer.

2. Of Real and Fantastical Ideas

Besides what we have already mentioned concerning ideas, other considerations belong to them, in reference to things from whence they are taken, or which they may be supposed to represent: and thus, I think, they may come under a threefold distinction; and are

First, either real or fantastical.

Secondly, adequate or inadequate.

Thirdly, true or false.

First, by real ideas, I mean such as have a foundation in nature; such as have a conformity with the real being and existence of things, or with their archetypes. Fantastical or chimerical I call such as have no foundation in nature, nor have any conformity with that reality of being to which they are tacitly referred as to their archetypes. If we examine the several sorts of ideas before-mentioned, we shall find, that,

First, our simple ideas are all real, all agree to the reality of things, not that they are all of them the images or representations of what does exist; the contrary whereof, in all but the primary qualities of bodies, hath been already shown. But though whiteness and coldness are no more in snow than pain is; yet those ideas of whiteness and coldness, pain, &c. being in us the effects of powers in things without us, ordained by our Maker to produce in us such sensations; they are real ideas in us, whereby we distinguish the qualities that are really in things themselves. For these several appearances being designed to be the mark, whereby we are to know and distinguish things which we have to do with, our ideas do as well serve us to that purpose, and are as real distinguishing characters, whether they be only constant effects, or else exact resemblances of something in the things themselves; the reality lying in that steady correspondence they have with the distinct constitutions of real beings. But whether they answer to those constitutions, as to causes or patterns, it matters not; it suffices that they are constantly produced by them. And thus our simple ideas are all real and true, because they answer and agree to those powers of things which produce them in our minds; that being all that is requisite to make them real, and not fictions at pleasure. For in simple ideas (as has been shown) the mind is wholly confined to the operation of things upon it and can make to itself no simple idea, more than what it has received.

Secondly, mixed modes and relations having no other reality but what they have in the minds of men, there is nothing more required to this kind of ideas to make them real, but that they be so framed, that there be a possibility of existing conformable to them. These ideas themselves, being archetypes, cannot differ from their archetypes, and so cannot be chimerical, unless any one will jumble together in them inconsistent ideas. Indeed, as any of them have the names of a known language assigned to them, by which he that has them in his mind would signify them to others, so bare possibility of existing is not enough; they must have a conformity to the ordinary signification of the name that is given them, that they may not be thought fantastical: as if a man would give the name of justice to that idea, which common use calls liberality. But this fantasticalness relates more to propriety of speech, than reality of ideas: for a man to be undisturbed in danger, sedately to consider what is fittest to be done, and to execute it steadily, is a mixed mode, or a complex idea of an action which may exist. But to be undisturbed in danger, without using one's reason or industry, is what is also possible to be; and so is as real an idea as the other. Though the first of these, having the name courage given to it, may, in respect of that name, be a right or wrong idea: but the other, whilst it has not a common received name of any known language assigned to it, is not capable of any deformity, being made with no reference to any thing but itself.

Thirdly, our complex ideas of substances being made all of them in reference to things existing without us, and intended to be representations of substances, as they really are; are no farther real, than as they are such combinations of simple ideas, as are really united, and co-exist in things without us. On the contrary, those are fantastical which are made up of such collections of simple ideas as were really never united, never were found together in any substance; v. g. a rational creature, consisting of a horse's head, joined to a body of human shape, or such as the centaurs are described: or, a body yellow, very malleable, fusible, and fixed; but lighter than common water: or an uniform, unorganized body, consisting, as to sense, all of similar parts, with perception and voluntary motion joined to it. Whether such substances as these can possibly exist or no, it is probable we do not know: but be that as it will, these ideas of substances being made conformable to no pattern existing that we know, and consisting of such collections of ideas, as no substance ever showed us united together, they ought to pass with us for barely imaginary: but much more are those complex ideas so, which contain in them any inconsistency or contradiction of their parts.

3. Of Adequate and Inadequate Ideas

Of our real ideas, some are adequate, and some are inadequate. Those I call adequate, which perfectly represent those achetypes which the mind supposes them taken from; which it intends them to stand for, and to which it refers them. Inadequate ideas are such, which are but a partial or incomplete representation of those archetypes to which they are referred. Upon which account it is plain,

First, that all our simple ideas are adequate. Because being nothing but the effects of certain powers in things, fitted and ordained by God to produce such sensations in us, they cannot but be correspondent and adequate to those powers: and we are sure they agree to the reality of things. For if sugar produce in us the ideas which we call whiteness and sweetness, we are sure there is a power in sugar to produce those ideas in our minds, or else they could not have been produced by it. And so each sensation answering the power that operates on any of our senses, the idea so produced is a real idea, (and not a fiction of the mind, which has no power to produce any simple ideas); and cannot but be adequate, since it ought only to answer that power: and so all simple ideas are adequate.

Secondly, our complex ideas of modes, being voluntary collections of simple ideas, which the mind puts together without reference to any real archetypes or standing patterns existing any where, are and cannot but be adequate ideas. Because they are not being intended for copies of things really existing, but for archetypes made by the mind to rank and denominate things by, cannot want any thing: they having each of them that combination of ideas, and thereby that perfection which the mind intended they should: so that the mind acquiesces in them, and can find nothing wanting. Thus by having the idea of a figure, with three sides meeting at three angles, I have a complete idea, wherein I require nothing else to make it perfect. That the mind is satisfied with the perfection of this its idea is plain, in that it does not conceive, that any understanding hath, or can have a more complete or perfect idea of that thing it signifies by the word triangle, supposing it to exist, than itself has in that complex idea of three sides and three angles; in which is contained all that is, or can be essential to it, or necessary to complete it, wherever or however it exists.

Thirdly, what ideas we have of substances, I have above showed. Now those ideas have in the mind a double reference: 1. Sometimes they are referred to a supposed real essence of each species of things. 2. Sometimes they are only designed to be pictures and representations in the mind of things that do exist by ideas of those qualities that are discoverable in them. In both which ways, these copies of those originals and archetypes are imperfect and inadequate.

The complex ideas we have of substances are, as it has been shown, certain collections of simple ideas that have been observed or supposed constantly to exist together. But such a complex idea cannot be the real essence of any substance; for then the properties we discover in that body would depend on that complex idea, and be deducible from it, and their necessary connection with it be known; as all properties of a triangle depend on, and, as far as they are discoverable, are deducible from the complex idea of three lines, including a space. But it is plain, that in our complex ideas of substances are not contained such ideas, on which all the other qualities, that are to be found in them do depend. The common idea men have of iron, is a body of a certain colour, weight and hardness; and a property that they look on as belonging to it, is malleableness. But yet this property has no necessary connection with that complex idea, or any part of it; and there is no more reason to think that malleableness depends on that colour, weight, and hardness, than that colour, or that weight depends on its malleableness. And yet, though we know nothing of these real essences, there is nothing more ordinary, than that men should attribute the sorts of things to such essences.

After all, if we would have, and actually had, in our complex idea, an exact collection of all the secondary qualities or powers of any substance, we should not yet thereby have an idea of the essence of that thing. For since the powers or qualities that are observable by us, are not the real essence of that substance, but depend on it, and flow from it, any collection whatsoever of these qualities cannot be the real essence of that thing. Whereby it is plain, that our ideas of substances are not adequate; are not what the mind intends them to be. Besides, a man has no idea of substance in general, nor knows what substance is in itself.

4. Of True and False Ideas

Though truth and falsehood belong, in propriety of speech, only to propositions; yet ideas are oftentimes termed true or false (as what words are there, that are not used with great latitude, and with some deviation from their strict and proper significations?) Though, I think, that when ideas themselves are termed true or false, there is still some secret or tacit proposition, which is the foundation of that denomination: as we shall see, if we examine the particular occasions wherein they come to be called true or false. In all which, we shall find some kind of affirmation or negation, which is the reason of that denomination. For our ideas, being nothing but bare appearances or perceptions in our minds, cannot properly and simply in themselves be said to be true or false, no more than a single name of any thing can be said to be true or false.

Whenever the mind refers any of its ideas to any thing extraneous to them, they are then capable to be called true or false. Because the mind in such a reference makes a tacit supposition of their conformity to that thing: which supposition, as it happens to be true or false, so the ideas themselves come to be denominated.

As to the truth and falsehood of our ideas, in reference to the real existence of things; when that is made the standard of their truth, none of them can be termed false, but only our complex ideas of substances.

First, our simple ideas being barely such perceptions as God has fitted us to receive, and given power to external objects to produce in us by established laws and ways, suitable to his wisdom and goodness, though incomprehensible to us, their truth consists in nothing else but in such appearances as are produced in us, and must be suitable to those powers he has placed in external objects, or else they could not be produced in us: and thus answering those powers, they are what they should be, true ideas. Nor do they become liable to any imputation of falsehood, if the mind (as in most men I believe it does) judges these ideas to be in the things themselves. For God, in his wisdom, having set them as marks of distinction in things, whereby we may be able to discern one thing from another, and so choose any of them for our uses, as we have occasion; it alters not the nature of our simple idea, whether we think that the idea of blue be in the violet itself, or in our mind only; and only the power of producing it by the texture of its parts, reflecting the particles of light after a certain manner, to be in the violet itself. For that texture in the object, by a regular and constant operation, producing the same idea of blue in us, it serves us to distinguish, by our eyes, that from any other thing, whether that distinguishing mark, as it is really in the violet, be only a peculiar texture of parts, or else that very colour, the idea whereof (which is in us) is the exact resemblance. And it is equally from that appearance to be denominated blue, whether it be that real colour, or only a peculiar texture in it, that causes in us that idea: since the name blue notes properly nothing but that mark of distinction that is in a violet, discernible only by our eyes, whatever it consists in: that being beyond our capacities distinctly to know, and perhaps would be of less use to us, if we had faculties to discern.

Secondly, neither can our complex ideas of modes, in reference to the essence of any thing really existing, be false. Because whatever complex idea I have of any mode, it hath no reference to any pattern existing, and made by nature: it is not supposed to contain in it any other ideas than what it hath; nor to represent any thing but such a complication of ideas as it does.

Thirdly, our complex ideas of substances, being all referred to patterns in things themselves, may be false. That they are all false, when looked upon as the representations of the unknown essences of things, is so evident that there needs nothing to be said of it.

THE DANGER OF THE ASSOCIATION OF IDEAS

SOME of our ideas have a natural correspondence and connexion one with another: it is the office and excellency of our reason to trace these, and hold them together in that union and correspondence which is founded in their peculiar beings. Besides this, there is another connexion of ideas wholly owing to chance or custom: ideas, that in themselves are not all of kin, come to be so united in some men's minds, that it is very hard to separate them; they always keep in company, and the one no sooner at any time comes into the understanding, but its associate appears with it; and if they are more than two, which are thus united, the whole gang, always inseparable, show themselves together.

This strong combination of ideas, not allied by nature, the mind makes in itself either voluntarily or by chance; and hence it comes in different men to be very different, according to their different inclinations, education, interests, &c. Custom settles habits of thinking in the understanding, as well as of determining in the will, and of motions in the body; all which seems to be but trains of motion in the animal spirits, which once set a-going, continue in the same steps they have been used to: which, by often treading, are worn into a smooth path, and the motion in it becomes easy, and as it were natural. As far as we can comprehend thinking, thus ideas seem to be produced in our minds; or if they are not, this may serve to explain their following one another in an habitual train, when once they are put into their track, as well as it does to explain such motions of the body. A musician used to any tune will find, that let it but once begin in his head, the ideas of the several notes of it will follow one another orderly in his understanding, without any care or attention, as regularly as his fingers move orderly over the keys of the organ to play out the tune he has begun, though his unattentive thoughts be elsewhere a wandering. Whether the natural cause of these ideas, as well as of that regular dancing of his fingers, be the motion of his animal spirits, I will not determine, how probable soever, by this instance, it appears to be so: but this may help us a little to conceive of intellectual habits, and of the tying together of ideas.

This wrong connexion in our minds of ideas in themselves loose and independent of one another, has such an influence, and is of so great force to set us awry in our actions, as well moral as natural, passions, reasonings, and notions themselves, that perhaps there is not any one thing that deserves more to be looked after.

Intellectual habits and defects this way contracted, are not less frequent and powerful, though less observed. Let the ideas of being and matter be strongly joined either by education or much thought, whilst these are still combined in the mind, what notions, what reasonings will there be about separate spirits? Let custom from the very childhood have joined figure and shape to the idea of God, and what absurdities will that mind be liable to about the Deity? Let the idea of infallibility be inseparably joined to any person, and these two constantly together possess the mind; and then one body, in two places at once, shall unexamined be swallowed for a certain truth by an implicit faith, whenever that imagined infallible person dictates and demands assent without inquiry.

Some such wrong and unnatural combinations of ideas will be found to establish the irreconcilable opposition between different sects of philosophy and religion; for we cannot imagine every one of their followers to impose wilfully on himself, and knowingly refuse truth offered by plain reason. Interest, though it does a great deal in the case, yet cannot be thought to work whole societies of men to so universal a perverseness, as that every one of them to a man should knowingly maintain falsehood: some at least must be allowed to do what all pretend to, i. e. to pursue truth sincerely; and therefore there must be something that blinds their understandings, and makes them not see the falsehood of what they embrace for real truth. That which thus captivates their reasons, and leads men of sincerity blindfold from common sense, will, when examined, be found to be what we are speaking of: some independent ideas, of no alliance to one another, are by education, custom, and the constant din of their party, so coupled in their minds, that they always appear there together; and they can no more separate them in their thoughts, than if there were but one idea, and they operate as if they were so. This gives sense to jargon, demonstration to absurdities, and consistency to nonsense, and is the foundation of the greatest, I had almost said of all the errours in the world; or if it does not reach so far, it is at least the most dangerous one, since so far as it obtains, it hinders men from seeing and examining. When two things in themselves disjoined, appear to the sight constantly united; if the eye sees these things riveted, which are loose, where will you begin to rectify the mistakes that follow in two ideas, that they have been accustomed so to join in their minds, as to substitute one for the other, and, as I am apt to think, often without perceiving it themselves? This, whilst they are under the deceit of it, makes them incapable of conviction, and they applaud themselves as zealous champions for truth, when indeed they are contending for errour; and the confusion of two different ideas, which a customary connexion of them in their minds hath to them made in effect but one, fills their heads with false views, and their reasonings with false consequences.[1]

[1] Cf. Locke's further comments on the association of ideas as a frequent cause of error, p. 331.

OF KNOWLEDGE AND PROBABILITY

THE NATURE OF KNOWLEDGE

SINCE the mind, in all its thoughts and reasonings, hath no other immediate object but its own ideas, which it alone does or can contemplate; it is evident, that our knowledge is only conversant about them.

Knowledge then seems to me to be nothing but the perception of the connexion and agreement, or disagreement and repugnancy, of any of our ideas. In this alone it consists. Where this perception is, there is knowledge; and where it is not, there, though we may fancy, guess, or believe, yet we always come short of knowledge. For when we know that white is not black, what do we else but perceive that these two ideas do not agree? When we possess ourselves with the utmost security of the demonstration, that the three angles of a triangle are equal to two right ones, what do we more but perceive, that equality to two right ones does necessarily agree to, and is inseparable from the three angles of a triangle?

But to understand a little more distinctly wherein this agreement or disagreement consists, I think we may reduce it all to these four sorts:

1. Identity, or diversity.
2. Relation.
3. Co-existence, or necessary connexion.
4. Real existence.

First, as to the first sort of agreement or disagreement, viz. identity or diversity. It is the first act of the mind, when it has any sentiments or ideas at all, to perceive its ideas; and so far as it perceives them, to know each what it is, and thereby also to perceive their difference, and that one is not another. This is so absolutely necessary, that without it there could be no knowledge, no reasoning, no imagination, no distinct thoughts, at all. By this the mind clearly and infallibly perceives each idea to agree with itself, and to be what it is; and all distinct ideas to disagree, i. e. the one not to be the other: and this it does without pains, labour, or deduction; but at first view, by its natural power of perception and distinction. And though men of art have reduced this into those general rules, "what is, is," and "it is impossible for the same thing to be and not to be," for ready application in all cases, wherein there may be occasion to reflect on it: yet it is certain, that the first exercise of this faculty is about particular ideas. A man infallibly knows, as soon as ever he has them in his mind, that the ideas he calls white and round, are the very ideas they are, and that they are not other ideas which he calls red or square. Nor can any maxim or proposition in the world make him know it clearer or surer than he did before, and without any such general rule. This then is the first agreement or disagreement, which the mind perceives in its ideas; which it always perceives at first sight: and if there ever happen any doubt about it, it will always be found to be about the names, and not the ideas themselves, whose identity and diversity will always be perceived, as soon and clearly as the ideas themselves are; nor can it possibly be otherwise.

Secondly, the next sort of agreement or disagreement, the mind perceives in any of its ideas, may, I think, be called relative, and is nothing but the perception of the relation between any two ideas, of what kind soever, whether substances, modes, or any other. For since all distinct ideas must eternally be known not to be the same, and so be universally and constantly denied one of another, there could be no room for any positive knowledge at all, if we could not perceive any relation between our ideas, and find out the agreement or disagreement they have one with another, in several ways the mind takes of comparing them.

Thirdly, the third sort of agreement, or disagreement, to be found in our ideas, which the perception of the mind is employed about, is co-existence, or non co-existence in the same subject; and this belongs particularly to substances. Thus when we pronounce concerning gold that it is fixed, our knowledge of this truth amounts to no more but this, that fixedness, or a power to remain in the fire unconsumed, is an idea that always accompanies, and is joined with that particular sort of yellowness, weight, fusibility, malleableness, and solubility in aqua regia, which make our complex idea, signified by the word gold.

Fourthly, the fourth and last sort is that of actual and real existence agreeing to any idea. Within these four sorts of agreement or disagreement, is, I suppose, contained all the knowledge we have, or are capable of: for all the inquiries we can make concerning any of our ideas, all that we know or can affirm concerning any of them, is, that it is, or is not, the same with some other; that it does or does not always co-exist with some other idea in the same subject; that it has this or that relation with some other idea; or that it has a real existence without the mind. Thus blue is not yellow; is of identity: two triangles upon equal bases between two parallels are equal; is of relation: iron is susceptible of magnetical impressions; is of co-existence: God is; is of real existence. Though identity and co-existence are truly nothing but relations, yet they are such peculiar ways of agreement or disagreement of our ideas, that they deserve well to be considered as distinct heads, and not under relation in general; since they are so different grounds of affirmation and negation, as will easily appear to any one, who will but reflect on what is said in several places of this essay. I should now proceed to examine the several degrees of our knowledge, but that it is necessary first to consider the different acceptations of the word knowledge.

THE DEGREES OF KNOWLEDGE

All our knowledge consisting, as I have said, in the view the mind has of its own ideas, which is the utmost light and greatest certainty we, with our faculties, and in our way of knowledge, are capable of; it may not be amiss to consider a little the degrees of its evidence. The different clearness of our knowledge seems to me to lie in the different way of perception the mind has of the agreement or disagreement of any of its ideas. For if we reflect on our own ways of thinking, we shall find that sometimes the mind perceives the agreement or disagreement of two ideas immediately by themselves, without the intervention of any other: and this, I think, we may call intuitive knowledge. For in this the mind is at no pains of proving or examining, but perceives the truth, as the eye doth light, only by being directed towards it. Thus the mind perceives, that white is not black, that a circle is not a triangle, that three are more than two, and equal to one and two. Such kind of truths the mind perceives at the first sight of the ideas together, by bare intuition, without the intervention of any other idea; and this kind of knowledge is the clearest and most certain, that human frailty is capable of. This part of knowledge is irresistible, and like bright sunshine forces itself immediately to be perceived, as soon as ever the mind turns its view that way; and leaves no room for hesitation, doubt, or examination, but the mind is presently filled with the clear light of it. It is on this intuition that depends all the certainty and evidence of all our knowledge; which certainty every one finds to be so great, that he cannot imagine, and therefore not require a greater: for a man cannot conceive himself capable of a greater certainty, than to know that any idea in his mind is such as he perceives it to be; and that two ideas wherein he perceives a difference, are different and not precisely the same. He that demands a greater certainty than this, demands he knows not what, and shows only that he has a mind to be a sceptick, without being able to be so. Certainty depends so wholly on this intuition, that in the next degree of knowledge, which I call demonstrative, this intuition is necessary in all the connexions of the intermediate ideas, without which we cannot attain knowledge and certainty.

The next degree of knowledge is, where the mind perceives the agreement or disagreement of any ideas, but not immediately. Though wherever the mind perceives the agreement or disagreement of any of its ideas, there be certain knowledge: yet it does not always happen, that the mind sees that agreement or disagreement which there is between them, even where it is discoverable: and in that case remains in ignorance, and at most gets no farther than a probable conjecture. The reason why the mind cannot always perceive presently the agreement or disagreement of two ideas, is, because those ideas, concerning whose agreement or disagreement the inquiry is made, cannot by the mind be so put together as to show it. In this case then, when the mind cannot so bring its ideas together, as by their immediate comparison, and as it were juxta-position or application one to another, to perceive their agreement or disagreement, it is fain, by the intervention of other ideas (one or more, as it happens) to discover the agreement or disagreement which it searches; and this is that which we call reasoning. Thus the mind being willing to know the agreement or disagreement in bigness, between the three angles of a triangle and two right ones, cannot by an immediate view and comparing them do it: because the three angles of a triangle cannot be brought at once, and be compared with any one or two angles; and so of this the mind has no immediate, no intuitive knowledge. In this case the mind is fain to find out some other angles, to which the three angles of a triangle have an equality; and, finding those equal to two right ones, comes to know their equality to two right ones.

Those intervening ideas which serve to show the agreement of any two others, are called proofs; and where the agreement and disagreement is by this means plainly and clearly perceived, it is called demonstration, it being shown to the understanding, and the mind made to see that it is so. A quickness in the mind to find out these intermediate ideas (that shall discover the agreement or disagreement of any other) and to apply them right, is, I suppose, that which is called sagacity.

This knowledge by intervening proofs, though it be certain, yet the evidence of it is not altogether so clear and bright, nor the assent so ready, as in intuitive knowledge. For though, in demonstration, the mind does at last perceive the agreement or disagreement of the ideas it considers; yet it is not without pains and attention: there must be more than one transient view to find it. A steady application and pursuit are required to this discovery: and there must be a progression by steps and degrees, before the mind can in this way arrive at certainty, and come to perceive the agreement or repugnancy between two ideas that need proofs and the use of reason to show it.

Now, in every step reason makes in demonstrative knowledge, there is an intuitive knowledge of that agreement or disagreement it seeks with the next intermediate idea, which it uses as a proof; for if it were not so, that yet would need a proof; since without the perception of such agreement or disagreement, there is no knowledge produced. If it be perceived by itself, it is intuitive knowledge: if it cannot be perceived by itself, there is need of some intervening idea, as a common measure to show their agreement or disagreement.

These two, viz. intuition and demonstration, are the degrees of our knowledge; whatever comes short of one of these, with what assurance soever embraced, is but faith, or opinion, but not knowledge, at least in all general truths. There is, indeed, another perception of the mind, employed about the particular existence of finite beings without us; which going beyond bare probability, and yet not reaching perfectly to either of the foregoing degrees of certainty, passes under the name of knowledge. There can be nothing more certain, than that the idea we receive from an external object is in our minds; this is intuitive knowledge. But whether there be any thing more than barely that idea in our minds, whether we can thence certainly infer the existence of any thing without us, which corresponds to that idea, is that, whereof some men think there may be a question made; because men may have such ideas in their minds, when no such thing exists, no such object affects their senses. But yet here, I think, we are provided with an evidence, that puts us past doubting: for I ask any one, whether he be not invincibly conscious to himself of a different perception, when he looks on the sun by day, and thinks on it by night; when he actually tastes wormwood, or smells a rose, or only thinks on that savour or odour? We as plainly find the difference there is between an idea revived in our minds by our own memory, and actually coming into our minds by our senses, as we do between any two distinct ideas. If any one say, a dream may do the same thing, and all these ideas may be produced in us without any external objects; he may please to dream that I make him this answer: 1. That it is no great matter, whether I remove this scruple or no: where all is but dream, reasoning and arguments are of no use, truth and knowledge nothing. 2. That I believe he will allow a very manifest difference between dreaming of being in the fire, and being actually in it. But yet if he be resolved to appear so sceptical, as to maintain, that what I call being actually in the fire is nothing but a dream; and we cannot thereby certainly know, that any such thing as fire actually exists without us: I answer, that we certainly finding that pleasure or pain follows upon the application of certain objects to us, whose existence we perceive, or dream that we perceive by our senses; this certainty is as great as our happiness or misery, beyond which we have no concernment to know or to be. So that, I think, we may add to the two former sorts of knowledge this also of the existence of particular external objects, by that perception and consciousness we have of the actual entrance of ideas from them, and allow these three degrees of knowledge, viz. intuitive, demonstrative, and sensitive: in each of which there are different degrees and ways of evidence and certainty.

THE EXTENT OF KNOWLEDGE

Knowledge, as has been said, lying in the perception of the agreement or disagreement of any of our ideas, it follows from hence, that,

First, we can have knowledge no farther than we have ideas.

Secondly, that we have no knowledge farther than we can have perception of their agreement or disagreement. Which perception being, 1. Either by intuition, or the immediate comparing any two ideas; or, 2. By reason, examining the agreement or disagreement of two ideas, by the intervention of some others; or, 3. By sensation, perceiving the existence of particular things: hence it also follows,

Thirdly, that we cannot have an intuitive knowledge, that shall extend itself to all our ideas, and all that we would know about them; because we cannot examine and perceive all the relations they have one to another by juxta-position, or an immediate comparison one with another. Thus having the ideas of an obtuse and an acute angled triangle, both drawn from equal bases, and between parallels, I can, by intuitive knowledge, perceive the one not to be the other, but cannot that way know whether they be equal or no; because their agreement or disagreement in equality can never be perceived by an immediate comparing them: the difference of figure makes their parts incapable of an exact immediate application; and therefore there is need of some intervening qualities to measure them by, which is demonstration, or rational knowledge.

Fourthly, it follows also, from what is above observed, that our rational knowledge cannot reach to the whole extent of our ideas: because between two different ideas we would examine, we cannot always find such mediums, as we can connect one to another with an intuitive knowledge, in all the parts of the deduction; and wherever that fails, we come short of knowledge and demonstration.

Fifthly, sensitive knowledge reaching no farther than the existence of things actually present to our senses, is yet much narrower than either of the former.

From all which it is evident, that the extent of our knowledge comes not only short of the reality of things, but even of the extent of our own ideas. Though our knowledge be limited to our ideas, and cannot exceed them either in extent or perfection; and though these be very narrow bounds, in respect of the extent of all being, and far short of what we may justly imagine to be in some even created understandings, not tied down to the dull and narrow information which is to be received from some few, and not very acute ways of perception, such as are our senses; yet it would be well with us if our knowledge were but as large as our ideas, and there were not many doubts and inquiries concerning the ideas we have, whereof we are not, nor I believe ever shall be in this world resolved. Nevertheless I do not question but that human knowledge, under the present circumstances of our beings and constitutions, may be carried much farther than it has hitherto been, if men would sincerely, and with freedom of mind, employ all that industry and labour of thought, in improving the means of discovering truth, which they do for the colouring or support of falsehood, to maintain a system, interest, or party, they are once engaged in. But yet after all, I think I may, without injury to human perfection, be confident, that our knowledge would never reach to all we might desire to know concerning those ideas we have: nor be able to surmount all the difficulties, and resolve all the questions that might arise concerning any of them. We have the ideas of a square, a circle, and equality; and yet, perhaps, shall never be able to find a circle equal to a square, and certainly know that it is so. We have the ideas of matter and thinking, but possibly shall never be able to know, whether any mere material being thinks, or no; it being impossible for us, by the contemplation of our own ideas, without revelation, to discover, whether omnipotency has not given to some systems of matter fitly disposed a power to perceive and think, or else joined and fixed to matter so disposed a thinking immaterial substance: it being, in respect of our notions, not much more remote from our comprehension to conceive, that God can, if he pleases, superadd to matter a faculty of thinking, than that he should superadd to it another substance, with a faculty of thinking; since we know not wherein thinking consists, nor to what sort of substances the Almighty has been pleased to give that power, which cannot be in any created being, but merely by the good pleasure and bounty of the Creator.[1] For I see no contradiction in it, that the first eternal thinking being should, if he pleased, give to certain systems of created senseless matter, put together as he thinks fit, some degrees of sense, perception, and thought: though, as I think, it is no less than a contradiction to suppose matter (which is evidently in its own nature void of sense and thought) should be that eternal first-thinking being. What certainty of knowledge can any one have that some perceptions, such as, v. g. pleasure and pain, should not be in some bodies themselves, after a certain manner modified and moved, as well as that they should be in an immaterial substance, upon the motion of the

[1] For a further discussion of whether God could confer upon matter a power to think, cf. p. 333.

parts of body? Body, as far as we can conceive, being able only to strike and affect body; and motion, according to the utmost reach of our ideas, being able to produce nothing but motion: so that when we allow it to produce pleasure or pain, or the idea of a colour or sound, we are fain to quit our reason, go beyond our ideas, and attribute it wholly to the good pleasure of our Maker. For since we must allow he has annexed effects to motion, which we can no way conceive motion able to produce, what reason have we to conclude, that he could not order them as well to be produced in a subject we cannot conceive capable of them, as well as in a subject we cannot conceive the motion of matter can any way operate upon? I say not this, that I would any way lessen the belief of the soul's immateriality: I am not here speaking of probability, but knowledge; and I think not only, that it becomes the modesty of philosophy not to pronounce magisterially, where we want that evidence that can produce knowledge; but also, that it is of use to us to discern how far our knowledge does reach; for the state we are at present in, not being that of vision, we must, in many things, content ourselves with faith and probability. It is past controversy, that we have in us something that thinks; our very doubts about what it is confirm the certainty of its being, though we must content ourselves in the ignorance of what kind of being it is: and it is in vain to go about to be sceptical in this, as it is unreasonable in most other cases to be positive against the being of any thing, because we cannot comprehend its nature. For I would fain know what substance exists, that has not something in it which manifestly baffles our understandings.

But to return to the argument in hand; our knowledge, I say, is not only limited to the paucity and imperfections of the ideas we have, and which we employ it about, but even comes short of that too. But how far it reaches, let us now inquire.

The affirmations or negations we make concerning the ideas we have, may, as I have before intimated in general, be reduced to these four sorts, viz. identity, co-existence, relation, and real existence. I shall examine how far our knowledge extends in each of these.

First, as to identity and diversity, in this way of agreement or disagreement of our ideas, our intuitive knowledge is as far extended as our ideas themselves; and there can be no idea in the mind, which it does not presently, by an intuitive knowledge, perceive to be what it is, and to be different from any other.

Secondly, as to the second sort, which is the agreement or disagreement of our ideas in co-existence; in this our knowledge is very short, though in this consists the greatest and most material part of our knowledge concerning substances. For our ideas of the species of substances being, as I have showed, nothing but certain collections of simple ideas united in one subject, and so co-existing together; v. g. our idea of flame is a body hot, luminous, and moving upward; of gold, a body heavy to a certain degree, yellow, malleable, and fusible: these, or some such complex ideas as these in men's minds, do these two names of the different substances, flame and gold, stand for. When we would know any thing farther concerning these, or any other sort of substances, what do we inquire, but what other qualities or power these substances have or have not? Which is nothing else but to know what other simple ideas do or do not co-exist with those that make up that complex idea.

This, how weighty and considerable a part soever of human science, is yet very narrow, and scarce any at all. The reason whereof is, that the simple ideas, whereof our complex ideas of substances are made up, are, for the most part, such as carry with them, in their own nature, no visible necessary connexion or inconsistency with any other simple ideas, whose co-existence with them we would inform ourselves about.

The ideas that our complex ones of substances are made up of, and about which our knowledge concerning substances is most employed, are those of their secondary qualities: which depending all (as has been shown) upon the primary qualities of their minute and insensible parts; or if not upon them, upon something yet more remote from our comprehension; it is impossible we should know which have a necessary union or inconsistency one with another: for not knowing the root they spring from, not knowing what size, figure, and texture of parts they are, on which depend, and from which result, those qualities which make our complex idea of gold; it is impossible we should know what other qualities result from, or are incompatible with, the same constitution of the insensible parts of gold, and so consequently must always co-exist with that complex idea we have of it, or else are inconsistent with it.

Besides this ignorance of the primary qualities of the insensible parts of bodies, on which depend all their secondary qualities, there is yet another and more incurable part of ignorance, which sets us more remote from a certain knowledge of the co-existence or in-co-existence (if I may so say) of different ideas in the same subject; and that is, that there is no discoverable connexion between any secondary quality and those primary qualities which it depends on.

That the size, figure, and motion of one body should cause a change in the size, figure, and motion of another body, is not beyond our conception: the separation of the parts of one body upon the intrusion of another;

and the change from rest to motion upon impulse; these and the like seem to have some connexion one with another. And if we knew these primary qualities of bodies, we might have reason to hope we might be able to know a great deal more of these operations of them one with another: but our minds not being able to discover any connexion betwixt these primary qualities of bodies and the sensations that are produced in us by them, we can never be able to establish certain and undoubted rules of the consequences or co-existence of any secondary qualities, though we could discover the size, figure, or motion of those invisible parts which immediately produce them. We are so far from knowing what figure, size, or motion of parts produce a yellow colour, a sweet taste, or a sharp sound, that we can by no means conceive how any size, figure, or motion of any particles, can possibly produce in us the idea of any colour, taste, or sound whatsoever; there is no conceivable connexion betwixt the one and the other.

In vain therefore shall we endeavour to discover by our ideas (the only true way of certain and universal knowledge) what other ideas are to be found constantly joined with that of our complex idea of any substance: since we neither know the real constitution of the minute parts on which their qualities do depend; nor, did we know them, could we discover any necessary connexion between them and any of the secondary qualities; which is necessary to be done before we can certainly know their necessary co-existence. So that let our complex idea of any species of substances be what it will, we can hardly, from the simple ideas contained in it, certainly determine the necessary co-existence of any other quality whatsoever. Our knowledge in all these inquiries reaches very little farther than our experience. Indeed, some few of the primary qualities have a necessary dependence and visible connexion one with another, as figure necessarily supposes extension: receiving or communicating motion by impulse, supposes solidity. But though these and perhaps some other of our ideas have, yet there are so few of them, that have a visible connexion one with another, that we can by intuition or demonstration discover the co-existence of very few of the qualities are to be found united in substances: and we are left only to the assistance of our senses, to make known to us what qualities they contain. For of all the qualities that are co-existent in any subject, without this dependence and evident connexion of their ideas one with another, we cannot know certainly any two to co-exist any farther than experience, by our senses, informs us. Thus though we see the yellow colour, and upon trial find the weight, malleableness, fusibility, and fixedness, that are united in a piece of gold; yet because no one of these ideas has any evident dependence, or necessary connexion with the other, we cannot certainly know, that where any four of these are, the fifth will be there also, how highly probable soever it may be; because the highest probability amounts not to certainty, without which there can be no true knowledge. For this co-existence can be no farther known than it is perceived; and it cannot be perceived but either in particular subjects, by the observation of our senses, or in general, by the necessary connexion of the ideas themselves.

As to the third sort of our knowledge, viz. the agreement or disagreement of any of our ideas in any other relation: this, as it is the largest field of our knowledge, so it is hard to determine how far it may extend: because the advances that are made in this part of knowledge, depending on our sagacity in finding intermediate ideas, that may show the relations and habitudes of ideas, whose co-existence is not considered, it is a hard matter to tell when we are at an end of such discoveries; and when reason has all the helps it is capable of, for the finding of proofs, or examining the agreement or disagreement of remote ideas. They that are ignorant of algebra cannot imagine the wonders in this kind are to be done by it: and what farther improvements and helps, advantageous to other parts of knowledge, the sagacious mind of man may yet find out, it is not easy to determine. This at least I believe, that the ideas of quantity are not those alone that are capable of demonstration and knowledge; and that other, and perhaps more useful parts of contemplation, would afford us certainty, if vices, passions, and domineering interest did not oppose or menace such endeavours.

The idea of a supreme being, infinite in power, goodness, and wisdom, whose workmanship we are, and on whom we depend; and the idea of ourselves, as understanding rational beings; being such as are clear in us, would, I suppose, if duly considered and pursued, afford such foundations of our duty and rules of action, as might place morality amongst the sciences capable of demonstration; wherein I doubt not but from self-evident propositions, by necessary consequences, as incontestable as those in mathematics, the measures of right and wrong might be made out to any one that will apply himself with the same indifferency and attention to the one, as he does to the other of these sciences. The relation of other modes may certainly be perceived, as well as those of number and extension: and I cannot see why they should not also be capable of demonstration, if due methods were thought on to examine or pursue their agreement or disagreement. "Where there is no property, there is no injustice," is a proposition as certain as any demonstration in Euclid:

for the idea of property being a right to any thing; and the idea to which the name injustice is given, being the invasion or violation of that right; it is evident, that these ideas, being thus established, and these names annexed to them, I can as certainly know this proposition to be true, as that a triangle has three angles equal to two right ones. Again, "no government allows absolute liberty:" the idea of government being the establishment of society upon certain rules or laws which require conformity to them; and the idea of absolute liberty being for any one to do whatever he pleases; I am as capable of being certain of the truth of this proposition, as of any in the mathematics.

Confident I am, that if men would, in the same method, and with the same indifferency, search after moral, as they do mathematical truths, they would find them have a stronger connexion one with another, and a more necessary consequence from our clear and distinct ideas, and to come nearer perfect demonstration than is commonly imagined. But much of this is not to be expected, whilst the desire of esteem, riches, or power, makes men espouse the well-endowed opinions in fashion, and then seek arguments either to make good their beauty, or varnish over and cover their deformity: nothing being so beautiful to the eye, as truth is to the mind; nothing so deformed and irreconcilable to the understanding as a lye. For though many a man can with satisfaction enough own a no very handsome wife in his bosom; yet who is bold enough openly to avow, that he has espoused a falsehood, and received into his breast so ugly a thing as a lye? Whilst the parties of men cram their tenets down all men's throats, whom they can get into their power, without permitting them to examine their truth or falsehood, and will not let truth have fair play in the world, nor men the liberty to search after it; what improvements can be expected of this kind? What greater light can be hoped for in the moral sciences? The subject part of mankind in most places might, instead thereof, with Egyptian bondage expect Egyptian darkness, were not the candle of the Lord set up by himself in men's minds, which it is impossible for the breath or power of man wholly to extinguish.

As to the fourth sort of our knowledge, viz., of the real actual existence of things, we have an intuitive knowledge of our own existence; and a demonstrative knowledge of the existence of a God; of the existence of any thing else, we have no other but a sensitive knowledge, which extends not beyond the objects present to our senses.

Our knowledge being so narrow, as I have showed, it will perhaps give us some light into the present state of our minds, if we look a little into the dark side, and take a view of our ignorance: which, being infinitely larger than our knowledge, may serve much to the quieting of disputes, and improvement of useful knowledge; if discovering how far we have clear and distinct ideas, we confine our thoughts within the contemplation of those things that are within the reach of our understandings, and launch not out into that abyss of darkness (where we have not eyes to see, nor faculties to perceive any thing) out of a presumption, that nothing is beyond our comprehension. But to be satisfied of the folly of such a conceit, we need not go far. He that knows any thing, knows this in the first place, that he need not seek long for instances of his ignorance. The meanest and most obvious things that come in our way, have dark sides, that the quickest sight cannot penetrate into. The clearest and most enlarged understandings of thinking men find themselves puzzled, and at a loss, in every particle of matter. We shall the less wonder to find it so, when we consider the causes of our ignorance; which, from what has been said, I suppose, will be found to be these three:

First, want of ideas.

Secondly, want of a discoverable connexion between the ideas we have.

Thirdly, want of tracing and examining our ideas.

There are some things, and those not a few, that we are ignorant of, for want of ideas.

First, all the simple ideas we have, are confined (as I have shown) to those we receive from corporeal objects by sensation, and from the operations of our own minds as the objects of reflection. But how much these few and narrow inlets are disproportionate to the vast whole extent of all beings, will not be hard to persuade those, who are not so foolish as to think their span the measure of all things. What other simple ideas it is possible the creatures in other parts of the universe may have, by the assistance of senses and faculties more, or perfecter, than we have, or different from ours, it is not for us to determine. But to say, or think there are no such, because we conceive nothing of them, is no better an argument, than if a blind man should be positive in it, that there was no such thing as sight and colours, because he had no manner of idea of any such thing, nor could by any means frame to himself any notions about seeing. The ignorance and darkness that is in us, no more hinders nor confines the knowledge that is in others, than the blindness of a mole is an argument against the quicksightedness of an eagle. He that will consider the infinite power, wisdom, and goodness of the Creator of all things, will find reason to think it was not all laid out upon so inconsiderable, mean, and impotent a creature as he will find man to be; who, in all probability, is one of the lowest of all intellectual beings. What faculties therefore other species of creatures have, to penetrate into the nature and inmost constitutions of things; what ideas they may receive of them, far different from ours; we know not. This we know, and certainly find, that we want several other views of them, besides those we have, to make discoveries of them more perfect. And we may be convinced that the ideas we can attain to by our faculties, are very disproportionate to things themselves, when a positive, clear, distinct one of substance itself, which is the foundation of all the rest, is concealed from us. But want of ideas of this kind being a part, as well as cause of our ignorance, cannot be described. Only this, I think, I may confidently say of it, that the intellectual and sensible world are in this perfectly alike; that that part, which we see of either of them, holds no proportion with what we see not; and whatsoever we can reach with our eyes, or our thoughts, of either of them, is but a point, almost nothing in comparison with the rest.

Secondly, another great cause of ignorance is the want of ideas we are capable of. As the want of ideas, which our faculties are not able to give us, shuts us wholly from those views of things, which it is reasonable to think other beings, perfecter than we, have, of which we know nothing; so the want of ideas I now speak of keeps us in ignorance of things we conceive capable of being known to us. Bulk, figure, and motion we have ideas of. But though we are not without ideas of these primary qualities of bodies in general, yet not knowing what is the particular bulk, figure, and motion, of the greatest part of the bodies of the universe; we are ignorant of the several powers, efficacies, and ways of operation, whereby the effects, which we daily see, are produced. These are hid from us in some things, by being too remote; and in others, by being too minute. When we consider the vast distance of the known and visible parts of the world, and the reasons we have to think, that what lies within our ken is but a small part of the universe, we shall then discover an huge abyss of ignorance. What are the particular fabrics of the great masses of matter, which make up the whole stupendous frame of corporeal beings, how far they are extended, what is their motion, and how continued or communicated, and what influence they have one upon another, are contemplations that at first glimpse our thoughts lose themselves in. If we narrow our contemplations, and confine our thoughts to this little canton, I mean this system of our sun, and the grosser masses of matter, that visibly move about it; what several sorts of vegetables, animals, and intellectual corporeal beings, infinitely different from those of our little spot of earth, may there probably be in the other planets, to the knowledge of which, even of their outward figures and parts, we can no way attain, whilst we are confined to this earth; there being no natural means, either by sensation or reflection, to convey their certain ideas into our minds? They are out of the reach of those inlets of all our knowledge: and what sorts of furniture and inhabitants those mansions contain in them, we cannot so much as guess, much less have clear and distinct ideas of them.

If a great, nay, far the greatest part of the several ranks of bodies in the universe, escape our notice by their remoteness, there are others that are no less concealed from us by their minuteness. These insensible corpuscles being the active parts of matter, and the great instruments of nature, on which depend not only all their secondary qualities, but also most of their natural operations; our want of precise distinct ideas of their primary qualities keeps us in an incurable ignorance of what we desire to know about them. I doubt not but if we could discover the figure, size, texture, and motion of the minute constituent parts of any two bodies, we should know without trial several of their operations one upon another, as we do now the properties of a square or a triangle. Did we know the mechanical affections of the particles of rhubarb, hemlock, opium, and a man; as a watch-maker does those of a watch, whereby it performs its operations, and of a file which by rubbing on them will alter the figure of any of the wheels; we should be able to tell before-hand, that rhubarb will purge, hemlock kill, and opium make a man sleep; as well as a watch-maker can, that a little piece of paper laid on the balance will keep the watch from going, till it be removed; or that, some small part of it being rubbed by a file, the machine would quite lose its motion, and the watch go no more. The dissolving of silver in aqua fortis, and gold in aqua regia, and not vice versa, would be then perhaps no more difficult to know, than it is to a smith to understand why the turning of one key will open a lock, and not the turning of another. But whilst we are destitute of senses acute enough to discover the minute particles of bodies, and to give us ideas of their mechanical affections, we must be content to be ignorant of their properties and ways of operation; nor can we be assured about them any farther, than some few trials we make are able to reach. But whether they will succeed again another time, we cannot be certain. This hinders our certain knowledge of universal truths concerning natural bodies; and our reason carries us herein very little beyond particular matter of fact.

And therefore I am apt to doubt, that how far soever human industry may advance useful and experimental philosophy in physical things, scientifical will still be out of our reach; because we want perfect and adequate ideas of those very bodies which are nearest to us, and most under our command. Those which we have ranked into classes under names, and we think ourselves best acquainted with, we have but very imperfect and incomplete ideas of. Distinct ideas of the several sorts of bodies that fall under the examination of our senses perhaps we may have: but adequate ideas, I suspect, we have not of any one amongst them. And though the former of these will serve us for common use and discourse, yet whilst we want the latter, we are not capable of scientifical knowledge; nor shall ever be able to discover general, instructive, unquestionable truths concerning them. Certainty and demonstration are things we must not, in these matters, pretend to. By the colour, figure, taste, and smell, and other sensible qualities, we have as clear and distinct ideas of sage and hemlock, as we have of a circle and a triangle: but having no ideas of the particular primary qualities of the minute parts of either of these plants, nor of other bodies which we would apply them to, we cannot tell what effects they will produce; nor when we see those effects, can we so much as guess, much less know, their manner of production. Thus having no ideas of the particular mechanical affections of the minute parts of bodies that are within our view and reach, we are ignorant of their constitutions, powers, and operations: and of bodies more remote we are yet more ignorant, not knowing so much as their very outward shapes, or the sensible and grosser parts of their constitutions.

Another cause of ignorance, of no less moment, is a want of a discoverable connexion between those ideas we have. For wherever we want that, we are utterly incapable of universal and certain knowledge; and are, in the former case, left only to observation and experiment: which, how narrow and confined it is, how far from general knowledge, we need not be told. I shall give some few instances of this cause of our ignorance, and so leave it. It is evident that the bulk, figure, and motion of several bodies about us, produce in us several sensations, as of colours, sounds, tastes, smells, pleasure and pain, &c. These mechanical affections of bodies having no affinity at all with those ideas they produce in us (there being no conceivable connexion between any impulse of any sort of body and any perception of a colour or smell, which we find in our minds) we can have no distinct knowledge of such operations beyond our experience; and can reason no otherwise about them, than as effects produced by the appointment of an infinitely wise agent, which perfectly surpass our comprehensions. As the ideas of sensible secondary qualities which we have in our minds, can by us be no way deduced from bodily causes, nor any correspondence or connexion be found between them and those primary qualities which (experience shows us) produce them in us; so on the other side, the operation of our minds upon our bodies is as inconceivable. How any thought should produce a motion in body is as remote from the nature of our ideas, as how any body should produce any thought in the mind. That it is so, if experience did not convince us, the consideration of the things themselves would never be able in the least to discover to us. These, and the like, though they have a constant and regular connexion, in the ordinary course of things; yet that connexion being not discoverable in the ideas themselves, which appearing to have no necessary dependence one on another, we can attribute their connexion to nothing else but the arbitrary determination of that all-wise agent, who has made them to be, and to operate as they do, in a way wholly above our weak understandings to conceive.

In some of our ideas there are certain relations, habitudes, and connexions, so visibly included in the nature of the ideas themselves, that we cannot conceive them separable from them by any power whatsoever. And in these only we are capable of certain and universal knowledge. Thus the idea of a right-lined triangle necessarily carries with it an equality of its angles to two right ones. Nor can we conceive this relation, this connexion of these two ideas, to be possibly mutable, or to depend on any arbitrary power, which of choice made it thus, or could make it otherwise. But the coherence and continuity of the parts of matter; the production of sensation in us of colours and sounds, &c. by impulse and motion; nay, the original rules and communication of motion being such, wherein we can discover no natural connexion with any ideas we have; we cannot but ascribe them to the arbitrary will and good pleasure of the wise architect. I need not, I think, here mention the resurrection of the dead, the future state of this globe of earth, and such other things, which are by every one acknowledged to depend wholly on the determination of a free agent. The things that, as far as our observation reaches, we constantly find to proceed regularly, we may conclude do act by a law set them; but yet by a law, that we know not: whereby, though causes work steadily, and effects constantly flow from them, yet their connexions and dependencies being not discoverable in our ideas, we can have but an experimental knowledge of them. From all which it is easy to perceive what a darkness we are involved in, how little it is of being, and the things that are, that we are capable to know. And therefore we shall do no injury to our knowledge, when we modestly think with ourselves, that we are so far from being able to comprehend the whole nature of the universe, and all the things contained in it, that we are not capable of a philosophical knowledge of the bodies that are about us, and make a part of us: concerning their secondary qualities, powers, and operations, we can have no universal certainty. Several effects come every day within the notice of our senses, of which we have so far sensitive knowledge; but the causes, manner, and certainty of their production, for the two foregoing reasons, we must be content to be very ignorant of. In these we can go no farther than particular experience informs us of matter of fact, and by analogy to guess what effects the like bodies are, upon other trials, like to produce. But as to a perfect science of natural bodies (not to mention spiritual beings) we are, I think, so far from being capable of any such thing, that I conclude it lost labour to seek after it.

THE REALITY OF KNOWLEDGE

I DOUBT not but my reader by this time may be apt to think, that I have been all this while only building a castle in the air; and be ready to say to me, "To what purpose all this stir? Knowledge, say you, is only the perception of the agreement or disagreement of our own ideas: but who knows what those ideas may be? Is there any thing so extravagant, as the imaginations of men's brains? Where is the head that has no chimeras in it? Or if there be a sober and a wise man, what difference will there be, by your rules, between his knowledge and that of the most extravagant fancy in the world? They both have their ideas, and perceive their agreement and disagreement one with another. If there be any difference between them, the advantage will be on the warm-headed man's side, as having the more ideas, and the more lively: and so, by your rules, he will be the more knowing. If it be true, that all knowledge lies only in the perception of the agreement or disagreement of our own ideas, the visions of an enthusiast, and the reasonings of a sober man, will be equally certain. It is no matter how things are; so a man observe but the agreement of his own imaginations, and talk conformably, it is all truth, all certainty. Such castles in the air will be as strong holds of truth, as the demonstrations of Euclid. That an harpy is not a centaur is by this way as certain knowledge, and as much a truth, as that a square is not a circle.

"But of what use is all this fine knowledge of men's own imaginations, to a man that inquires after the reality of things? It matters not what men's fancies are, it is the knowledge of things that is only to be prized; it is this alone gives a value to our reasonings, and preference to one man's knowledge over another's, that it is of things as they really are, and not of dreams and fancies."

To which I answer, that if our knowledge of our ideas terminate in them, and reach no farther, where there is something farther intended, our most serious thoughts will be of little more use than the reveries of a crazy brain; and the truths built thereon of no more weight, than the discourse of a man, who sees things clearly in a dream, and with great assurance utters them. But, I hope, before I have done, to make it evident, that this way of certainty, by the knowledge of our own ideas, goes a little farther than bare imagination: and I believe it will appear, that all the certainty of general truths a man has, lies in nothing else.[1]

It is evident the mind knows not things immediately, but only by the intervention of the ideas it has of them. Our knowledge therefore is real, only so far as there is a conformity between our ideas and the reality of things. But what shall be here the criterion? How shall the mind, when it perceives nothing but its own ideas, know that they agree with things themselves? This, though it seems not to want difficulty, yet, I think, there be two sorts of ideas, that, we may be assured, agree with things.

First, the first are simple ideas, which since the mind, as has been showed, can by no means make to itself, must necessarily be the product of things operating on the mind in a natural way, and producing therein those perceptions which by the wisdom and will of our Maker they are ordained and adapted to. From whence it follows, that simple ideas are not fictions of our fancies, but the natural and regular productions of things without us, really operating upon us, and so carry with them all the conformity which is intended, or which our state requires: for they represent to us things under those appearances which they are fitted to produce in us, whereby we are enabled to distinguish the sorts of particular substances, to discern the states they are in, and so to take them for our necessities, and to apply them to our uses. Thus the idea of whiteness, or bitterness, as it is in the mind, exactly answering that power, which is in any body to produce it there, has all the real conformity it can, or ought to have, with things without us. And this

[1] That knowledge is "real" in the sense that all rational beings, competent to judge, would ofttimes agree, Locke clearly states elsewhere. Cf. p. 338.

conformity between our simple ideas, and the existence of things, is sufficient for real knowledge.

Secondly, all our complex ideas, except those of substances, being archetypes of the mind's own making, not intended to be the copies of any thing, nor referred to the existence of any thing, as to their originals; cannot want any conformity necessary to real knowledge. For that which is not designed to represent any thing but itself, can never be capable of a wrong representation, nor mislead us from the true apprehension of any thing, by its dislikeness to it; and such, excepting those of substances, are all our complex ideas.

I doubt not but it will be easily granted, that the knowledge we have of mathematical truths, is not only certain, but real knowledge; and not the bare empty vision of vain insignificant chimeras of the brain: and yet, if we will consider, we shall find that it is only of our own ideas. The mathematician considers the truth and properties belonging to a rectangle, or circle, only as they are in idea in his own mind. For it is possible he never found either of them existing mathematically, i. e. precisely true, in his life. But yet the knowledge he has of any truths or properties belonging to a circle, or any other mathematical figure, are nevertheless true and certain, even of real things existing; because real things are no farther concerned, nor intended to be meant by any such propositions, than as things really agree to those archetypes in his mind. Is it true of the idea of a triangle, that its three angles are equal to two right ones? It is true also of a triangle, wherever it really exists. Whatever other figure exists, that is not exactly answerable to the idea of a triangle in his mind, is not at all concerned in that proposition: and therefore he is certain all his knowledge concerning such ideas is real knowledge; because intending things no farther than they agree with those his ideas, he is sure what he knows concerning those figures, when they have barely an ideal existence in his mind, will hold true of them also, when they have real existence in matter; his consideration being barely of those figures, which are the same, wherever or however they exist.

And hence it follows that moral knowledge is as capable of real certainty, as mathematics. For certainty being but the perception of the agreement or disagreement of our ideas; and demonstration nothing but the perception of such agreement, by the intervention of other ideas, or mediums; our moral ideas, as well as mathematical, being archetypes themselves, and so adequate and complete ideas; all the agreement or disagreement, which we shall find in them, will produce real knowledge, as well as in mathematical figures.[1]

For the attaining of knowledge and certainty, it is requisite that we have determined ideas; and, to make our knowledge real, it is requisite that the ideas answer their archetypes. Nor let it be wondered, that I place the certainty of our knowledge in the consideration of our ideas, with so little care and regard (as it may seem) to the real existence of things: since most of those discourses, which take up the thoughts, and engage the disputes of those who pretend to make it their business to enquire after truth and certainty, will, I presume, upon examination be found to be general propositions, and notions in which existence is not at all concerned. All the discourses of the mathematicians about the squaring of a circle, conic sections, or any other part of mathematics, concern not the existence of any of those figures; but their demonstrations, which depend on their

[1] Locke frequently recurs to the question of how ideas in the mind give knowledge of objects outside of the mind. Cf. the passage on p. 339.

ideas, are the same, whether there be any square or circle existing in the world, or no. In the same manner the truth and certainty of moral discourses abstracts from the lives of men, and the existence of those virtues in the world whereof they treat. Nor are Tully's offices less true, because there is nobody in the world that exactly practises his rules, and lives up to that pattern of a virtuous man which he has given us, and which existed no where, when he writ, but in idea. If it be true in speculation, i. e. in idea, that murder deserves death, it will also be true in reality of any action that exists conformable to that idea of murder. As for other actions, the truth of that proposition concerns them not. And thus it is of all other species of things, which have no other essences but those ideas, which are in the minds of men.

Thirdly, there is another sort of complex ideas, which being referred to archetypes without us, may differ from them, and so our knowledge about them may come short of being real. Such are our ideas of substances, which consisting of a collection of simple ideas, supposed taken from the works of nature, may yet vary from them, by having more or different ideas united in them, than are to be found united in the things themselves. From whence it comes to pass, that they may, and often do, fail of being exactly conformable to things themselves.

I say then, that to have ideas of substances, which, by being conformable to things, may afford us real knowledge, it is not enough, as in modes, to put together such ideas as have no inconsistence, though they did never before so exist; v. g. the ideas of sacrilege or perjury, &c. were as real and true ideas before, as after the existence of any such fact. But our ideas of substances being supposed copies, and referred to archetypes without us, must still be taken from something that does or has existed; they must not consist of ideas put together at the pleasure of our thoughts, without any real pattern they were taken from, though we can perceive no inconsistence in such a combination. The reason whereof is, because we knowing not what real constitution it is of substances, whereon our simple ideas depend, and which really is the cause of the strict union of some of them one with another, and the exclusion of others; there are very few of them, that we can be sure are, or are not, inconsistent in nature, any farther than experience and sensible observation reach. Herein therefore is founded the reality of our knowledge concerning substances, that all our complex ideas of them must be such, and such only, as are made up of such simple ones, as have been discovered to co-exist in nature. And our ideas being thus true: though not, perhaps, very exact copies, are yet the subjects of real (as far as we have any) knowledge of them. Which (as has been already shown) will not be found to reach very far: but so far as it does, it will still be real knowledge. Whatever ideas we have, the agreement we find they have with others, will still be knowledge. If those ideas be abstract, it will be general knowledge. But, to make it real concerning substances, the ideas must be taken from the real existence of things. Whatever simple ideas have been found to co-exist in any substance, these we may with confidence join together again, and so make abstract ideas of substances. For whatever have once had an union in nature, may be united again.

KNOWLEDGE OF OUR OWN EXISTENCE

LET us proceed now to inquire concerning our knowledge of the existence of things, and how we come by it. I say then, that we have the knowledge of our own existence by intuition; of the existence of God by demonstration; and of other things by sensation.

As for our own existence, we perceive it so plainly, and so certainly, that it neither needs nor is capable of any proof. For nothing can be more evident to us, than our own existence; I think, I reason, I feel pleasure and pain: can any of these be more evident to me, than my own existence? if I doubt of all other things, that very doubt makes me perceive my own existence, and will not suffer me to doubt of that. For if I know I feel pain, it is evident I have as certain perception of my own existence, as of the existence of the pain I feel: or if I know I doubt, I have as certain perception of the existence of the thing doubting, as of that thought which I call doubt. Experience then convinces us, that we have an intuitive knowledge of our own existence, and an internal infallible perception that we are. In every act of sensation, reasoning, or thinking, we are conscious to ourselves of our own being; and, in this matter, come not short of the highest degree of certainty.

KNOWLEDGE OF THE EXISTENCE OF GOD

THOUGH God has given us no innate ideas of himself; though he has stamped no original characters on our minds, wherein we may read his being; yet having furnished us with those faculties our minds are endowed with, he hath not left himself without witness: since we have sense, perception, and reason, and cannot want a clear proof of him, as long as we carry ourselves about us. Nor can we justly complain of our ignorance in this great point, since he has so plentifully provided us with the means to discover and know him, so far as is necessary to the end of our being, and the great concernment of our happiness. But though this be the most obvious truth that reason discovers; and though its evidence be (if I mistake not) equal to mathematical certainty: yet it requires thought and attention, and the mind must apply itself to a regular deduction of it from some part of our intuitive knowledge, or else we shall be as uncertain and ignorant of this as of other propositions, which are in themselves capable of clear demonstration. To show therefore that we are capable of knowing, i. e. being certain that there is a God, and how we may come by this certainty, I think we need go no farther than ourselves, and that undoubted knowledge we have of our own existence.

I think it is beyond question, that man has a clear idea of his own being; he knows certainly he exists, and that he is something. He that can doubt, whether he be any thing or no, I speak not to; no more than I would argue with pure nothing, or endeavour to convince non-entity, that it were something. If any one pretends to be so sceptical, as to deny his own existence (for really to doubt of it is manifestly impossible) let him for me enjoy his beloved happiness of being nothing, until hunger, or some other pain, convince him of the contrary. This then, I think, I may take for a truth, which every one's certain knowledge assures him of, beyond the liberty of doubting, viz. that he is something that actually exists.

In the next place, man knows by an intuitive certainty, that bare nothing can no more produce any real being, than it can be equal to two right angles. If a man knows not that non-entity, or the absence of all being, cannot be equal to two right angles, it is impossible he should know any demonstration in Euclid. If therefore we know there is some real being, and that non-entity cannot produce any real being, it is an evident demonstration, that from eternity there has been something; since what was not from eternity had a beginning; and what had a beginning must be produced by something else.

Next, it is evident, that what had its being and beginning from another, must also have all that which is in, and belongs to its being, from another too. All the powers it has must be owing to, and received from, the same source. This eternal source then of all being must also be the source and original of all power; and so this eternal being must be also the most powerful.

Again, a man finds in himself perception and knowledge. We have then got one step farther; and we are certain now, that there is not only some being, but some knowing intelligent being in the world.

There was a time then, when there was no knowing being, and when knowledge began to be; or else there has been also a knowing being from eternity. If it be said, there was a time when no being had any knowledge, when that eternal being was void of all understanding, I reply, that then it was impossible there should ever have been any knowledge: it being as impossible that things wholly void of knowledge, and operating blindly, and without any perception, should produce a knowing being, as it is impossible that a triangle should make itself three angles bigger than two right ones. For it is as repugnant to the idea of senseless matter, that it should put into itself, sense, perception, and knowledge, as it is repugnant to the idea of a triangle, that it should put into itself greater angles than two right ones.

Thus from the consideration of ourselves, and what we infallibly find in our own constitutions,[1] our reason leads us to the knowledge of this certain and evident truth, that there is an eternal, most powerful, and most knowing being; which whether any one will please to call God, it matters not. The thing is evident, and from this idea duly considered, will easily be deduced all those other attributes, which we ought to ascribe to this eternal being. If nevertheless any one should be found so senselessly arrogant, as to suppose man alone knowing and wise, but yet the product of mere ignorance and chance; and that all the rest of the universe acted only by that blind hap-hazard: I shall leave with him that very rational and emphatical rebuke of Tully, (l. ii. De Leg.) to be considered at his leisure: "What can be more sillily arrogant and misbecoming, than for a man to think that he has a mind and understanding in him, but yet in all the universe besides there is no such thing? Or that those things which with the utmost stretch of his reason he can scarce comprehend, should be moved and managed without any reason at all?"

Though our own being furnishes us, as I have shown, with an evident and incontestible proof of a deity; and I believe nobody can avoid the cogency of it, who will but as carefully attend to it, as to any other demonstration of so many parts: yet this being so fundamental a truth, and of that consequence, that all religion and genuine morality depend thereon, I doubt not but I shall be forgiven by my reader, if I go over some parts of

[1] A still clearer statement of this proof for the existence of God was made in another place. Cf. p. 340.

this argument again, and enlarge a little more upon them.

There is no truth more evident, than that something must be from eternity. I never yet heard of any one so unreasonable, or that could suppose so manifest a contradiction, as a time wherein there was perfectly nothing: this being of all absurdities the greatest, to imagine that pure nothing, the perfect negation and absence of all beings, should ever produce any real existence.

It being then unavoidable for all rational creatures to conclude, that something has existed from eternity; let us next see what kind of thing that must be.

There are but two sorts of beings in the world, that man knows or conceives.

First, such as are purely material, without sense, perception, or thought, as the clippings of our beards, and parings of our nails.

Secondly, sensible, thinking, perceiving beings, such as we find ourselves to be, which, if you please, we will hereafter call cogitative and incogitative beings, which to our present purpose, if for nothing else, are, perhaps, better terms than material and immaterial.

If then there must be something eternal, let us see what sort of being it must be. And to that, it is very obvious to reason, that it must necessarily be a cogitative being. For it is as impossible to conceive, that ever bare incogitative matter should produce a thinking intelligent being, as that nothing should of itself produce matter. Let us suppose any parcel of matter eternal, great or small, we shall find it, in itself, able to produce nothing. For example; let us suppose the matter of the next pebble we meet with eternal, closely united, and the parts firmly at rest together; if there were no other being in the world, must it not eternally remain so, a dead inactive lump? Is it possible to conceive it can add motion to itself, being purely matter, or produce any thing? Matter then, by its own strength, cannot produce in itself so much as motion: the motion it has must also be from eternity, or else be produced, and added to matter by some other being more powerful than matter; matter, as is evident, having not power to produce motion in itself. But let us suppose motion eternal too; yet matter, incogitative matter and motion, whatever changes it might produce of figure and bulk, could never produce thought: knowledge will still be as far beyond the power of motion and matter to produce, as matter is beyond the power of nothing or non-entity to produce. And I appeal to every one's own thoughts, whether he cannot as easily conceive matter produced by nothing, as thought to be produced by pure matter, when before there was no such thing as thought, or an intelligent being existing? Divide matter into as minute parts as you will (which we are apt to imagine a sort of spiritualizing, or making a thinking thing of it) vary the figure and motion of it as much as you please; a globe, cube, cone, prism, cylinder, &c. whose diameters are but 1000000th part of a gry *, will operate no otherwise upon other bodies of proportionable bulk, than those of an inch or foot diameter; and you may as rationally expect to produce sense, thought, and knowledge, by

* A gry is $\frac{1}{10}$ of a line, a line $\frac{1}{10}$ of an inch, an inch $\frac{1}{10}$ of a philosophical foot, a philosophical foot $\frac{1}{3}$ of a pendulum, whose diadroms, in the latitude of 45 degrees, are each equal to one second of time, or $\frac{1}{60}$ of a minute. I have affectedly made use of this measure here, and the parts of it, under a decimal division, with names to them; because, I think, it would be of general convenience, that this should be the common measure, in the commonwealth of letters. (Locke's own footnote.)

putting together, in a certain figure and motion, gross particles of matter, as by those that are the very minutest, that do any where exist. They knock, impel, and resist one another, just as the greater do, and that is all they can do. So that if we will suppose nothing first, or eternal; matter can never begin to be: if we suppose bare matter, without motion, eternal motion can never begin to be: if we suppose only matter and motion first, or eternal; thought can never begin to be. For it is impossible to conceive that matter, either with or without motion, could have originally in and from itself sense, perception, and knowledge; as is evident from hence, that then sense, perception, and knowledge must be a property eternally inseparable from matter and every particle of it. Not to add, that though our general or specific conception of matter makes us speak of it as one thing, yet really all matter is not one individual thing, neither is there any such thing existing as one material being, or one single body that we know or can conceive. And therefore if matter were the eternal first cogitative being, there would not be one eternal infinite cogitative being, but an infinite number of eternal finite cogitative beings, independent one of another, of limited force and distinct thoughts, which could never produce that order, harmony and beauty which are to be found in nature. Since therefore whatsoever is the first eternal being must necessarily be cogitative; and whatsoever is first of all things must necessarily contain in it, and actually have, at least, all the perfections that can ever after exist; nor can it ever give to another any perfection that it hath not, either actually in itself, or at least in a higher degree; it necessarily follows, that the first eternal being cannot be matter.

If therefore it be evident, that something necessarily

must exist from eternity, it is also as evident, that that something must necessarily be a cogitative being: for it is as impossible that incogitative matter should produce a cogitative being, as that nothing, or the negation of all being, should produce a positive being or matter.

Perhaps it will be said, that though it be as clear as demonstration can make it, that there must be an eternal being, and that being must also be knowing; yet it does not follow, but that thinking being may also be material. Let it be so; it equally still follows, that there is a God. For if there be an eternal, omniscient, omnipotent being, it is certain that there is a God, whether you imagine that being to be material or no. But herein, I suppose, lies the danger and deceit of that supposition: there being no way to avoid the demonstration, that there is an eternal knowing being, men, devoted to matter, would willingly have it granted, that this knowing being is material; and then letting slide out of their minds, or the discourse, the demonstration whereby an eternal knowing being was proved necessarily to exist, would argue all to be matter, and so deny a God, that is, an eternal cogitative being; whereby they are so far from establishing, that they destroy their own hypothesis. For if there can be, in their opinion, eternal matter, without any eternal cogitative being, they manifestly separate matter and thinking, and suppose no necessary connexion of the one with the other, and so establish the necessity of an eternal spirit, but not of matter; since it has been proved already, that an eternal cogitative being is unavoidably to be granted. Now if thinking and matter may be separated, the eternal existence of matter will not follow from the eternal existence of a cogitative being, and they suppose it to no purpose.

But now let us suppose they can satisfy themselves or others, that this eternal thinking being is material.

First, I would ask them, Whether they imagine, that all matter, every particle of matter, thinks? This, I suppose, they will scarce say; since then there would be as many eternal thinking beings as there are particles of matter, and so an infinity of gods. And yet if they will not allow matter as matter, that is, every particle of matter to be as well cogitative as extended, they will have as hard a task to make out to their own reasons a cogitative being out of incogitative particles, as an extended being out of unextended parts, if I may so speak.

Secondly, if all matter does not think, I next ask, "Whether it be only one atom that does so?" That has as many absurdities as the other; for then this atom of matter must be alone eternal or not. If this alone be eternal, then this alone, by its powerful thought or will, made all the rest of matter. And so we have the creation of matter by a powerful thought, which is that the materialists stick at. For if they suppose one single thinking atom to have produced all the rest of matter, they cannot ascribe that pre-eminency to it upon any other account than that of its thinking, the only supposed difference. But allow it to be by some other way, which is above our conception, it must still be creation, and these men must give up their great maxim, "ex nihilo nil fit." If it be said, that all the rest of matter is equally eternal, as that thinking atom, it will be to say any thing at pleasure, though ever so absurd; for to suppose all matter eternal, and yet one small particle in knowledge and power infinitely above all the rest, is without any the least appearance of reason to frame an hypothesis. Every particle of matter, as matter, is capable of all the same figures and motions of any other;

and I challenge any one, in his thoughts, to add any thing else to one above another.

If then neither one peculiar atom alone can be this eternal thinking being; nor all matter as matter, i. e. every particle of matter, can be; it only remains that it is some certain system of matter duly put together, that is this thinking eternal being. This is that, which, I imagine, is that notion which men are aptest to have of God; who would have him a material being, as most readily suggested to them, by the ordinary conceit they have of themselves, and other men, which they take to be material thinking beings. But this imagination, however more natural, is no less absurd than the other: for to suppose the eternal thinking being to be nothing else but a composition of particles of matter each whereof is cogitative, is to ascribe all the wisdom and knowledge of that eternal being only to the juxta-position of parts; than which nothing can be more absurd. For unthinking particles of matter, however put together, can have nothing thereby added to them, but a new relation of position, which it is impossible should give thought and knowledge to them.

Others would have matter to be eternal, notwithstanding that they allow an eternal, cogitative, immaterial being. This, though it take not away the being of a God, yet since it denies one and the first great piece of his workmanship, the creation, let us consider it a little. Matter must be allowed eternal: Why? because you cannot conceive how it can be made out of nothing: why do you not also think yourself eternal? You will answer perhaps, because about twenty or forty years since you began to be. But if I ask you what that you is, which began then to be, you can scarce tell me. The matter whereof you are made, began not then to be; for if it did, then it is not eternal: but it began to be put together in such a fashion and frame as makes up your body; but yet that frame of particles is not you, it makes not that thinking thing you are; (for I have now to do with one who allows an eternal, immaterial thinking being, but would have unthinking matter eternal too) therefore when did that thinking being begin to be? If it did never begin to be, then have you always been a thinking thing from eternity; the absurdity whereof I need not confute, till I meet with one who is so void of understanding as to own it. If therefore you can allow a thinking thing to be made out of nothing (as all things that are not eternal must be) why also can you not allow it possible, for a material being to be made out of nothing, by an equal power, but that you have the experience of the one in view, and not of the other?

But you will say, is it not impossible to admit of the making any thing out of nothing, since we cannot possibly conceive it? I answer, No; because it is not reasonable to deny the power of an infinite being, because we cannot comprehend its operations. We do not deny other effects upon this ground, because we cannot possibly conceive the manner of their production. It is an overvaluing ourselves to reduce all to the narrow measure of our capacities; and to conclude all things impossible to be done, whose manner of doing exceeds our comprehension. This is to make our comprehension infinite, or God finite, when what we can do is limited to what we can conceive of it. If you do not understand the operations of your own finite mind, that thinking thing within you, do not deem it strange, that you cannot comprehend the operations of that eternal infinite mind, who made and governs all things, and whom the heaven of heavens cannot contain.

KNOWLEDGE OF THE EXISTENCE OF OTHER THINGS

THE knowledge of our own being we have by intuition. The existence of a God reason clearly makes known to us, as has been shown.

The knowledge of the existence of any other thing we can have only by sensation: for there being no necessary connexion of real existence with any idea a man hath in his memory, nor of any other existence but that of God, with the existence of any particular man; no particular man can know the existence of any other being, but only when by actual operating upon him, it makes itself perceived by him. For the having the idea of any thing in our mind, no more proves the existence of that thing, than the picture of a man evidences his being in the world, or the visions of a dream make thereby a true history.

It is therefore the actual receiving of ideas from without, that gives us notice of the existence of other things, and makes us know that something doth exist at that time without us, which causes that idea in us, though perhaps we neither know nor consider how it does it: for it takes not from the certainty of our senses, and the ideas we receive by them, that we know not the manner wherein they are produced: v. g. whilst I write this, I have, by the paper affecting my eyes, that idea produced in my mind, which whatever object causes, I call white; by which I know that that quality or accident (i. e. whose appearance before my eyes always causes that idea) doth really exist, and hath a being without me. And of this, the greatest assurance I can possibly have, and to which my faculties can attain, is the testimony of my eyes, which are the proper and sole judges of this thing, whose testimony I have reason to rely on as so certain, that I can no more doubt, whilst I write this, that I see white and black, and that something really exists, that causes that sensation in me, than that I write or move my hand; which is a certainty as great as human nature is capable of, concerning the existence of any thing, but a man's self alone, and of God.

The notice we have by our senses, of the existence of things without us, though it be not altogether so certain as our intuitive knowledge, or the deductions of our reason employed about the clear abstract ideas of our own minds; yet it is an assurance that deserves the name of knowledge. If we persuade ourselves, that our faculties act and inform us right, concerning the existence of those objects that affect them, it cannot pass for an ill-grounded confidence: for I think nobody can, in earnest, be so sceptical, as to be uncertain of the existence of those things which he sees and feels. At least, he that can doubt so far (whatever he may have with his own thoughts) will never have any controversy with me; since he can never be sure I say any thing contrary to his own opinion. As to myself, I think God has given me assurance enough of the existence of things without me; since by their different application I can produce in myself both pleasure and pain, which is one great concernment of my present state. This is certain, the confidence that our faculties do not herein deceive us is the greatest assurance we are capable of, concerning the existence of material beings. For we cannot act any thing, but by our faculties; nor talk of knowledge itself, but by the helps of those faculties, which are fitted to apprehend even what knowledge is. But besides the assurance we have from our senses themselves, that they do not err in the information they give us, of the existence of things without us, when they are affected by them, we are farther confirmed in this assurance by other concurrent reasons.

First, it is plain those perceptions are produced in us by exterior causes affecting our senses; because those that want the organs of any sense, never can have the ideas belonging to that sense produced in their minds. This is too evident to be doubted: and therefore we cannot but be assured, that they come in by the organs of that sense, and no other way. The organs themselves, it is plain, do not produce them; for then the eyes of a man in the dark would produce colours, and his nose smell roses in the winter: but we see nobody gets the relish of a pine-apple, till he goes to the Indies, where it is, and tastes it.

Secondly, because sometimes I find, that I cannot avoid the having those ideas produced in my mind. For though when my eyes are shut, or windows fast, I can at pleasure recall to my mind the ideas of light, or the sun, which former sensations had lodged in my memory; so I can at pleasure lay by that idea, and take into my view that of the smell of a rose, or taste of sugar. But, if I turn my eyes at noon towards the sun, I cannot avoid the ideas, which the light, or sun, then produces in me. So that there is a manifest difference between the ideas laid up in my memory, (over which, if they were there only, I should have constantly the same power to dispose of them, and lay them by at pleasure) and those which force themselves upon me, and I cannot avoid having. And therefore it must needs be some exterior cause, and the brisk acting of some objects without me, whose efficacy I cannot resist, that produces those ideas in my mind, whether I will or no. Besides, there is nobody who doth not perceive the difference in himself between contemplating the sun, as he hath the idea of it in his memory, and actually looking upon it: of which two, his perception is so distinct, that few of his ideas are more distinguishable one from another. And therefore he hath certain knowledge, that they are not both memory, or the actions of his mind, and fancies only within him; but that actual seeing hath a cause without.

Thirdly, add to this, that many of those ideas are produced in us with pain, which afterwards we remember without the least offence. Thus the pain of heat or cold, when the idea of it is revived in our minds, gives us no disturbance; which, when felt, was very troublesome, and is again, when actually repeated; which is occasioned by the disorder the external object causes in our bodies when applied to it. And we remember the pains of hunger, thirst, or the head-ache without any pain at all; which would either never disturb us, or else constantly do it, as often as we thought of it, were there nothing more but ideas floating in our minds and appearances entertaining our fancies, without the real existence of things affecting us from abroad. The same may be said of pleasure, accompanying several actual sensations.

Fourthly, our senses in many cases bear witness to the truth of each other's report, concerning the existence of sensible things without us. He that sees a fire, may, if he doubt whether it be any thing more than a bare fancy, feel it too; and be convinced by putting his hand in it. Which certainly could never be put into such exquisite pain, by a bare idea or phantom, unless that the pain be a fancy too: which yet he cannot, when the burn is well, by raising the idea of it, bring upon himself again. So that this evidence is as great as we can desire, being as certain to us as our pleasure or pain, i. e. happiness or misery; beyond which we have no concernment, either of knowing or being. Such an assurance of the existence of things without us, is sufficient to direct us in the attaining the good, and avoiding the evil, which is caused by them; which is the important concernment we have of being made acquainted with them.

In fine then, when our senses do actually convey into our understandings any idea, we cannot but be satisfied that there doth something at that time really exist without us, which doth affect our senses, and by them give notice of itself to our apprehensive faculties, and actually produce that idea which we then perceive: and we cannot so far distrust their testimony, as to doubt, that such collections of simple ideas, as we have observed by our senses to be united together, do really exist together. But this knowledge extends as far as the present testimony of our senses, employed about particular objects that do then affect them, and no farther. For if I saw such a collection of simple ideas, as is wont to be called man, existing together one minute since, and am now alone, I cannot be certain that the same man exists now, since there is no necessary connexion of his existence a minute since, with his existence now: by a thousand ways he may cease to be, since I had the testimony of my senses for his existence. And if I cannot be certain, that the man I saw last to-day is now in being, I can less be certain that he is so, who hath been longer removed from my senses, and I have not seen since yesterday, or since the last year; and much less can I be certain of the existence of men that I never saw. And therefore though it be highly probable, that millions of men do now exist, yet, whilst I am alone writing this, I have not that certainty of it which we strictly call knowledge; though the great likelihood of it puts me past doubt, and it be reasonable for me to do several things upon the confidence that there are men (and men also of my acquaintance, with whom I have to do) now in the world: but this is but probability, not knowledge.

As when our senses are actually employed about any object, we do know that it does exist; so by our memory we may be assured, that heretofore things that affected our senses have existed. And thus we have knowledge of the past existence of several things, whereof our senses having informed us, our memories still retain the ideas; and of this we are past all doubt, so long as we remember well. But this knowledge also reaches no farther than our senses have formerly assured us.

KNOWLEDGE OF THE NATURE OR ESSENCE OF THE SUBSTANCES ABOUT US

SINCE the essences of things are thought, by some, (and not without reason) to be wholly unknown: it may not be amiss to consider the several significations of the word essence.

First, essence may be taken for the being of any thing, whereby it is what it is. And thus the real internal, but generally, in substances, unknown constitution of things, whereon their discoverable qualities depend, may be called their essence. This is the proper original signification of the word, as is evident from the formation of it; *essentia,* in its primary notation, signifying properly being. And in this sense it is still used, when we speak of the essence of particular things, without giving them any name.

Secondly, the learning and disputes of the schools having been much busied about genus and species, the word essence has almost lost its primary signification: and instead of the real constitution of things, has been almost wholly applied to the artificial constitution of genus and species. It is true, there is ordinarily supposed a real constitution of the sorts of things; and it is past doubt, there must be some real constitution, on which any collection of simple ideas co-existing must depend. But it being evident, that things are ranked under names into sorts or species, only as they agree to certain abstract ideas, to which we have annexed those names: the essence of each genus, or sort, comes to be nothing but that abstract idea, which the general, or sortal (if I may have leave so to call it from sort, as I do general from genus) name stands for. And this we shall find to be that which the word essence imports in its most familiar use. These two sorts of essences, I suppose, may not unfitly be termed, the one the *real*, the other *nominal* essence.

Between the nominal essence and the name, there is so near a connexion, that the name of any sort of things cannot be attributed to any particular being but what has this essence, whereby it answers that abstract idea, whereof that name is the sign.

Concerning the real essences of corporeal substances, (to mention these only) there are, if I mistake not, two opinions. The one is of those, who using the word essence for they know not what, suppose a certain number of those essences, according to which all natural things are made, and wherein they do exactly every one of them partake, and so become of this or that species. The other, and more rational opinion, is of those who look on all natural things to have a real, but unknown constitution of their insensible parts; from which flow those sensible qualities, which serve us to distinguish them one from another, according as we have occasion to rank them into sorts under common denominations. The former of these opinions, which supposes these essences, as a certain number of forms or moulds, wherein all natural things, that exist, are cast, and do equally partake, has, I imagine, very much perplexed the knowledge of natural things. The frequent productions of monsters, in all the species of animals, and of changelings, and other strange issues of human birth, carry with them difficulties, not possible to consist with this hypothesis: since it is as impossible, that two things, partaking exactly of the same real essence, should have different properties, as that two figures partaking of the same real essence of a circle should have different properties. But were there no other reason against it, yet the supposition of essences that cannot be known, and the making of them nevertheless to be that which distinguishes the species of things, is so wholly useless, and unserviceable to any part of our knowledge, that that alone were sufficient to make us lay it by, and content ourselves with such essences of the sorts or species of things as come within the reach of our knowledge: which, when seriously considered, will be found, as I have said, to be nothing else but those abstract complex ideas, to which we have annexed distinct general names.

Essences being thus distinguished into nominal and real, we may farther observe, that in the species of simple ideas and modes, they are always the same; but in substances always quite different. Thus a figure including a space between three lines, is the real as well as nominal essence of a triangle; it being not only the abstract idea to which the general name is annexed, but the very *essentia* or being of the thing itself, that foundation from which all its properties flow, and to which they are all inseparably annexed. But it is far otherwise concerning that parcel of matter, which makes the ring on my finger, wherein these two essences are apparently different. For it is the real constitution of its insensible parts, on which depend all those properties of colour, weight, fusibility, fixedness, &c. which are to be found in it, which constitution we know not, and so having no particular idea of, have no name that is the sign of it. But yet it is its colour, weight, fusibility, fixedness, &c. which makes it to be gold, or gives it a right to that name, which is therefore its nominal essence: since nothing can be called gold but what has a conformity of qualities to that abstract complex idea, to which that name is annexed.

In the next place, these essences of the species of mixed modes are not only made by the mind, but made very arbitrarily, made without patterns, or reference to any real existence. Wherein they differ from those of substances, which carry with them the supposition of some real being, from which they are taken, and to which they are conformable. But in its complex ideas of mixed modes, the mind takes a liberty not to follow the existence of things exactly. It unites and retains certain collections, as so many distinct specific ideas, whilst others, that as often occur in nature, and are as plainly suggested by outward things, pass neglected, without particular names or specifications. Nor does the mind, in these of mixed modes, as in the complex idea of substances, examine them by the real existence of things; or verify them by patterns, containing such peculiar compositions in nature. To know whether his idea of adultery or incest be right, will a man seek it any where amongst things existing? Or is it true, because any one has been witness to such an action? No: but it suffices here, that men have put together such a collection into one complex idea, that makes the archetype and specific idea, whether ever any such action were committed *in rerum natura* or no.

To understand this right, we must consider wherein this making of these complex ideas consists; and that is not in the making any new idea, but putting together those which the mind had before. Wherein the mind does these three things: first, it chooses a certain number: secondly, it gives them connexion, and makes them into one idea: thirdly, it ties them together by a name. If we examine how the mind proceeds in these, and what liberty it takes in them, we shall easily observe how these essences of the species of mixed modes are the workmanship of the mind; and consequently, that the species themselves are of men's making.

No body can doubt but that these ideas of mixed modes are made by a voluntary collection of ideas put together in the mind, independent from any original patterns in nature, who will but reflect that this sort of complex ideas may be made, abstracted, and have names given them, and so a species be constituted, before any one individual of that species ever existed. Who can doubt but the ideas of sacrilege or adultery might be framed in the minds of men, and have names given them; and so these species of mixed modes be constituted, before either of them was ever committed; and might be as well discoursed of and reasoned about, and as certain truths discovered of them, whilst yet they had no being but in the understanding, as well as now, that they have but too frequently a real existence? Whereby it is plain, how much the sorts of mixed modes are the creatures of the understanding, where they have a being as subservient to all the ends of real truth and knowledge, as when they really exist: and we cannot doubt but law-makers have often made laws about species of actions, which were only the creatures of their own understandings; beings that had no other existence but in their own minds. And I think nobody can deny, but that the resurrection was a species of mixed modes in the mind, before it really existed.

To see how arbitrarily these essences of mixed modes are made by the mind, we need but take a view of almost any of them. A little looking into them will satisfy us, that it is the mind that combines several scattered independent ideas into one complex one, and, by the common name it gives them, makes them the essence of a certain species, without regulating itself by any connexion they have in nature. For what greater connexion in nature has the idea of a man, than the idea of a sheep, with killing; that this is made a particular species of action, signified by the word murder, and the other not? Or what union is there in nature between the idea of the relation of a father with killing, than that of a son, or neighbour; that those are combined into one complex idea, and thereby made the essence of the distinct species parricide, whilst the other make no distinct species at all? But though they have made killing a man's father, or mother, a distinct species from killing his son, or daughter; yet in some other cases, son and daughter are taken in too, as well as father and mother: and they are all equally comprehended in the same species, as in that of incest. Thus the mind in mixed modes arbitrarily unites into complex ideas such as it finds convenient; whilst others that have altogether as much union in nature, are left loose, and never combined into one idea, because they have no need of one name. It is evident then, that the mind by its free choice gives a connexion to a certain number of ideas, which in nature have no more union with one another, than others that it leaves out: why else is the part of the weapon, the beginning of the wound is made with, taken notice of to make the distinct species called stabbing, and the figure and matter of the weapon left out? I do not say, this is done without reason, as we shall see more by and by; but this I say, that it is done by the free choice of the mind, pursuing its own ends; and that therefore these species of mixed modes are the workmanship of the understanding: and there is nothing more evident, than that, for the most part, in the framing these ideas the mind searches not its patterns in nature, nor refers the ideas it makes to the real existence of things; but puts such together, as may best serve its own purposes, without tying itself to a precise imitation of any thing that really exists.[1]

The way also wherein the names of mixed modes are ordinarily learned, does not a little contribute to the doubtfulness of their signification. For if we will observe how children learn languages, we shall find that to make them understand what the names of simple ideas, or substances, stand for, people ordinarily show them the thing, whereof they would have them have the idea; and then repeat to them the name that stands for it, as white, sweet, milk, sugar, cat, dog. But as for mixed modes, especially the most material of them, moral words, the sounds are usually learned first; and then to know what complex ideas they stand for, they are either beholden to the explication of others, or (which happens for the most part) are left to their own observation and industry; which being little laid out in the search of the true and precise meaning of names, these moral words are in most men's mouths little more than bare sounds; or when they have any, it is for the most part but a very loose and undetermined, and consequently obscure and confused signification. And even those themselves who have with more attention settled

[1] Locke was here aiming at those who in any field of investigation mistook their own abstract ideas or "mixed modes" for real beings. Particularly perhaps he was attacking those who spun theological dogmas out of their private ideas and then tried to impose these dogmas on others. Cf. on this point, p. 341.

their notions, do yet hardly avoid the inconvenience, to have them stand for complex ideas, different from those which other, even intelligent and studious men, make them the signs of. Where shall one find any, either controversial debate, or familiar discourse, concerning honour, faith, grace, religion, church, &c. wherein it is not easy to observe the different notions men have of them? which is nothing but this, that they are not agreed in the signification of those words, nor have in their minds the same complex ideas which they make them stand for: and so all the contests that follow thereupon, are only about the meaning of a sound. And hence we see, that in the interpretation of laws, whether divine or human, there is no end; comments beget comments, and explications make new matter for explications; and of limiting, distinguishing, varying the signification of these moral words, there is no end. These ideas of men's making are, by men still having the same power, multiplied *in infinitum.* Many a man who was pretty well satisfied of the meaning of a text of scripture, or clause in the code at first reading, has by consulting commentators quite lost the sense of it, and by these elucidations given rise or increase to his doubts, and drawn obscurity upon the place. I say not this, that I think commentaries needless; but to show how uncertain the names of mixed modes naturally are, even in the mouths of those who had both the intention and the faculty of speaking as clearly as language was capable to express their thoughts.

If the signification of the names of mixed modes are uncertain, because there be no real standards existing in nature, to which those ideas are referred, and by which they may be adjusted; the names of substances are of a doubtful signification, for a contrary reason, viz. because the ideas they stand for are supposed conformable to the reality of things, and are referred to standards made by nature. In our ideas of substances we have not the liberty, as in mixed modes, to frame what combinations we think fit, to be the characteristical notes to rank and denominate things by. In these we must follow nature, suit our complex ideas to real existences, and regulate the signification of their names by the things themselves, if we will have our names to be signs of them, and stand for them. Here, it is true, we have patterns to follow; but patterns that will make the signification of their names very uncertain: for names must be of a very unsteady and various meaning, if the ideas they stand for be referred to standards without us, that either cannot be known at all, or can be known but imperfectly and uncertainly.

The measure and boundary of each sort, or species, whereby it is constituted that particular sort, and distinguished from others, is that we call its essence, which is nothing but that abstract idea to which the name is annexed; so that every thing contained in that idea is essential to that sort. This, though it be all the essence of natural substances that we know, or by which we distinguish them into sorts; yet I call it by a peculiar name, the nominal essence, to distinguish it from the real constitution of substances, upon which depends this nominal essence, and all the properties of that sort; which therefore, as has been said, may be called the real essence: v. g. the nominal essence of gold is that complex idea the word gold stands for, let it be, for instance, a body yellow, of a certain weight, malleable, fusible, and fixed. But the real essence is the constitution of the insensible parts of that body, on which those qualities, and all the other properties of gold depend. How far these two are different, though they are both called essence, is obvious at first sight to discover.[1]

It is true, I have often mentioned a real essence, distinct in substances from those abstract ideas of them, which I call their nominal essence. By this real essence I mean the real constitution of any thing, which is the foundation of all those properties that are combined in, and are constantly found to co-exist with the nominal essence; that particular constitution which every thing has within itself, without any relation to any thing without it. But essence, even in this sense, relates to a sort, and supposes a species; for being that real constitution, on which the properties depend, it necessarily supposes a sort of things, properties belonging only to species, and not to individuals; v. g. supposing the nominal essence of gold to be a body of such a peculiar colour and weight, with malleability and fusibility, the real essence is that constitution of the parts of matter, on which these qualities and their union depend: and is also the foundation of its solubility in aqua regia and other properties accompanying that complex idea. Here are essences and properties, but all upon supposition of a sort, or general abstract idea, which is considered as immutable; but there is no individual parcel of matter, to which any of these qualities are so annexed, as to be essential to it, or inseparable from it. That which is essential belongs to it as a condition, whereby it is of this or that sort; but take away the consideration of its being ranked under the name of some abstract idea, and then there is nothing necessary to it, nothing inseparable from it. Indeed, as to the real essences of substances, we only suppose their being, without precisely knowing what they are: but

[1] Locke further discusses the value of the nominal essence for making classifications of objects. Cf. p. 343.

that which annexes them still to the species, is the nominal essence, of which they are the supposed foundation and cause.

Nor indeed can we rank and sort things, and consequently (which is the end of sorting) denominate them by their real essences, because we know them not. Our faculties carry us no farther towards the knowledge and distinction of substances, than a collection of those sensible ideas which we observe in them; which, however made with the greatest diligence and exactness we are capable of, yet is more remote from the true internal constitution, from which those qualities flow, than, as I said, a countryman's idea is from the inward contrivance of that famous clock at Strasburgh, whereof he only sees the outward figure and motions. There is not so contemptible a plant or animal, that does not confound the most enlarged understanding. Though the familiar use of things about us take off our wonder; yet it cures not our ignorance. When we come to examine the stones we tread on, or the iron we daily handle, we presently find we know not their make, and can give no reason of the different qualities we find in them. It is evident the internal constitution, whereon their properties depend, is unknown to us. For to go no farther than the grossest and most obvious we can imagine amongst them, what is that texture of parts, that real essence, that makes lead and antimony fusible; wood and stones not? What makes lead and iron malleable, antimony and stones not? And yet how infinitely these come short of the fine contrivances, and unconceivable real essences of plants or animals, every one knows. The workmanship of the all-wise and powerful God, in the great fabric of the universe, and every part thereof, farther exceeds the capacity and comprehension of the most inquisitive and intelligent man, than the best contrivance of the most ingenious man doth the conceptions of the most ignorant of rational creatures. Therefore we in vain pretend to range things into sorts, and dispose them into certain classes, under names, by their real essences, that are so far from our discovery or comprehension. A blind man may as soon sort things by their colours, and he that has lost his smell, as well distinguish a lily and a rose by their odours, as by those internal constitutions which he knows not. He that thinks he can distinguish sheep and goats by their real essences, that are unknown to him, may be pleased to try his skill in those species, called cassiowary and querechinchio; and by their internal real essences determine the boundaries of those species, without knowing the complex idea of sensible qualities, that each of those names stands for, in the countries where those animals are to be found.

Those therefore who have been taught, that the several species of substances had their distinct internal substantial forms; and that it was those forms which made the distinction of substances into their true species and genera; were led yet farther out of the way, by having their minds set upon fruitless inquiries after substantial forms, wholly unintelligible, and whereof we have scarce so much as any obscure or confused conception in general.

That our ranking and distinguishing natural substances into species, consists in the nominal essences the mind makes, and not in the real essences to be found in the things themselves, is farther evident from our ideas of spirits. For the mind getting, only by reflecting on its own operations, those simple ideas which it attributes to spirits, it hath, or can have no other notion of spirit, but by attributing all those operations, it finds in itself, to a sort of beings, without consideration of matter. And even the most advanced notion we have of God is but attributing the same simple ideas which we have got from reflection on what we find in ourselves, and which we conceive to have more perfection in them, than would be in their absence; attributing, I say, those simple ideas to him in an unlimited degree. Thus having got, from reflecting on ourselves, the idea of existence, knowledge, power, and pleasure, each of which we find it better to have than to want; and the more we have of each, the better: joining all these together, with infinity to each of them, we have the complex idea of an eternal, omniscient, omnipotent, infinitely wise and happy Being. And though we are told, that there are different species of angels; yet we know not how to frame distinct specific ideas of them; not out of any conceit that the existence of more species than one of spirits is impossible, but because having no more simple ideas (nor being able to frame more) applicable to such beings, but only those few taken from ourselves, and from the actions of our own minds in thinking, and being delighted, and moving several parts of our bodies, we can no otherwise distinguish in our conceptions the several species of spirits one from another, but by attributing those operations and powers, we find in ourselves, to them in a higher or lower degree; and so have no very distinct specific ideas of spirits, except only of God, to whom we attribute both duration, and all those other ideas with infinity; to the other spirits, with limitation. Nor as I humbly conceive do we, between God and them in our ideas, put any difference by any number of simple ideas, which we have of one, and not of the other, but only that of infinity. All the particular ideas of existence, knowledge, will, power, and motion, &c. being ideas derived from the operations of our minds, we attribute all of them to all sorts of spirits, with the difference only of degrees, to the utmost we can imagine, even infinity, when we would frame, as well as we can, an idea of the first being; who yet, it is certain, is infinitely more remote, in the real excellency of his nature, from the highest and perfectest of all created beings, than the greatest man, nay purest seraph, is from the most contemptible part of matter; and consequently must infinitely exceed what our narrow understandings can conceive of him.

It is not impossible to conceive, nor repugnant to reason, that there may be many species of spirits, as much separated and diversified one from another by distinct properties whereof we have no ideas, as the species of sensible things are distinguished one from another by qualities which we know, and observe in them. That there should be more species of intelligent creatures above us, than there are of sensible and material below us, is probable to me from hence; that in all the visible corporeal world, we see no chasms or gaps. All quite down from us the descent is by easy steps, and a continued series of things, that in each remove differ very little one from the other. There are fishes that have wings, and are not strangers to the airy region; and there are some birds that are inhabitants of the water, whose blood is cold as fishes, and their flesh so like in taste, that the scrupulous are allowed them on fish-days. There are animals so near of kin both to birds and beasts, that they are in the middle between both: amphibious animals link the terrestrial and aquatic together; seals live at land and sea, and porpoises have the warm blood and entrails of a hog, not to mention what is confidently reported of mermaids or sea-men. There are some brutes, that seem to have as much knowledge and reason, as some that are called men; and the animal and vegetable kingdoms are so nearly joined, that if you will take the lowest of one, and the highest of the other, there will scarce be perceived any great difference between them; and so on, till we come to the lowest and the most inorganical parts of matter, we shall find everywhere, that the several species are linked together, and differ but in almost insensible degrees. And when we consider the infinite power and wisdom of the Maker, we have reason to think, that it is suitable to the magnificent harmony of the universe, and the great design and infinite goodness of the architect, that the species of creatures should also, by gentle degrees, ascend upward from us toward his infinite perfection, as we see they gradually descend from us downwards: which if it be probable, we have reason then to be persuaded, that there are far more species of creatures above us, than there are beneath: we being, in degrees of perfection, much more remote from the infinite being of God, than we are from the lowest state of being, and that which approaches nearest to nothing. And yet of all those distinct species, for the reasons abovesaid, we have no clear distinct ideas.

But to return to the species of corporeal substances. If I should ask any one, whether ice and water were two distinct species of things, I doubt not but I should be answered in the affirmative: and it cannot be denied, but he that says they are two distinct species is in the right. But if an Englishman, bred in Jamaica, who perhaps had never seen nor heard of ice, coming into England in the winter, find the water, he put in his basin at night, in a great part frozen in the morning, and not knowing any peculiar name it had, should call it hardened water; I ask, whether this would be a new species to him different from water? And, I think, it would be answered here, it would not be to him a new species, no more than congealed jelly, when it is cold, is a distinct species from the same jelly fluid and warm; or than liquid gold, in the furnace, is a distinct species from hard gold in the hands of a workman. And if this be so, it is plain, that our distinct species are nothing but distinct complex ideas, with distinct names annexed to them.

By all which it is clear, that our distinguishing substances into species by names, is not at all founded on their real essences; nor can we pretend to range and determine them exactly into species, according to internal essential differences.[1]

But though these nominal essences of substances are made by the mind, they are not yet made so arbitrarily as those of mixed modes. To the making of any nomi nal essence, it is necessary, First, that the ideas whereof it consists have such an union as to make but one idea, how compounded soever. Secondly, that the particular idea so united be exactly the same, neither more nor less. For if two abstract complex ideas differ either in number or sorts of their component parts, they make two different, and not one and the same essence. In the first of these, the mind, in making its complex ideas of substances, only follows nature; and puts none together, which are not supposed to have an union in nature. Nobody joins the voice of a sheep with the shape of a horse; nor the colour of lead, with the weight and fixedness of gold; to be the complex ideas of any real substances: unless he has a mind to fill his head with chimeras, and his discourse with unintelligible words. Men observing certain qualities always joined and existing together, therein copied nature; and of ideas so united, made their complex ones of substances. For though men may make what complex ideas they please,

[1] For Locke's defence of this point against the attacks of his critics, cf. p. 345.

and give what names to them they will: yet if they will be understood, when they speak of things really existing, they must in some degree conform their ideas to the things they would speak of: or else men's language will be like that of Babel; and every man's words being intelligible only to himself, would no longer serve to conversation, and the ordinary affairs of life, if the ideas they stand for be not some way answering the common appearances and agreement of substances, as they really exist.

The more, indeed, of these co-existing qualities we unite into one complex idea, under one name, the more precise and determinate we make the signification of that word; but never yet make it thereby more capable of universal certainty, in respect of other qualities not contained in our complex idea; since we perceive not their connexion or dependence on one another, being ignorant both of that real constitution in which they are all founded, and also how they flow from it. For the chief part of our knowledge concerning substances is not, as in other things, barely of the relation of two ideas that may exist separately; but is of the necessary connexion and co-existence of several distinct ideas in the same subject, or of their repugnancy so to co-exist. Could we begin at the other end, and discover what it was, wherein that colour consisted, what made a body lighter or heavier, what texture of parts made it malleable, fusible, and fixed, and fit to be dissolved in this sort of liquor, and not in another; if (I say) we had such an idea as this of bodies, and could perceive wherein all sensible qualities originally consist, and how they are produced; we might frame such ideas of them, as would furnish us with matter of more general knowledge, and enable us to make universal propositions, that should carry general truth and certainty with them. But whilst our complex ideas of the sorts of substances are so remote from that internal real constitution, on which their sensible qualities depend, and are made up of nothing but an imperfect collection of those apparent qualities our senses can discover; there can be few general propositions concerning substances, of whose real truth we can be certainly assured: since there are but few simple ideas, of whose connexion and necessary co-existence we can have certain and undoubted knowledge. I imagine, amongst all the secondary qualities of substances, and the powers relating to them, there cannot any two be named, whose necessary co-existence, or repugnance to co-exist, can certainly be known, unless in those of the same sense, which necessarily exclude one another, as I have elsewhere showed. No one, I think, by the colour that is in any body, can certainly know what smell, taste, sound, or tangible qualities it has, nor what alterations it is capable to make or receive, on or from other bodies. The same may be said of the sound or taste, &c. Our specific names of substances standing for any collections of such ideas, it is not to be wondered, that we can with them make very few general propositions of undoubted real certainty. But yet so far as any complex idea, of any sort of substances, contains in it any simple idea, whose necessary co-existence with any other may be discovered, so far universal propositions may with certainty be made concerning it: v. g. could any one discover a necessary connexion between malleableness, and the colour or weight of gold, or any other part of the complex idea signified by that name, he might make a certain universal proposition concerning gold in this respect; and the real truth of this proposition, "that all gold is malleable," would be as certain as of this, "the three angles of all right-lined triangles are all equal to two right ones."

Had we such ideas of substances as to know what real constitutions produce those sensible qualities we find in them, and how those qualities flowed from thence, we could, by the specific ideas of their real essences in our own minds, more certainly find out their properties, and discover what qualities they had or had not, than we can now by our senses: and to know the properties of gold, it would be no more necessary that gold should exist, and that we should make experiments upon it, than it is necessary for the knowing the properties of a triangle, that a triangle should exist in any matter; the idea in our minds would serve for the one as well as the other. But we are so far from being admitted into the secrets of nature, that we scarce so much as ever approach the first entrance towards them.

In our search after the knowledge of substances, the bare contemplation of their abstract ideas will carry us but a very little way in the search of truth and certainty. What then are we to do for the improvement of our knowledge in substantial beings? The want of ideas of their real essences, sends us from our own thoughts to the things themselves, as they exist.[1] Experience here must teach me what reason cannot; and it is by trying alone, that I can certainly know, what other qualities co-exist with those of my complex idea, v. g. whether that yellow, heavy, fusible body, I call gold, be malleable, or no. Our reasonings from these ideas will carry us but a little way in the certain discovery of the other properties in those masses of matter wherein all these are to be found. Because the other properties of such bodies, depending not on these, but on that unknown real essence, on which these also depend, we cannot by them discover the rest; we can go no

[1] For a concrete instance of going "from our own thoughts to the things themselves," cf. p. 347.

farther than the simple ideas of our nominal essence will carry us, which is very little beyond themselves; and so afford us but very sparingly any certain, universal, and useful truths. For upon trial having found that particular piece (and all others of that colour, weight, and fusibility, that I ever tried) malleable, that also makes now perhaps a part of my complex idea, part of my nominal essence of gold: whereby though I make my complex idea, to which I affix the name gold, to consist of more simple ideas than before; yet still it not containing the real essence of any species of bodies, it helps me not certainly to know (I say to know, perhaps it may to conjecture) the other remaining properties of that body, farther than they have a visible connexion with some or all of the simple ideas, that make up my nominal essence. For example, I cannot be certain from this complex idea, whether gold be fixed, or no; because, as before, there is no necessary connexion or inconsistence to be discovered betwixt a complex idea of a body yellow, heavy, fusible, malleable; betwixt these, I say, and fixedness; so that I may certainly know, that in whatsoever body these are found, there fixedness is sure to be. Here again for assurance, I must apply myself to experience; as far as that reaches, I may have certain knowledge, but no farther.

I deny not, but a man, accustomed to rational and regular experiments, shall be able to see farther into the nature of bodies, and guess righter at their yet unknown properties, than one that is a stranger to them: but yet, as I have said, this is but judgment and opinion, not knowledge and certainty. This way of getting and improving our knowledge in substances only by experience and history, which is all that the weakness of our faculties in this state of mediocrity, which we are in in this world, can attain to; makes me suspect, that natural philosophy is not capable of being made a science. We are able, I imagine, to reach very little general knowledge concerning the species of bodies, and their several properties. Experiments and historical observations we may have, from which we may draw advantages of ease and health, and thereby increase our stock of conveniences for this life; but beyond this I fear our talents reach not, nor are our faculties, as I guess, able to advance.

From whence it is obvious to conclude, that since our faculties are not fitted to penetrate into the internal fabric and real essences of bodies; but yet plainly discover to us the being of a God, and the knowledge of ourselves, enough to lead us into a full and clear discovery of our duty and great concernment; it will become us, as rational creatures, to employ those faculties we have about what they are most adapted to, and follow the direction of nature, where it seems to point us out the way. For it is rational to conclude that our proper employment lies in those inquiries, and in that sort of knowledge which is most suited to our natural capacities, and carries in it our greatest interest, i. e. the condition of our eternal estate. Hence I think I may conclude, that morality is the proper science and business of mankind in general; (who are both concerned, and fitted to search out their *summum bonum*) as several arts, conversant about several parts of nature, are the lot and private talent of particular men, for the common use of human life, and their own particular subsistence in this world.

I would not therefore be thought to disesteem, or dissuade the study of nature. I readily agree the contemplation of his works gives us occasion to admire, revere, and glorify their Author: and, if rightly directed, may be of greater benefit to mankind, than the monuments of exemplary charity, that have at so great charge been raised by the founders of hospitals and alms-houses. He that first invented printing, discovered the use of the compass, or made public the virtue and right use of quinine, did more for the propagation of knowledge, for the supply and increase of useful commodities, and saved more from the grave, than those who built colleges, work-houses, and hospitals. All that I would say, is, that we should not be too forwardly possessed with the opinion, or expectation of knowledge, where it is not to be had; or by ways that will not attain to it: that we should not take doubtful systems for complete sciences, nor unintelligible notions for scientifical demonstrations. In the knowledge of bodies, we must be content to glean what we can from particular experiments; since we cannot, from a discovery of their real essences, grasp at a time whole sheaves, and in bundles comprehend the nature and properties of whole species together. Where our inquiry is concerning co-existence, or repugnancy to co-exist, which by contemplation of our ideas we cannot discover; there experience, observation, and natural history must give us by our senses, and by retail, an insight into corporeal substances. The knowledge of bodies we must get by our senses, warily employed in taking notice of their qualities and operations on one another: and what we hope to know of separate spirits in this world, we must, I think, expect only from revelation. He that shall consider how little general maxims, precarious principles, and hypotheses laid down at pleasure, have promoted true knowledge, or helped to satisfy the inquiries of rational men after real improvements; how little, I say, the setting out at that end has, for many ages together, advanced men's progress towards the knowledge of natural philosophy; will think we have reason to thank those, who in this latter age have taken another course, and have trod out to us, though not an easier way to learned ignorance, yet a surer way to profitable knowledge.

Not that we may not, to explain any phænomena of nature, make use of any probable hypothesis whatsoever: hypotheses, if they are well made, are at least great helps to the memory, and often direct us to new discoveries. But my meaning is, that we should not take up any one too hastily (which the mind, that would always penetrate into the causes of things, and have principles to rest on, is very apt to do) till we have very well examined particulars, and made several experiments, in that thing which we would explain by our hypothesis, and see whether it will agree to them all; whether our principles will carry us quite through, and not be as inconsistent with one phænomenon of nature, as they seem to accommodate and explain another. And at least that we take care, that the name of principles deceive us not, nor impose on us, by making us receive that for an unquestionable truth, which is really at best but a very doubtful conjecture, such as are most (I had almost said all) of the hypotheses in natural philosophy.

But whether natural philosophy be capable of certainty or no, the ways to enlarge our knowledge, as far as we are capable, seem to me, in short, to be these two:

First, the first is to get and settle in our minds determined ideas of those things, whereof we have general or specific names; at least so many of them as we would consider and improve our knowledge in, or reason about.

Secondly, the other is the art of finding out those intermediate ideas, which may show us the agreement or repugnancy of our ideas, which cannot be immediately compared.

JUDGMENT AND PROBABILITY

THE understanding faculties being given to man, not barely for speculation, but also for the conduct of his life, man would be at a great loss, if he had nothing to direct him but what has the certainty of true knowledge. For that being very short and scanty, as we have seen, he would be often utterly in the dark, and in most of the actions of his life, perfectly at a stand, had he nothing to guide him in the absence of clear and certain knowledge. He that will not eat, till he has demonstration that it will nourish him; he that will not stir, till he infallibly knows the business he goes about will succeed; will have little else to do, but to sit still and perish.

Therefore as God has set some things in broad daylight; as he has given us some certain knowledge, though limited to a few things in comparison, probably, as a taste of what intellectual creatures are capable of, to excite in us a desire and endeavour after a better state: so in the greatest part of our concernments he has afforded us only the twilight, as I may so say, of probability; suitable, I presume, to that state of mediocrity and probationership, he has been pleased to place us in here; wherein, to check our over-confidence and presumption, we might by every day's experience be made sensible of our short-sightedness and liableness to errour; the sense whereof might be a constant admonition to us, to spend the days of this our pilgrimage with industry and care, in the search and following of that way, which might lead us to a state of greater perfection:

it being highly rational to think, even were revelation silent in the case, that as men employ those talents God has given them here, they shall accordingly receive their rewards at the close of the day, when their sun shall set, and night shall put an end to their labours.

The faculty which God has given man to supply the want of clear and certain knowledge, in cases where that cannot be had, is judgment: whereby the mind takes its ideas to agree or disagree; or which is the same, any proposition to be true or false, without perceiving a demonstrative evidence in the proofs. The mind sometimes exercises this judgment out of necessity, where demonstrative proofs and certain knowledge are not to be had; and sometimes out of laziness, unskilfulness, or haste, even where demonstrative and certain proofs are to be had. Men often stay not warily to examine the agreement or disagreement of two ideas, which they are desirous or concerned to know; but either incapable of such attention as is requisite in a long train of gradations, or impatient of delay, lightly cast their eyes on, or wholly pass by the proofs; and so without making out the demonstration, determine of the agreement or disagreement of two ideas, as it were by a view of them as they are at a distance, and take it be the one or the other, as seems most likely to them upon such a loose survey. This faculty of the mind, when it is exercised immediately about things, is called judgment: when about truths delivered in words, is most commonly called assent or dissent: which being the most usual way, wherein the mind has occasion to employ this faculty, I shall under these terms treat of it, as least liable in our language to equivocation.

Thus the mind has two faculties, conversant about truth and falsehood.

First, knowledge, whereby it certainly perceives, and

is undoubtedly satisfied of the agreement or disagreement of any ideas.

Secondly, judgment, which is the putting ideas together, or separating them from one another in the mind, when their certain agreement or disagreement is not perceived, but presumed to be so; which is, as the word imports, taken to be so before it certainly appears. And if it so unites, or separates them, as in reality things are, it is right judgment.

As demonstration is the showing the agreement or disagreement of two ideas, by the intervention of one or more proofs, which have a constant, immutable, and visible connexion one with another; so probability is nothing but the appearance of such an agreement or disagreement, by the intervention of proofs, whose connexion is not constant and immutable, or at least is not perceived to be so, but is, or appears for the most part to be so, and is enough to induce the mind to judge the proposition to be true or false, rather than the contrary.

Our knowledge, as has been shown, being very narrow, and we not happy enough to find certain truth in every thing which we have occasion to consider; most of the propositions we think, reason, discourse, nay act upon, are such, as we cannot have undoubted knowledge of their truth; yet some of them border so near upon certainty, that we make no doubt at all about them; but assent to them as firmly, and act, according to that assent, as resolutely, as if they were infallibly demonstrated, and that our knowledge of them was perfect and certain. But there being degrees herein from the very neighbourhood of certainty and demonstration, quite down to improbability and unlikeness, even to the confines of impossibility; and also degrees of assent from full assurance and confidence, quite down to conjecture, doubt, and distrust: I shall come now, (having, as I think, found out the bounds of human knowledge and certainty) in the next place, to consider the several degrees and grounds of probability, and assent or faith.

Probability is likeliness to be true, the very notation of the word signifying such a proposition, for which there be arguments or proofs, to make it pass or be received for true. The entertainment the mind gives this sort of propositions, is called belief, assent, or opinion, which is the admitting or receiving any proposition for true, upon arguments or proofs that are found to persuade us to receive it as true, without certain knowledge that it is so. And herein lies the difference between probability and certainty, faith and knowledge, that in all the parts of knowledge there is intuition; each immediate idea, each step has its visible and certain connexion; in belief, not so. That which makes me believe is something extraneous to the thing I believe; something not evidently joined on both sides to, and so not manifestly showing the agreement or disagreement of those ideas that are under consideration.

Probability then, being to supply the defect of our knowledge, and to guide us where that fails, is always conversant about propositions, whereof we have no certainty, but only some inducements to receive them for true. The grounds of it are, in short, these two following.

First, the conformity of any thing with our own knowledge, observation, and experience.

Secondly, the testimony of others, vouching their observation and experience. In the testimony of others, is to be considered, 1. The number. 2. The integrity. 3. The skill of the witnesses. 4. The design of the author, where it is a testimony out of a book cited. 5. The consistency of the parts, and circumstances of the relation. 6. Contrary testimonies.

The propositions we receive upon inducements of probability, are of two sorts; either concerning some particular existence, or, as it is usually termed, matter of fact, which falling under observation, is capable of human testimony; or else concerning things, which being beyond the discovery of our senses, are not capable of any such testimony.

Concerning the first of these, viz. particular matter of fact.

First, where any particular thing, consonant to the constant observation of ourselves and others in the like case, comes attested by the concurrent reports of all that mention it, we receive it as easily, and build as firmly upon it, as if it were certain knowledge: and we reason and act thereupon with as little doubt, as if it were perfect demonstration. Thus, if all Englishmen who have occasion to mention it, should affirm that it froze in England the last winter, or that there were swallows seen there in the summer; I think a man could almost as little doubt of it, as that seven and four are eleven. The first therefore, and highest degree of probability, is, when the general consent of all men, in all ages, as far as it can be known, concurs with a man's constant and never failing experience in like cases, to confirm the truth of any particular matter of fact attested by fair witnesses; such are all the stated constitutions and properties of bodies, and the regular proceedings of causes and effects in the ordinary course of nature. This we call an argument from the nature of things themselves. For what our own and other men's constant observation has found always to be after the same manner, that we with reason conclude to be the effect of steady and regular causes, though they came not within the reach of our knowledge. Thus, that fire warmed a man, made lead fluid, and changed the colour or consistency in wood or charcoal; that iron sunk in water, and swam in quicksilver: these and the like propositions about particular facts, being agreeable to our constant experience, as often as we have to do with these matters: and being generally spoke of (when mentioned by others) as things found constantly to be so, and therefore not so much as controverted by any body; we are put past doubt, that a relation affirming any such thing to have been, or any predication that it will happen again in the same manner, is very true. These probabilities rise so near to a certainty, that they govern our thoughts as absolutely, and influence all our actions as fully, as the most evident demonstration; and in what concerns us, we make little or no difference between them and certain knowledge. Our belief, thus grounded, rises to assurance.

Secondly, the next degree of probability is, when I find by my own experience, and the agreement of all others that mention it, a thing to be, for the most part, so; and that the particular instance of it is attested by many and undoubted witnesses, v. g. history giving us such an account of men in all ages; and my own experience, as far as I had an opportunity to observe, confirming it, that most men prefer their private advantage to the public: if all historians that write of Tiberius say that Tiberius did so, it is extremely probable. And in this case, our assent has a sufficient foundation to raise itself to a degree which we may call confidence.

Thirdly, in things that happen indifferently, as that a bird should fly this or that way; that it should thunder on a man's right or left hand, &c. when any particular matter of fact is vouched by the concurrent testimony of unsuspected witnesses, there our assent is also unavoidable. Thus, that there is such a city in Italy as Rome; that, about one thousand seven hundred years ago, there lived in it a man, called Julius Cæsar; that he was a general, and that he won a battle against another, called Pompey: this, though in the nature of the thing there be nothing for nor against it, yet being related by historians of credit, and contradicted by no one writer, a man cannot avoid believing it, and can as little doubt of it, as he does of the being and actions of his own acquaintance, whereof he himself is a witness.

Thus far the matter goes easy enough. Probability upon such grounds carries so much evidence with it, that it naturally determines the judgment, and leaves us as little liberty to believe, or disbelieve, as a demonstration does, whether we will know, or be ignorant. The difficulty is, when testimonies contradict common experience, and the reports of history and witnesses clash with the ordinary course of nature, or with one another; there it is, where diligence, attention, and exactness are required, to form a right judgment, and to proportion the assent to the different evidence and probability of the thing; which rises and falls, according as those two foundations of credibility, viz. common observation in like cases, and particular testimonies in that particular instance, favour or contradict it. These are liable to so great variety of contrary observations, circumstances, reports, different qualifications, tempers, designs, oversights, &c. of the reporters, that it is impossible to reduce to precise rules the various degrees wherein men give their assent. This only may be said in general, that as the arguments and proofs pro and con, upon due examination, nicely weighing every particular circumstance, shall to any one appear, upon the whole matter, in a greater or less degree, to preponderate on either side; so they are fitted to produce in the mind such different entertainment, as we call belief, conjecture, guess, doubt, wavering, distrust, disbelief, &c.

The probabilities we have hitherto mentioned are only such as concern matter of fact, and such things as are capable of observation and testimony. There remains that other sort, concerning which men entertain opinions with variety of assent, though the things be such, that, falling not under the reach of our senses, they are not capable of testimony. Such are, 1. The existence, nature, and operations of finite immaterial beings without us; as spirits, angels, devils, &c. or the existence of material beings; which either for their smallness in themselves, or remoteness from us, our senses cannot take notice of; as whether there be any plants, animals, and intelligent inhabitants in the planets, and other mansions of the vast universe. 2. Concerning the manner of operation in most parts of the works of nature: wherein though we see the sensible effects, yet their causes are unknown, and we perceive not the ways and manner how they are produced. We see animals are generated, nourished, and move; the loadstone draws iron; and the parts of a candle, successively melting, turn into flame, and give us both light and heat. These and the like effects we see and know: but the causes that operate, and the manner they are produced in, we can only guess and probably conjecture. For these and the like, coming not within the scrutiny of human senses, cannot be examined by them, or be attested by any body; and therefore can appear more or less probable, only as they more or less agree to truths that are established in our minds, and as they hold proportion to other parts of our knowledge and observation. Analogy in these matters is the only help we have, and it is from that alone we draw all our grounds of probability. Thus observing that the bare rubbing of two bodies violently one upon another produces heat, and very often fire itself, we have reason to think, that what we call heat and fire consists in a violent agitation of the imperceptible minute parts of the burning matter: observing likewise that the different refractions of pellucid bodies produce in our eyes the different appearances of several colours; and also that the different ranging and laying the superficial parts of several bodies, as of velvet, watered silk, &c. does the like, we think it probable that the colour and shining of bodies is in them nothing but the different arrangement and refraction of their minute and insensible parts. Thus finding in all parts of the creation, that fall under human observation, that there is a gradual connexion of one with another, without any great or discernible gaps between, in all that great variety of things we see in the world, which are so closely linked together, that in the several ranks of beings, it is not easy to discover the bounds betwixt them; we have reason to be persuaded, that by such gentle steps things ascend upwards in degrees of perfection. It is a hard matter to say where sensible and rational begin, and where insensible and irrational end: and who is there quick-sighted enough to determine precisely, which is the lowest species of living things, and which the first of those which have no life? Things, as far as we can observe, lessen and augment, as the quantity does in a regular cone; where though there be a manifest odds betwixt the bigness of the diameter at a remote distance, yet the difference between the upper and under, where they touch one another, is hardly discernible. The difference is exceeding great between some men, and some animals; but if we will compare the understanding and abilities of some men and some brutes, we shall find so little difference, that it will be hard to say, that that of the man is either clearer or larger. Observing, I say, such gradual and gentle descents downwards in those parts of the creation that are beneath man, the rule of analogy may make it probable, that it is so also in things above us and our observation; and that there are several ranks of intelligent beings, excelling us in several degrees of perfection, ascending upwards towards the infinite perfection of the Creator, by gentle steps and differences, that are every one at no great distance from the next to it. This sort of probability, which is the best conduct of rational experiments, and the rise of hypothesis, has also its use and influence; and a wary reasoning from analogy leads us often into the discovery of truths and useful productions, which would otherwise lie concealed.

Though the common experience and the ordinary course of things have justly a mighty influence on the minds of men, to make them give or refuse credit to any thing proposed to their belief; yet there is one case, wherein the strangeness of the fact lessens not the assent to a fair testimony given of it. For where such supernatural events are suitable to ends aimed at by him, who has the power to change the course of nature, there, under such circumstances, they may be the fitter to procure belief, by how much the more they are beyond, or contrary to ordinary observation. This is the proper case of miracles, which well attested do not only find credit themselves, but give it also to other truths, which need such confirmation.

REASONING

THE word reason in the English language has different significations: sometimes it is taken for true and clear principles; sometimes for clear and fair deductions from those principles; and sometimes for the cause, and particularly the final cause. But the consideration I shall have of it here, is in a signification different from all these: and that is, as it stands for a faculty in man, that faculty whereby man is supposed to be distinguished from beasts, and wherein it is evident he much surpasses them.

If general knowledge, as has been shown, consists in a perception of the agreement or disagreement of our own idea; and the knowledge of the existence of all things without us (except only of a God, whose existence every man may certainly know and demonstrate to himself from his own existence) be had only by our senses: what room is there for the exercise of any other faculty, but outward sense and inward perception? What need is there of reason? Very much; both for the enlargement of our knowledge, and regulating our assent: for it hath to do both in knowledge and opinion, and is necessary and assisting to all our other intellectual faculties, and indeed contains two of them, viz. sagacity and illation. By the one, it finds out; and by the other, it so orders the intermediate ideas, as to discover what connexion there is in each link of the chain, whereby the extremes are held together; and thereby, as it were, to draw into view the truth sought for, which is that which we call illation or inference, and consists in nothing but the perception of the connexion there is between the ideas, in each step of the deduction, whereby the mind comes to see either the certain agreement or disagreement of any two ideas, as in demonstration, in which it arrives at knowledge; or their probable connexion, on which it gives or withholds its assent, as in opinion. Sense and intuition reach but a very little way. The greatest part of our knowledge depends upon deductions and intermediate ideas: and in those cases, where we are fain to substitute assent instead of knowledge, and take propositions for true, without being certain they are so, we have need to find out, examine, and compare the grounds of their probability. In both these cases, the faculty which finds out the means, and rightly applies them to discover certainty in the one, and probability in the other, is that which we call reason. For as reason perceives the necessary and indubitable connexion of all the ideas or proofs one to another, in each step of any demonstration that produces knowledge: so it likewise perceives the probable connexion of all the ideas or proofs one to another, in every step of a discourse, to which it will think assent due. This is the lowest degree of that which can be truly called reason. For where the mind does not perceive this probable connexion, where it does not discern whether there be any such connexion or no; there men's opinions are not the product of judgment, or the consequence of reason, but the effects of chance and hazard, of a mind floating at all adventures, without choice and without direction.

There is one thing more, which I shall desire to be considered concerning reason; and that is, whether syllogism, as is generally thought, be the proper instrument of it, and the usefullest way of exercising this faculty. The causes I have to doubt are these.

First, because syllogism serves our reason but in one only of the forementioned parts of it; and that is, to show the connexion of the proofs in any one instance, and no more; but in this it is of no great use, since the mind can conceive such connexion where it really is, as easily, nay perhaps better, without it. If we will observe the actings of our own minds, we shall find that we reason best and clearest, when we only observe the connexion of the proof, without reducing our thoughts to any rule of syllogism. And therefore we may take notice, that there are many men that reason exceeding clear and rightly, who know not how to make a syllogism. He that will look into many parts of Asia and America, will find men reason there perhaps as acutely as himself, who yet never heard of a syllogism, nor can reduce any one argument to those forms: and I believe scarce any one makes syllogisms in reasoning within himself.

But God has not been so sparing to men to make them barely two-legged creatures, and left it to Aristotle to make them rational, i. e. those few of them that he could get so to examine the grounds of syllogisms, as to see, that in above threescore ways, that three propositions may be laid together, there are but about fourteen, wherein one may be sure that the conclusion is right; and upon what grounds it is, that in these few the conclusion is certain, and in the other not. God has been more bountiful to mankind than so. He has given them a mind that can reason, without being instructed in methods of syllogizing: the understanding is not taught to reason by these rules; it has a native faculty to perceive the coherence or incoherence of its ideas, and can range them right, without any such perplexing repetitions.

Secondly, another reason that makes me doubt whether syllogism be the only proper instrument of reason in the discovery of truth, is, that of whatever use, mode and figure is pretended to be in the laying open of fallacy (which has been above considered) those scholastic forms of discourse are not less liable to fallacies than the plainer ways of argumentation: and for this I appeal to common observation, which has always found these artificial methods of reasoning more adapted to catch and entangle the mind, than to instruct and inform the understanding. And hence it is that men, even when they are baffled and silenced in this scholastic way, are seldom or never convinced, and so brought over to the conquering side: they perhaps acknowledge their adversary to be the more skilful disputant; but rest nevertheless persuaded of the truth on their side: and go away, worsted as they are, with the same opinion they brought with them, which they could not do, if this way of argumentation carried light and conviction with it, and made men see where the truth lay. And therefore syllogism has been thought more proper for the attaining victory in dispute, than for the discovery or confirmation of truth in fair inquiries. And if it be certain, that fallacies can be couched in syllogism, as it cannot be denied; it must be something else, and not syllogism, that must discover them.

The rules of syllogism serve not to furnish the mind with those intermediate ideas that may show the connexion of remote ones. This way of reasoning discovers no new proofs, but is the art of marshalling and ranging the old ones we have already. The forty-seventh proposition of the first book of Euclid is very true; but the discovery of it, I think, not owing to any rules of common logic. A man knows first, and then he is able to prove syllogistically. So that syllogism comes after knowledge, and then a man has little or no need of it. But it is chiefly by the finding out those ideas that show the connexion of distant ones, that our stock of knowledge is increased, and that useful arts and sciences are advanced. Syllogism at best is but the art of fencing with the little knowledge we have, without making any addition to it.

THE RELATION OF FAITH AND REASON

Besides those we have hitherto mentioned, there is one sort of propositions that challenge the highest degree of our assent upon bare testimony, whether the thing proposed agree or disagree with common experience, and the ordinary course of things, or no. The reason whereof is, because the testimony is of such an one, as cannot deceive, nor be deceived, and that is of God himself. This carries with it an assurance beyond doubt, evidence beyond exception. This is called by a peculiar name, *revelation;* and our assent to it, *faith:* which as absolutely determines our minds, and as perfectly excludes all wavering, as our knowledge itself; and we may as well doubt of our own being, as we can, whether any revelation from God be true. So that faith is a settled and sure principle of assent and assurance, and leaves no manner of room for doubt or hesitation. Only we must be sure, that it be a divine revelation, and that we understand it right: else we shall expose ourselves to all the extravagancy of enthusiasm, and all the errour of wrong principles, if we have faith and assurance in what is not divine revelation.

It has been above shown, 1. That we are of necessity ignorant, and want knowledge of all sorts, where we want ideas. 2. That we are ignorant, and want rational knowledge where we want proofs. 3. That we want certain knowledge and certainty, as far as we want clear and determined specific ideas. 4. That we want probability to direct our assent in matters where we have neither knowledge of our own, nor testimony of other men, to bottom our reason upon.

From these things thus premised, I think we may come to lay down the measures and boundaries between faith and reason; the want whereof may possibly have been the cause, if not of great disorders, yet at least of great disputes, and perhaps mistakes in the world. For till it be resolved, how far we are to be guided by reason, and how far by faith, we shall in vain dispute, and endeavour to convince one another in matters of religion.

However faith be opposed to reason, faith is nothing but a firm assent of the mind: which if it be regulated, as is our duty, cannot be afforded to any thing but upon good reason; and so cannot be opposite to it. He that believes, without having any reason for believing, may be in love with his own fancies; but neither seeks truth as he ought, nor pays the obedience due to his Maker, who would have him use those discerning faculties he has given him, to keep him out of mistake and errour. He that does not this to the best of his power, however he sometimes lights on truth, is in the right but by chance; and I know not whether the luckiness of the accident will excuse the irregularity of his proceeding. This at least is certain, that he must be accountable for whatever mistakes he runs into: whereas he that makes use of the light and faculties God has given him, and seeks sincerely to discover truth by those helps and abilities he has, may have this satisfaction in doing his duty as a rational creature, that, though he should miss truth, he will not miss the reward of it. For he governs his assent right, and places it as he should, who, in any case or matter whatsoever, believes or disbelieves, according as reason directs him. He that doth otherwise transgresses against his own light, and misuses those faculties which were given him to no other end, but to search and follow the clearer evidence and greater probability.

I find every sect, as far as reason will help them, make use of it gladly: and where it fails them, they cry out, it is matter of faith, and above reason. And I do not see how they can argue, with any one, or ever convince a gainsayer who makes use of the same plea, without setting down strict boundaries between faith and reason; which ought to be the first point established in all questions, where faith has any thing to do.

Reason therefore here, as contradistinguished to faith,

I take to be the discovery of the certainty or probability of such propositions or truths, which the mind arrives at by deduction made from such ideas, which it has got by the use of its natural faculties; viz. by sensation or reflection.

Faith, on the other side, is the assent to any proposition, not thus made out by the deductions of reason; but upon the credit of the proposer, as coming from God, in some extraordinary way of communication. This way of discovering truths to men we call revelation.

Whatsoever truth we come to the clear discovery of, from the knowledge and contemplation of our own ideas, will always be certainer to us, than those which are conveyed to us by traditional revelation. For the knowledge we have, that this revelation came at first from God, can never be so sure, as the knowledge we have from the clear and distinct perception of the agreement or disagreement of our own ideas; v. g. if it were revealed some ages since, that the three angles of a triangle were equal to two right ones, I might assent to the truth of that proposition, upon the credit of the tradition, that it was revealed; but that would never amount to so great a certainty, as the knowledge of it, upon the comparing and measuring my own ideas of two right angles, and the three angles of a triangle. The like holds in matter of fact, knowable by our senses; v. g. the history of the deluge is conveyed to us by writings, which had their original from revelation: and yet nobody, I think, will say he has as certain and clear a knowledge of the flood, as Noah that saw it; or that he himself would have had, had he then been alive and seen it. For he has no greater assurance than that of his senses, that it is writ in the book supposed writ by Moses inspired: but he has not so great an assurance that Moses writ that book, as if he had seen Moses write it. So that the assurance of its being a revelation is less still than the assurance of his senses.

In propositions then, whose certainty is built upon the clear perception of the agreement or disagreement of our ideas, attained either by immediate intuition, as in self-evident propositions, or by evident deductions of reason in demonstrations, we need not the assistance of revelation, as necessary to gain our assent, and introduce them into our minds. Because the natural ways of knowledge could settle them there, or had done it already; which is the greatest assurance we can possibly have of any thing, unless where God immediately reveals it to us: and there too our assurance can be no greater, than our knowledge is, that it is a revelation from God. But yet nothing, I think, can, under that title, shake or over-rule plain knowledge; or rationally prevail with any man to admit it for true, in a direct contradiction to the clear evidence of his own understanding. For since no evidence of our faculties, by which we receive such revelations, can exceed, if equal, the certainty of our intuitive knowledge, we can never receive for a truth any thing that is directly contrary to our clear and distinct knowledge: v. g. the ideas of one body, and one place, do so clearly agree, and the mind has so evident a perception of their agreement, that we can never assent to a proposition, that affirms the same body to be in two distant places at once, however it should pretend to the authority of a divine revelation: since the evidence, first, that we deceive not ourselves, in ascribing it to God; secondly, that we understand it right; can never be so great, as the evidence of our own intuitive knowledge, whereby we discern it impossible for the same body to be in two places at once. And therefore no proposition can be received for divine revelation, or obtain the assent due to all such, if it be contradictory to our clear intuitive knowledge. Because this would be to subvert the principles and foundations of all knowledge, evidence, and assent whatsoever: and there would be left no difference between truth and falsehood, no measures of credible and incredible in the world, if doubtful propositions shall take place before self-evident; and what we certainly know give way to what we may possibly be mistaken in. In propositions therefore contrary to the clear perception of the agreement or disagreement of any of our ideas, it will be in vain to urge them as matters of faith. They cannot move our assent, under that or any other title whatsoever. For faith can never convince us of any thing that contradicts our knowledge.

There being many things, wherein we have very imperfect notions, or none at all; and other things, of whose past, present, or future existence, by the natural use of our faculties, we can have no knowledge at all; these, as being beyond the discovery of our natural faculties, and above reason, are, when revealed, the proper matter of faith. Thus, that part of the angels rebelled against God, and thereby lost their first happy state; and that the dead shall rise, and live again; these and the like, being beyond the discovery of reason, are purely matters of faith; with which reason has directly nothing to do.

But since God in giving us the light of reason has not thereby tied up his own hands from affording us, when he thinks fit, the light of revelation in any of those matters, wherein our natural faculties are able to give a probable determination; revelation, where God has been pleased to give it, must carry it against the probable conjectures of reason. Because the mind not being certain of the truth of that it does not evidently know, but only yielding to the probability that appears in it, is bound to give up its assent to such a testimony; which, it is satisfied, comes from one who cannot err, and will not deceive. But yet it still belongs to reason to judge of the truth of its being a revelation, and of the signification of the words wherein it is delivered. Indeed, if any thing shall be thought revelation, which is contrary to the plain principles of reason, and the evident knowledge the mind has of its own clear and distinct ideas; there reason must be hearkened to, as to a matter within its province: since a man can never have so certain a knowledge, that a proposition which contradicts the clear principles and evidence of his own knowledge, was divinely revealed, or that he understands the words rightly wherein it is delivered; as he has, that the contrary is true: and so is bound to consider and judge of it as a matter of reason, and not swallow it, without examination, as a matter of faith.

Whatever God hath revealed is certainly true; no doubt can be made of it. This is the proper object of faith: but whether it be a divine revelation or no, reason must judge; which can never permit the mind to reject a greater evidence to embrace what is less evident, nor allow it to entertain probability in opposition to knowledge and certainty. There can be no evidence, that any traditional revelation is of divine original, in the words we receive it, and in the sense we understand it, so clear and so certain, as that of the principles of reason; and therefore nothing that is contrary to, and inconsistent with, the clear and self-evident dictates of reason, has a right to be urged or assented to as a matter of faith, wherein reason hath nothing to do.

Reason is natural revelation, whereby the Eternal Father of light, and Fountain of all knowledge, communicates to mankind that portion of truth which he has laid within the reach of their natural faculties:

revelation is natural reason enlarged by a new set of discoveries communicated by God immediately, which reason vouches the truth of, by the testimony and proofs it gives, that they come from God. So that he that takes away reason, to make way for revelation, puts out the light of both, and does much-what the same, as if he would persuade a man to put out his eyes, the better to receive the remote light of an invisible star by a telescope.

He therefore that will not give himself up to all the extravagancies of delusion and errour, must bring this guide of his light within to the trial. God, when he makes the prophet, does not unmake the man. He leaves all his faculties in the natural state, to enable him to judge of his inspirations, whether they be of divine original or no. When he illuminates the mind with supernatural light, he does not extinguish that which is natural. If he would have us assent to the truth of any proposition, he either evidences that truth by the usual methods of natural reason, or else makes it known to be a truth which he would have us assent to, by his authority; and convinces us that it is from him, by some marks which reason cannot be mistaken in. Reason must be our last judge and guide in everything.

LOCKE'S LETTERS AND CONTROVERSIAL WRITINGS
WHICH PROVIDE
AN EXPLANATION OF POINTS IN THE ESSAY

THE NATURE OF IDEAS

(Locke was accused by some of his contemporaries and by many of his critics in later years for dealing with the *origin of ideas* before making clear what the *nature of ideas* is. He seems to have failed to appreciate the point of criticism on this score. In reply to John Norris's remarks on his *Essay* he wrote as follows.)

I AM complained of for not having "given an account of or defined the nature of our ideas." By "giving an account of the nature of ideas" is not meant that I should make known to men their ideas; for I think nobody can imagine that any articulate sounds of mine, or anybody else, can make known to another what his ideas, that is, what his perceptions are, better than what he himself knows and perceives them to be; which is enough for affirmations or negations about them. By the "nature of ideas," therefore, is meant here their causes and manner of production in the mind, i.e. in what alteration of the mind this perception consists. And as to that, I answer, no man can tell; for which I not only appeal to experience, which were enough, but shall add this reason, viz. because no man can give any account of any alteration made in any simple substance whatsoever; all the alteration we can conceive being only of the alteration of compounded substances, and that only by a transposition of parts. For what difference a man finds in himself when he sees a marygold, and sees not a marygold, has no difficulty and needs not be inquired after: he has the idea now which he had not before.

Ideas may be real beings, though not substances, as motion is a real being, though not a substance. And it seems probable that in us ideas depend on and are some way or other the effect of motion, since they are so fleeting; it being, as I have elsewhere observed, so hard, and almost impossible, to keep in our minds the same unvaried ideas long together, unless when the object that produces it is present to the senses; from which the same motion that first produced it being continued, the idea itself may continue.

This therefore may be a sufficient excuse of the ignorance I have owned of what our ideas are, any farther than as they are perceptions we experiment in ourselves; and the dull unphilosophical way I have taken of examining their production, only so far as experience and observation lead me; wherein my dim sight went not beyond sensation and reflection.

THE FACULTY OF REASON

(Locke was attacked in his own day and frequently since for reducing reason to a mere succession of ideas. Such reduction was actually done later by some members of the British school of empiricism. But Locke never did so. Reason was for him a faculty which we possessed prior to and independently of experience. Reason could not, to be sure, generate knowledge out of itself, as rationalists sometimes supposed. Rather it needed material to work upon, and it obtained this material through the ideas which experience brought to it. But ideas were only the *materials* for reason, the *materials* which reason used to get knowledge. And the activity of reason upon these materials was as indispensable for knowledge as the presence of the materials. Perhaps it was the long discussion of the origin of ideas which led Locke's readers to suppose that he reduced reason to a mere succession of ideas. But the whole tone of the *Essay,* as well as the explicit description of knowledge in the later pages of the *Essay,* is hostile to such an interpretation. Reason must, in order to furnish us with knowledge, perceive the agreement or disagreement of our ideas. And the reason which so acts is not produced by the ideas, but is an activity expended upon the ideas. The following passages are taken from Locke's controversy with the Bishop of Worcester.)

I KNOW nobody that does not think that reason, or the faculty of reasoning, is distinct from the ideas it makes use of or is employed about.

Reason being a faculty of the mind, nothing, in my poor opinion, can properly be said to be necessary to that faculty, but what is required to its being. As nothing is necessary to sight in a man, but such a constitution of the body and organ, that a man may have the power of seeing, so I submit it to your lordship, whether anything can properly be said to be necessary to reason in a man, but such a constitution of body or mind or both, as may give him the power of reasoning. Indeed such a particular sort of objects or instruments may be sometimes said to be necessary to the eye, but it is never said in reference to the faculty of seeing, but in reference to some particular end of seeing; and then a microscope and a mite may be necessary to the eye, if the end proposed be to know the shape and parts of that animal. And so if a man would reason about substance, then the idea of substance is necessary to his reason; but yet I doubt not but that many a rational creature has been, who in all his life never bethought himself of any necessity his reason had of an idea of substance.

My new way by ideas, or my way by ideas, which often occurs in your lordship's letter, is, I confess, a very large and doubtful expression, and may, in the full latitude, comprehend my whole *Essay*. For treating in it of the understanding, which is nothing but the faculty of thinking, I could not well treat of that faculty of the mind which consists in thinking, without considering the immediate objects of the mind in thinking which I call ideas. And therefore in treating of the understanding, I guess it will not be thought strange that the greatest part of my book has been taken up in considering what these objects of the mind in thinking are, whence they come, what use the mind makes of them in its several ways of thinking, and what are the outward marks whereby it signifies them to others or records them for its own use. And this in short is my way by ideas, that which your lordship calls my new way by ideas; which, my lord, if it be new, it is but a new history of an old thing. For I think it will not be doubted that men always performed the actions of thinking, reasoning, believing, and knowing, just after the same manner that they do now; though whether the same account has heretofore been given of the way how they performed these actions, or wherein they consisted, I do not know.

Let reason, taken for principles of reason, be as different as it will from ideas, reason, taken as a faculty, is as different from them, in my apprehension. And in both senses of the word reason, either as taken for a faculty or for the principles of reason allowed by mankind, reason and ideas may consist together.

THE RELATION OF REASON AND IDEAS IN OBTAINING KNOWLEDGE

(Locke shows in the following paragraphs the relation of the faculty of reason to the ideas, both these being necessary if knowledge is to be obtained. Ideas constitute the materials without which reason has nothing to operate upon; and reason is the activity which so grasps the agreements and disagreements of ideas to each other as to formulate knowledge. These paragraphs throw light upon the passage in the *Essay* in which Locke speaks of "the materials of reason and knowledge." Cf. above, p. iii.)

THE thing signified by ideas is nothing but the immediate objects of our minds in thinking. Your lordship says that a certain knowledge is placed in good and sound reason, not in the idea. But it may be placed in ideas, and in good and sound reason too, i.e. in reason rightly managing those ideas so as to produce evidence by them. So that, my lord, I must own I see not the force of the argument which says 'not in ideas but in sound reason,' since I see no such opposition between them, but that ideas and sound reason may consist together. For instance, when a man would show the certainty of this truth, that the three angles of a triangle are equal to two right ones, the first thing probably that he does is to draw a diagram. What is the use of that diagram but steadily to suggest to his mind those several ideas he would make use of in that demonstration? The considering and laying these together in such order and with such connection as to make the agreement of the ideas of the three angles of the triangle with the ideas of two right ones to be perceived is called right reasoning, and the business of that faculty which we call reason, which when it operates rightly by considering and comparing ideas so as to produce certainty, this showing or demonstration that the thing is so, is called good and sound reason. The ground of this certainty lies in ideas themselves, and their agreement or disagreement, which reason neither does nor can alter, but only lays them so together as to make it perceivable. Without such a due consideration and ordering of the ideas, certainty could not be had. And thus certainty is placed both in ideas and in good and sound reason.

Nothing is truer than that it is not the idea that makes us certain without reason, or without the understanding. But it is as true that it is not reason, it is not the understanding, that makes us certain without ideas. It is not the sun makes me certain it is day, without my eyes, nor it is not my sight makes me certain it is day, without the sun; but the one employed about the other.

Nor is it one idea by itself that in this or any case makes us certain. But certainty consists in the perceived agreement or disagreement of all the ideas that serve to show the agreement or disagreement of distinct ideas, as they stand in the proposition whose truth or falsehood we would be certain of.

This, whether your lordship will call placing of certainty in the idea or placing the certainty in reason, whether your lordship will say it is not the idea that gives us the certainty but the argument, is indifferent to me. I shall not be so unmannerly as to prescribe the way you should speak, in this or any other matter. But this your lordship will give me leave to say, that let it be called how your lordship pleases, there is no contradiction in it to what I have said concerning certainty, or the way how we came by it, or the ground on which I place it.

Your lordship indeed here again seems to oppose reason and ideas. And to that I say that mere ideas are the objects of the understanding, and reason is one of the faculties of the understanding employed upon them; and that the understanding, or reason—whichever your lordship pleases to call it—makes or forms, out of the simple ones that come in by sensation and reflection, all the other ideas, whether general, relative, or complex, by abstracting, comparing, and compounding its positive simple ideas, whereof it cannot make or frame any one, but what it receives by sensation or reflection. And therefore I never denied that reason was employed about our particular simple ideas, to make out of them ideas general, relative, and complex; nor about all our ideas, whether simple, or complex, positive or relative, general or particular: it being the proper business of reason, in the search after truth and knowledge, to find out the relations between all these sorts of ideas, in the perception whereof knowledge and certainty of truth consists.

These, my lord, are, in short, my notions about ideas, their original and formation, and of the use the mind, or reason, makes of them in knowledge. Whether your lordship thinks fit to call this a new way of reasoning must be left to your lordship. Whether it be a right way is that alone which I am concerned for. But your lordship seems all along (I crave leave here once for all to take notice of it) to have some particular exception against ideas, and particularly clear and distinct ideas, as if they were not to be used or were of no use in reason and knowledge; or as if reason were opposed to them, or leads us into the knowledge and certainty of things without them; or the knowledge of things did not at all depend on them. I beg your lordship's pardon for expressing myself so variously and doubtfully in this matter. The reason whereof is because I must own that I do not everywhere clearly understand what your lordship means when you speak, as you do, of ideas, as if I ascribed more to them than belonged to them, or expected more of them than they could do.

I never said nor thought ideas, nor anything else, could bring us to the certainty of reason, without the exercise of reason. And I do not see but your lordship yourself and everybody else must make use of my way of ideas, unless they can find out a way that will bring them to certainty by thinking on nothing. So that let certainty be placed as much as it will on reason, let the nature of things belong as properly as it will to our reason, it will nevertheless be true that certainty consists in the perception of the agreement or disagreement of ideas, and that the complex idea the word nature stands for is ultimately made up of the simple ideas of sensation and reflection. I must own that I think certainty grounded on ideas. All the satisfaction men's minds can have in their inquiries after truth and certainty is to be had only from considering, observing, and rightly laying together of ideas, so as to find out their agreement or disagreement, and no other way. When you can prove that we can have a certainty by a consequence of reason, which certainty shall not also be by the immediate objects of the mind in using its reason, you may say such certainty is not by ideas but by consequence of reason. But that I believe will not be till you can show that the mind can think or reason or know without immediate objects of thinking, reasoning, or knowing, all which objects, as your lordship knows, I call ideas.

THE IDEA OF SUBSTANCE

(Locke was accused by the Bishop of Worcester of having "almost discarded substance out of the reasonable part of the world." Locke's insistence upon the unknowability of the real nature of substance was mistakenly taken to be a denial of the real existence of substance. Locke replied to the charge as follows.)

IF BY almost discarding substance out of the reasonable part of the world your lordship means that I have destroyed and almost discarded the true idea we have of it by calling it "a substratum, a supposition of we know not what support of such qualities as are capable of producing simple ideas in us; an obscure and relative idea; that without knowing what it is, it is that which supports accidents; so that of substance we have no idea of what it is, but only a confused and obscure one of what it does;" I must confess this, and the like I have said of our idea of substance, and should be very glad to be convinced by your lordship or any body else that I have spoken too meanly of it. He that would show me a more clear and distinct idea of substance would do me a kindness I should thank him for. But this is the best I can hitherto find, either in my own thoughts or in the books of logicians. For their account or idea of it is that it is *ens* or *res per se subsistens et substans accidentibus,* which in effect is no more but that substance is a being or thing, or in short something they know not what or of which they have no clearer idea than that it is something which supports accidents or other simple ideas or modes and is not supported itself as a mode or an accident.

But supposing, my lord, that I should own that we have a very imperfect, obscure, inadequate idea of substance. Would it not be a little too hard to charge us with discarding substance out of the world? For what "almost discarding" and "reasonable part of the world" signify, I must confess I do not clearly comprehend. But let "almost" and "reasonable part" signify here what they will, (for I dare say your lordship meant something by them,) would not your lordship think you were a little too hardly dealt with, if for acknowledging yourself to have a very imperfect and inadequate idea of God, or of several other things which, in this very treatise, you confess our understandings come short in and cannot comprehend, you should be accused to be one of these gentlemen that have almost discarded God, or those other mysterious things, whereof you contend we have very imperfect and inadequate ideas, out of the reasonable world? For I suppose your lordship means by "almost discarding out of the reasonable world" something that is blameable; for it seems not to be inserted for a commendation.

Your lordship's next words are to tell the world that my simile about the elephant and tortoise "is to ridicule the notion of substance and the European philosophers for asserting it." But if your lordship please to turn again to my *Essay,* you will find those passages were not intended to ridicule the notion of substance or those who asserted it; but to show that though substance did support accidents, yet philosophers, who had found such a support necessary, had no more a clear idea of what that support was, than the Indian had of that which supported his tortoise, though sure he was it was something. Had your pen, which quoted so much of the nineteenth section of the thirteenth chapter of my second book, but set down the remaining line and a half of that paragraph, you would by these words which follow there, "so that of substance we have no idea of what it is, but only a confused, obscure one of what it does," have put it past doubt what I meant.

THE IDEA OF CAUSATION

"Everything must have a cause" is not a true principle of reason, nor a true proposition, but the contrary. The certainty whereof we attain by the contemplation of our ideas, and by perceiving that the idea of eternity and the idea of the existence of something do agree; and the idea of existence from eternity and of having a cause do not agree or are inconsistent within the same thing. But "everything that has a beginning must have a cause" is a true principle of reason or a proposition certainly true; which we come to know by the same way, i.e. by contemplating our ideas and perceiving that the idea of beginning to be is necessarily connected with the idea of some operation; and the idea of operation with the idea of something operating which we call a cause. And so the beginning to be is perceived to agree with the idea of a cause, as is expressed in the proposition, and thus it comes to be a certain proposition, and so may be called a principle of reason, as every true proposition is to him that perceives the certainty of it.

THE ASSOCIATION OF IDEAS

(Locke treated the association of ideas in the *Essay,* and there regarded it as the cause of much erroneous thinking. A few years later he returned to the same topic in the forty-first chapter of *The Conduct of the Understanding.* The following passage is taken from the latter source.)

THOUGH I have, in the second book of my Essay concerning Human Understanding, treated of the association of ideas; yet having done it there historically, as giving a view of the understanding in this as well as its several other ways of operating, rather than designing there to inquire into the remedies that ought to be applied to it; it will, under this latter consideration, afford other matter of thought to those who have a mind to instruct themselves thoroughly in the right way of conducting their understandings; and that the rather, because this, if I mistake not, is as frequent a cause of mistake and errour in us, as perhaps any thing else that can be named; and is a disease of the mind as hard to be cured as any; it being a very hard thing to convince any one that things are not so, and naturally so, as they constantly appear to him.

By this one easy and unheeded miscarriage of the understanding, sandy and loose foundations become infallible principles, and will not suffer themselves to be touched or questioned; such unnatural connexions become by custom as natural to the mind as sun and light, fire and warmth go together, and so seem to carry with them as natural an evidence as self-evident truths themselves. And where then shall one with hopes of success begin the cure? Many men firmly embrace falsehood for truth; not only because they never thought otherwise; but also because, thus blinded as they have been from the beginning, they never could think otherwise; at least without a vigour of mind able to contest the empire of habit, and look into its own principles; a freedom which few men have the notion of in themselves, and fewer are allowed the practice of by others; it being the great art and business of the teachers and guides in most sects to suppress, as much as they can, this fundamental duty which every man owes himself, and is the first steady step towards right and truth in the whole train of his actions and opinions.

As to the ingenuous part of mankind, whose condition allows them leisure, and letters, and inquiry after truth; I can see no other right way of principling them, but to take heed, as much as may be, that in their tender years, ideas, that have no natural cohesion, come not to be united in their heads; and that this rule be often inculcated to them to be their guide in the whole course of their lives and studies, viz. that they never suffer any ideas to be joined in their understandings, in any other or stronger combination than what their own nature and correspondence give them; and that they often examine those that they find linked together in their minds; whether this association of ideas be from the visible agreement that is in the ideas themselves, or from the habitual and prevailing custom of the mind joining them thus together in thinking.

This is for caution against this evil, before it be thoroughly riveted by custom in the understanding; but he that would cure it when habit has established it, must nicely observe the very quick and almost imperceptible motions of the mind in its habitual actions. What I have said in another place about the change of the ideas of sense into those of judgment, may be proof of this.

Let any one not skilled in painting be told when he sees bottles and tobacco-pipes, and other things so painted, as they are in some places shown; that he does not see protuberances, and you will not convince him but by the touch: he will not believe that by an instantaneous legerdemain of his own thoughts, one idea is substituted for another. How frequent instances may one meet with of this in the arguings of the learned, who not seldom, in two ideas that they have been accustomed to join in their minds, substitute one for the other; and, I am apt to think, often without perceiving it themselves? This, whilst they are under the deceit of it, makes them incapable of conviction, and they applaud themselves as zealous champions for truth, when indeed they are contending for errour. And the confusion of two different ideas, which a customary connexion of them in their minds hath made to them almost one, fills their head with false views, and their reasonings with false consequences.

WHETHER MATTER CAN THINK

(Locke believed that thinking is carried on by the soul or thinking substance of which each man is intuitively aware in himself. But on theoretical grounds, as a deduction from his belief in the omnipotence of God, he also affirmed that God had the power to make matter think. The question is in Locke wholly hypothetical. For he never maintained that God had anywhere exercised this power which he attributed to God. But the question became important in later philosophical developments of Locke's thought. The following passages therefore derive their importance from the use to which in the next century Locke's thought was put.)

The idea of matter is an extended solid substance. Wherever there is such a substance, there is matter and the essence of matter, whatever other qualities not contained in that essence it shall please God to superadd to it. For example, God creates an extended solid substance, without the superadding anything else to it, and so we may consider it at rest. To some parts of it he superadds motion, but it has still the essence of matter. Other parts of it he frames into plants, with all the excellencies of vegetation, life, and beauty, which are to be found in a rose or a peach-tree, &c. above the essence of matter in general; but it is still matter. To other parts he adds sense and spontaneous motion, and those other properties that are to be found in an elephant. Hitherto it is not doubted but the power of God may go, and that the properties of a rose, a peach, or an elephant, superadded to matter, change not the properties of matter. But matter is in these things matter still. But if one venture to go on one step further and say, God may give to matter thought, reason, and volition, as well as sense and spontaneous motion, there are men ready presently to limit the power of the omnipotent creator and tell us he cannot do it, because it destroys the essence, "changes the essential properties of matter." To make good which assertion they have no more to say but that thought and reason are not included in the essence of matter. I grant it. But whatever excellency not contained in its essence be superadded to matter, it does not destroy the essence of matter if it leaves it an extended solid substance. Wherever that is, there is the essence of matter. And if everything of greater perfection, superadded to such a substance, destroys the essence of matter, what will become of the essence of matter in a plant or an animal whose properties far exceed those of a mere extended solid substance?

To keep within the present subject of the power of thinking and self-motion, bestowed by omnipotent power on some parts of matter, the objection to this is, I cannot conceive how matter should think. What is the consequence? *Ergo,* God cannot give it a power to think. Let this stand for a good reason, and then proceed in other cases by the same. You cannot conceive how matter can attract matter at any distance, much less at the distance of 1,000,000 miles; *ergo,* God cannot give it such a power. You cannot conceive how matter should feel or move itself, or affect an immaterial being or be moved by it; *ergo,* God cannot give it such powers: which is in effect to deny gravity and the revolution of the planets about the sun, to make brutes mere machines without sense of spontaneous motion, and to allow man neither sense nor voluntary motion.

Let us apply this rule one degree farther. You cannot conceive how an extended solid substance should think; therefore God cannot make it think. Can you conceive how your own soul or any substance thinks? You find indeed that you do think, and so do I; but I want to be told how the action of thinking is performed. This, I confess, is beyond my conception; and I would be glad any one who conceives it would explain it to me. God, I find, has given me this faculty; and since I cannot but be convinced of his power in this instance, (which, though I every moment experiment in myself, yet I cannot conceive the manner of,) what would it be less than an insolent absurdity to deny his power in other like cases only for this reason, because I cannot conceive the manner how?

To explain this matter a little farther. God has created a substance, let it be for example a solid extended substance. Is God bound to give it, besides being, a power of action? That, I think, nobody will say. He therefore may leave it in a state of inactivity, and it will be nevertheless a substance; for action is not necessary to the being of any substance that God does create. God has likewise created and made to exist, *de novo,* an immaterial substance which will not lose its being of a substance, though God should bestow on it nothing more but this bare being, without giving it any activity at all. Here are now two distinct substances, the one material, the other immaterial, both in a state of perfect inactivity. Now, I ask, what power God can give to one of these substances (supposing them to retain the same distinct natures, that they had as substances in their state of inactivity) which he cannot give to the other? In that state, it is plain, neither of them thinks; for thinking being an action, it cannot be denied that God can put an end to any action of any created substance without annihilating of the substance whereof it is an action. And if it be so, he can also create or give existence to such a substance without giving that substance any action at all. Now I would ask, why omnipotency cannot give to either of these substances, which are equally in a state of perfect inactivity, the same power that it can give to the other? Let it be, for example, that of spontaneous or self-motion, which is a power that it is supposed God can give to an unsolid substance, but denied that he can give to a solid substance.

If it be asked why they limit the omnipotency of God in reference to the one rather than the other of these substances, all that can be said to it is that they cannot conceive how the solid substance should ever be able to move itself. And as little, say I, are they able to conceive how a created unsolid substance should move itself. But there may be something in an immaterial substance that you do not know. I grant it; and in a material one too: for example, gravitation of matter towards matter, and in the several proportions observable, inevitably shows that there is something in matter that we do not understand unless we can conceive self-motion in matter, or an inexplicable and inconceivable attraction in matter, at immense and almost incomprehensible distances. It must therefore be confessed that there is something in solid as well as unsolid substances that we do not understand. But this we know, that they may each of them have their distinct beings without any activity superadded to them, unless you will deny that God can take from any being its power of acting, which it is probable will be thought too presumptuous for any one to do. And I say, it is as hard to conceive self-motion in a created immaterial as in a material being, consider it how you will. And therefore this is no reason to deny omnipotency to be able to give a power of self-motion to a material substance if he pleases, as well as to an immaterial; since neither of them can have it from themselves nor can we conceive how it can be in either of them.

The same is visible in the other operation of thinking. Both these substances may be made and exist without thought. Neither of them has or can have the power of thinking from itself. God may give it to either of them, according to the good pleasure of his omnipotency. And in whichever of them it is, it is equally beyond our capacity to conceive how either of those substances thinks. But for that reason, to deny that God, who had power enough to give them both a being out of nothing, can, by the same omnipotency, give them what other powers and perfections he pleases, has no better a foundation than to deny his power of creation, because we cannot conceive how it is performed. And there at last this way of reasoning must terminate.

THE OBJECTIVITY OF KNOWLEDGE

(Though Locke defined knowledge as perception of the agreements and disagreements of our ideas, he also maintained that the knowledge thus obtained has objective value. Knowledge is not mere fancy. Knowledge is what all informed men will alike consent to, when they have the necessary ideas. Men do not, to be sure, have the necessary ideas to give them knowledge of many matters of fact. But all men who are properly informed will hold to such necessary truths as those of mathematics.)

Universal reason, which enlightens every one, whereof all men partake, seems to me nothing else but the power men have to consider the ideas they have one with another, and, by this comparing them, find out the relations that are between them. And therefore if an intelligent being at one end of the world and another at the other end of the world will consider twice two and four together, he cannot but find them to be equal, i. e. to be the same number. These relations, it is true, are infinite, and God who knows all things and their relations as they are knows them all, and so his knowledge is infinite. But men are able to discover more or less of these relations, only as they apply their minds to consider any sort of ideas and to find out intermediate ones which can show the relation of those ideas which cannot be immediately compared by juxtaposition.

We cannot say God reasons at all; for he has at once a view of all things. But reason is very far from such an intuition. It is a laborious and gradual progress in the knowledge of things, by comparing one idea with a second, and a second with a third, and that with a fourth, &c. to find the relation between the first and the last of these in this train, and in search for such intermediate ideas, as may show us the relation we desire to know, which sometimes we find and sometimes not.

THE REALITY OF KNOWLEDGE

(Locke sought constantly to escape the subjectivistic and sceptical implications of his theory of knowledge. He was not very successful. The following passage is characteristic of the effort to maintain that the perception of the relation of ideas gave knowledge of the real relations of external things.)

MATHEMATICAL demonstrations do afford a certainty of the knowledge of things as really existing, as much as any other demonstrations whatsoever. And therefore they afford your lordship no ground upon that account to separate them, as you do here, from demonstrations in other subjects.

Your lordship indeed thinks I have given you sufficient grounds to charge me with the contrary. For you say I grant that those ideas on which mathematical demonstrations proceed are wholly in the mind, (this indeed I grant), and do not relate to the existence of things. But these latter words I do not remember that I anywhere say. And I wish you had quoted the place where I grant any such thing. I am sure it is not in that place where it is likeliest to be found: I mean where I examine whether the knowledge we have of mathematical truths be the knowledge of things as really existing. There I say (and I think I have proved) that it is, though it consists in the perception of the agreement or disagreement of ideas that are only in the mind, because it takes in all those things really existing which answer those ideas. Upon which grounds it was that I there affirmed moral knowledge also capable of certainty. And pray, my lord, what other way can your lordship proceed, in any demonstration you would make, about any other thing but figures and numbers, but the same that you do in demonstrations about figures and numbers? If you would demonstrate anything concerning man or murder, must you not first settle in your mind the idea or notion you have of that animal or that action, and then show what you would demonstrate necessarily to belong to that idea in your mind, and to those things existing only as they correspond with and answer that idea in your mind? How else you can make any general proposition that shall contain the knowledge of things as really existing, I that am ignorant should be glad to learn when your lordship shall do me the favour to show me any such.

I grant that those ideas on which mathematical demonstrations proceed are wholly in the mind. I say the same of all other demonstrations. For the ideas that other demonstrations proceed on are wholly in the mind. And no demonstration whatsoever concerns things really existing any farther than as they correspond with and answer those ideas in the mind which the demonstration proceeds on.

PROOF FOR THE EXISTENCE OF GOD

(This argument repeats that given in the *Essay* itself.)

The proposition of whose truth I would be certain is this: a knowing being has eternally existed. Here the ideas joined are *eternal existence* with *a knowing being.* But does not my mind perceive any immediate connexion or repugnancy in those ideas? No. The proposition then at first view affords me no certainty; or, as our English idiom phrases it, it is not certain, or I am not certain of it. But though I am not, yet I would be certain whether it be true or not. What then must I do? Find arguments to prove that it is true, or the contrary. And what is that, but to cast about and find out intermediate ideas which may show me the necessary connexion or inconsistency of the ideas in the proposition? Either of which, when by these intervening ideas I am brought to perceive, I am then certain that the proposition is true, or I am certain that it is false. As, in the present case, I perceive in myself thought and perception, the idea of actual perception has an evident connexion with an actual being that doth perceive and think. The idea of an actual thinking being hath a perceivable connexion with the eternal existence of some knowing being, by the intervention of the negation of all being, or the idea of nothing, which has a necessary connexion with no power, no operation, no causality, no effect, i. e. with nothing. So that the idea of once actually nothing has a visible connexion with nothing to eternity for the future; and hence the idea of an actual being is perceived to have a necessary connexion with some actual being from eternity. And by the like way of ideas may be perceived the actual existence of a knowing being to have a connexion with the existence of an actual knowing being from eternity; and the idea of an eternal, actual, knowing being, with the idea of immateriality, by the intervention of the idea of matter, and of its actual division, divisibility, and want of perception, &c., which are the ideas I make use of in this proof.

CRITICISM OF THEOLOGICAL SPECULATION

(Locke drew a sharp distinction between mixed modes which the mind made without any pattern in nature and the objective reality of things. He used this distinction to undermine the tendency to dogmatize in theology and metaphysics. The following passage discloses the way in which Locke recurrently and insistently enforced the theological implications of his theory of knowledge.)

There is in the world a great and fierce contest about nature and grace. It would be very hard for me if I must be brought in as a party on either side, because a disputant in that controversy should think the clear and distinct apprehensions of nature and grace come not into our minds by the simple ideas of sensation and reflection. If this be so, I may be reckoned among the objectors against all sorts and points of orthodoxy, whenever any one pleases. I may be called to account as one heterodox in the points of free-grace, free-will, predestination, original sin, justification by faith, transubstantiation, the pope's supremacy, and what not, as well as in the doctrine of the trinity; and all because they cannot be furnished with clear and distinct notions of grace, free-will, transubstantiation, &c. by sensation and reflection. For in all these, or any other points, I do not see but there may be complaint made, that they have not always right understanding and clear notions of those things on which the doctrine they dispute of depends. And it is not altogether unusual for men to talk unintelligibly to themselves and others, in these and other points of controversy, for want of clear and distinct apprehensions or ideas. For all which unintelligible talking I do not think myself accountable, though it should so fall out that my way by ideas would not help them to what it seems is wanting, clear and distinct notions.

To own a doctrine as received by others when I do not know how these others received it is perhaps a short way to orthodoxy, that may satisfy some men. But he that takes this way to give satisfaction, in my opinion makes a little bold with truth. And it may be questioned whether such a profession be pleasing to that God who requires truth in the inward parts, however acceptable it may in any man be to his diocesan.

I have been pretty large in making this matter plain,

that they who are so forward to bestow hard censures or names on the opinions of those who differ from them, may consider whether sometimes they are not more due to their own; and that they may be persuaded a little to temper that heat which supposing the truth in their current opinions, gives them (as they think) a right to lay what imputations they please on those who would fairly examine the grounds they stand upon. For talking with a supposition and insinuations that truth and knowledge, nay and religion too, stand and fall with their systems, is at best but an imperious way of begging the question and assuming to themselves under the pretence of zeal for the cause of God a title to infallibility. It is very becoming that men's zeal for truth should go so far as their proofs, but not go for proofs themselves. He that attacks received opinions with anything but fair arguments may, I own, be justly suspected not to mean well, nor to be led by the love of truth; but the same may be said of him too who so defends them. An errour is not the better for being common, nor truth the worse for having lain neglected. And if it were put to the vote anywhere in the world, I doubt, as things are managed, whether truth would have the majority, at least whilst the authority of men, and not the examination of things, must be its measure.

NOMINAL ESSENCE

(Locke's treatment of the nominal essence in the *Essay* seemed to some critics to involve a denial of the practical and scientific value of the classification of objects into species. That no such denial was intended or implied Locke went out of his way to make clear.)

In the objection you raise about species I fear you are fallen into the same difficulty I often found myself under, when I was writing on that subject, where I was very apt to suppose distinct species I could talk of without names. For pray, sir, consider what it is you mean when you say that "we can no more doubt of a sparrow's being a bird and a horse's being a beast than we can of this colour being black and the other white," &c. but this, that the combination of simple ideas which the word bird stands for is to be found in that particular thing we call a sparrow. And therefore I hope I have nowhere said there is no such sort of creature in nature as birds. If I have, it is both contrary to truth and to my opinion. This I do say, that there are real constitutions in things, from whence these simple ideas flow which we observe combined in them. And this I farther say, that there are real distinctions and differences in those real constitutions, one from another, whereby they are distinguished one from another, whether we think of them or name them or no; but that that whereby we distinguish and rank particular substances into sorts or genera and species is not those real essences or internal constitutions, but such combinations of simple ideas as we observe in them. This I designed to show. If you find anything contrary to this, I beg the favour of you to mark it to me, that I may correct it; for it is not what I think true. Some parts of that third book concerning words, though the thoughts were easy and clear enough, yet cost me more pains to express than all the rest of my *Essay*. And therefore I shall not much wonder if there be in some places of it obscurity and doubtfulness. It would be a great kindness from my readers to oblige me, as you have done, by telling me anything they find amiss. For the printed book being more for others' use than my own, it is fit I should accommodate it to that as much as I can; which truly is my intention.

CONTRAST BETWEEN NOMINAL AND REAL ESSENCE

(Locke's contrast between nominal and real essence is closely connected with his use of an empirical method. It was just because we know, not the real inner constitution of things, but the appearances of things in experience, that Locke was forced theoretically to defend an empirical method. We cannot proceed by necessary deductions since our knowledge does not penetrate to the real natures of things on which all their properties and powers depend. We must proceed by inductive generalizations since our knowledge is confined to what experience discloses of objects. We use methods of classification which are useful to us in our affairs. We believe in real natures, but we must recognize we do not know real natures.)

There is an internal constitution of things on which their properties depend. This your lordship and I are agreed of, and this we call the real essence. There are also certain complex ideas or combinations of these properties in men's minds, to which they commonly annex specific names, or names of sorts or kinds of things. This, I believe, your lordship does not deny. These complex ideas, for want of a better name, I have called nominal essences; how properly, I will not dispute. But if any one will help me to a better name for them, I am ready to receive it; till then I must, to express myself, use this. Now my lord, body, life, and the power of reasoning, being not the real essence of a man, as I believe your lordship will agree, will your lordship say, that they are not enough to make the thing wherein they are found of the kind called man, and not of the kind called baboon, because the difference of these kinds is real? If this be not real enough to make the thing of one kind and not of another, I do not see how *animal rationale* can be enough to distinguish a man from an horse; for that is but the nominal, not real, essence of that kind, designed by the name man. And yet, I suppose, every one thinks it real enough to make a real difference between that and other kinds. And if nothing will serve the turn to make things of one kind and not of another (which, as I have showed, signifies no more but ranking of them under different specific names) but their real, unknown constitutions which are the real essences we are speaking of, I fear it would be a long while before we should have really different kinds of substances, or distinct names for them, unless we could distinguish them by these differences of which we have no distinct conceptions. For I think it would not be readily answered me, if I should demand, wherein lies the real difference in the internal constitution of a stag from that of a buck, which are each of them very well known to be of one kind and not of the other. And nobody questions but that the kinds whereof each of them is are really different.

From these simple ideas which are knowable by us, we know as much of the powers and internal constitutions of things as these powers discover; and if we can know so much as that there are such powers and that there are certain beings in the world, endued with such powers and properties, that, by these simple ideas that are but the effects of these powers, we can as certainly distinguish the beings wherein those powers are and receive as certain advantage from them as if those simple ideas were resemblances: what is it we complain of the want of, in order to our certainty of things? But we do not see that internal constitution from whence those powers flow. Suppose we be ignorant of this (as we are like to be for any discoveries that have been yet made); that is a good argument to show how short our philosophical speculations are about the real, internal constitutions of things, but is no prejudice to us who by those simple ideas search out, find, and distinguish things for our uses. For though by those ideas which are not resemblances we cannot comprehend the internal frame or constitution of things, nor in what manner these ideas are produced in us by these powers, yet by them we certainly know that there are such essences or constitutions of these substances, that have those powers whereby they regularly produce those ideas in us, and that they are distinguished from each other by those powers.

These, and the like fashions of speaking, intimate that the substance is supposed always something besides the extension, figure, solidity, motion, thinking, or other observable idea, though we know not what it is.

Knowing the colour, figure, and smell of hyssop, I can when I see hyssop know so much as that there is a certain being in the world endued with such distinct powers and properties. And yet I may justly complain that I want something in order to certainty that hyssop will cure a bruise or a cough, or that it will kill moths, or, used in a certain way, harden iron, or an hundred other useful properties that may be in it which I shall never know, and yet might be certain of if I knew the real essences or internal constitutions of things on which their properties depend.

AN INSTANCE OF EMPIRICISM

(In spite of the technical difficulties into which Locke found himself plunged as the *Essay* developed, he remained firmly confident of the superiority of direct observation of facts to fine-spun theorizing. In a letter of Nov. 1, 1692, he contrasted "the way of accurate practical observation" with the "useless though pleasing visions" of "speculative hypotheses." In another letter of Jan. 20, 1693, he commended the empirical procedure in connection with the practice of medicine. The Dr. Sydenham whose name comes into the passage was so outstanding in his medical practice that he was sometimes called "the English Hippocrates"; he was a friend of Locke, Boyle, and others in the Royal Academy of the seventeenth century.)

I PERFECTLY agree with you concerning general theories, that they are for the most part but a sort of waking dreams, with which, when men have warmed their own heads, they pass into unquestionable truths, and then the ignorant world must be set right by them. Though this be, as you rightly observe, beginning at the wrong end, when men lay the foundation in their own fancies, and then endeavour to suit the phenomena of diseases and the cure of them to those fancies. I wonder that, after the pattern Dr. Sydenham has set them of a better way, men should return again to that romance way of physic. But I see it is easier and more natural for men to build castles in the air of their own than to survey well those that are to be found standing. Nicely to observe the history of diseases in all their changes and circumstances is a work of time, accurateness, attention, and judgment, and wherein if men, through prepossession or oscitancy, mistake, they may be convinced of their errour by unerring nature and matter of fact, which leaves less room for the subtlety and dispute of words, which serves very much instead of knowledge in the learned world, where, methinks, wit and invention has much the preference to truth. Upon such grounds as are the established history of diseases, hypotheses might with less danger be erected, which I think are so far useful as they serve as an art of memory to direct the physician in particular cases, but not to be relied on as foundations of reasoning or verities to be contended for; they being, I think I may say all of them, suppositions taken up *gratis,* and will so remain, till we can discover how the natural functions of the body are performed, and by what alteration of the humours, or defects in the parts, they are hindered or disordered. To which purpose, I fear the Galenists' four humours, or the chemist's sal, sulphur, and mercury, or the late prevailing invention of acid and alcali, or whatever hereafter shall be substituted to these with new applause, will upon examination be found to be but so many learned empty sounds with no precise determinate signification. What we know of the works of nature, especially in the constitution of health, and the operations of our own bodies, is only by the sensible effects, but not by any certainty we can have of the tools she uses, or the ways she works by. So that there is nothing left for a physician to do but to observe well, and so by analogy argue to like cases, and thence make to himself rules of practice. And he that is this way most sagacious will, I imagine, make the best physician, though he should entertain distinct hypotheses concerning distinct species of diseases, subservient to this end, that were inconsistent one with another; they being made use of in those several sorts of diseases, but as distinct arts of memory, in those cases. And I the rather say this, that they might be relied on only as artificial helps to a physician and not as philosophical truths to a naturalist. But, sir, I run too far, and must beg your pardon for talking so freely on a subject you understand so much better than I do. I hoped the way of treating diseases, which, with so much approbation, Dr. Sydenham had introduced into the world, would have beaten the other out and turned men from visions and wrangling to observation, and endeavouring after settled practices in more diseases such as I think he has given us in some. If my zeal for the saving men's lives and preserving their health (which is infinitely to be preferred to any speculations ever so fine in physic) has carried me too far, you will excuse it in one who wishes well to the practice of physic, though he meddles not with it.